Over at Uncle Joe's

Moscow and Me

(A Glimpse at Post-WWII Soviet Union from an American Traveler and Correspondent)

By ORIANA ATKINSON

The Only Edition Approved by the Atkinson Family

The Women War Correspondents Series

Over at Uncle Joe's

Moscow and Me

(A Glimpse at Post-WWII Soviet Union from an American Traveler and Correspondent)

By ORIANA ATKINSON

Second Edition Reprint with commentary, 2019
First Edition Publication, 1947

The Women War Correspondents Series

The Ardent Writer Press
Brownsboro, Alabama

Visit Oriana's Author Page at
www.ArdentWriterPress.com

For general information about publishing with The Ardent Writer Press contact *steve@ardentwriterpress.com* or forward mail to:
The Ardent Writer Press,
Box 25
Brownsboro, Alabama 35741.

Cover and interior composition © by Steve Gierhart, The Ardent Writer Press, using Photoshop techniques. Photo of Oriana from the author's family.

Library of Congress Cataloging-in-Publication Data

Oriana Atkinson

Over at Uncle Joe's: Moscow and Me (A Glimpse at Post WWII Soviet Union from an American Traveler and Correspondent)

p. cm. (Ardent Writer Press -2019) ISBN 978-1-64066-003-8 (paperback); ISBN 978-1-64066-004-5 (hardback); eBook mobi Kindle version ISBN 978-1-64066-005-2

Library of Congress Control Number 2019945748
- Russia.
- Travel--Humor.
- Russia--Civilization--Humor.
- Russia--Social life and customs--20th century.
- Russia--Description and travel--20th century.
- Russia--Foreign relations--United States.
- HUM026000 HUMOR / Topic / Travel (BISAC)
- TRV023000   TRAVEL / Russia (BISAC)

Second Edition © 2019 (Oriana Atkinson © Original Copyright 1947)

CONTENTS

Acknowledgments

SOME of the material in this book has appeared in articles which I wrote for the *New York Times*, the *Woman's Home Companion, McCall's Magazine* and *Holiday*. The editors of these publications have kindly given me permission to use it here.

I acknowledge a debt of gratitude to Mrs. Joseph Phillips. Tracy is the lovely, red-haired English girl who was my first guide to Moscow. It was she who led me through the mazes of the "Dipstores" and the Gastronoms. It was she who sketched vividly for me what the primary pitfalls of that city were sure to be. It was she who conducted me on my first excursions around the town. Although she left Russia about three months after I arrived, while she was there her kindness to me went far over and above the call of duty.

Dedication

**For Heather MacIlveen and Andrew MacIlveen
with love**

Chapter 1

Introduction

AMERICANS who have been for any length of time in the U.S.S.R. usually return home with one resolve firmly in mind: "Never discuss Russia with anybody who has never been there." This is an extremely sensible resolution, but like many other good ones, almost impossible to keep. As Jimmy Durante says, "Everybody wants to get into the act!" I used to think that the theatre, as a topic of conversation, could engender more bad temper than anything else in the world. I know better now. As a topic, Russia can make lifelong enemies of good friends in the twinkling of an eye.

When I returned home after ten months in Moscow, I too had the same high resolve, but it soon went glimmering. So many people seemed to be so deeply interested in my Russian adventure that I was persuaded to answer questions about it. My countrymen's ideas and attitude bewildered me, and instead of quietly withdrawing from the ensuing fracas, I found myself yelling, "But listen a minute, you don't understand!" Nearly everybody looked at me with scorn. Not understand? Of course, they understood! Hadn't they read every word about Russia that appeared in the papers? Listened to everything about Russia on the radio? Read hundreds of books about Russia? What did I think they were, dopes?

Ten months in Russia does not make a Russian expert. Paul Winterton, an Englishman who went to Russia and who wrote a book about his experiences there, said one thing which has become a classic among Americans who have been to Russia. He said, "There are no experts on Russia. There

1

are only degrees of ignorance." I was never outside Moscow from the time I arrived there until we flew to Odessa and took ship from there to come home. If you will look at an up-to-date map of the USSR, you will see what a vast amount of territory it covers. By comparison, the U.S.A. looks like a postage stamp. Russia is the biggest country in the world and Moscow is only a pin point on that sprawling expanse. But after ten months in Moscow I do claim this: I know more about Russia than anybody who has ever been there.

World War II tossed a lot of Americans into a lot of places where they never expected to find themselves. I was no exception. My husband was appointed foreign correspondent for the *New York Times* in Moscow and I accompanied him there. We had been in Russia once before. In 1936, at the invitation of the Soviet government, we attended a Soviet Theatrical Festival there. That was the sum total of my knowledge of Russia and my interest in it. I knew nothing about Russian politics and very little about American politics, either. The American Communists I had met convinced me that whatever they were for, I was against.

Seriously, however, I really went to Russia with an open mind about Communism. I figured that anything I had heard about it in America was probably pretty far removed from the real thing. That proved to be true. Yet nothing that I saw in the ten grubby, tiresome, frustrated and fascinating months that I spent over at Uncle Joe Stalin's made me want to relinquish my American citizenship and cast my lot with the hammer-and-sickle boys. I came home deeply convinced that democracy, the American brand, is for me.

Chapter 2

Moscow and Me

YOU CANNOT LIVE in Moscow without hearing politics discussed day after day, all day long. All the foreign correspondents have offices in the Metropole Hotel or come there every day, and it is safe to say that ninety-nine and seventy-eight hundredths percent of their conversation is about politics. Politics is the chief subject of conversation of every other English-speaking person in Moscow. You can no more live there without discussing politics than you can breathe without using air.

But aside from listening to political discussions, I had plenty to do. I studied the Russian language with Russian teachers; I "kept house," by which I mean that I shopped for food in the Moscow stores and cooked three meals a day on a hot plate in our room at the Metropole. I had looked forward to being free from household cares during the Russian experiment and thought that living in the Metropole Hotel would ensure that. But little did I know. We simply were unable to eat the food at the hotel and that meant that I had to get back into harness and establish a household in a foreign city.

Of course, in the beginning I understood no Russian at all. The business of getting the ration cards under control was no easy matter. Locating and buying food with the aid of a courier who understood no English was a little complicated. Cooking on a stove about as big around as a fifty-cent piece took a bit of doing. But after a little while all these tangles untangled and gradually I felt as though our way of life there, although rugged, was endurable. Of course I sputtered and griped all the time, but I really got so I could handle the situation and that was all that counted.

I found plenty of time to give to other affairs besides my domestic ones. When we first arrived, we did not have a car of our own, and so I walked around the city a good deal. Sometimes I went alone, but usually I had a Russian guide or secretary. I went to the theatre, to the ballet, to concerts and recitals. I met Russians daily whose business it was to associate with me whether they wanted to or not—secretaries, couriers, chambermaids and so on. I met a few Russians at the homes of my American friends. I knew all the American newspapermen, of course, and listened to them curse the censorship and plot how to outwit it. I met American diplomats and American engineers who had been in distant parts of the Soviet Union helping to establish various industries at the request of the Russians. These men were usually a bundle of nerves on their way home, full of their adventures and with the firm conviction that the Russian workman is the most careless and shoddy in the world. American engineers have told me tall tales of the lack of pride in workmanship all over Russia. "I won't say that everything in the whole U.S.S.R. is put together with safety pins and paper clips," said one engineer, "but the only reason I won't say it is because they haven't got enough safety pins or clips."

I met American fur buyers who told me that all the best furs in Russia were being bought by American furriers but that they seldom saw the skins they were buying; they had some sort of system by which the lists of graded skins were presented to them and they bought on paper. I met American agricultural experts, full of admiration for the Russian people and full of conflicting and exasperating statistics which they were always trying to assemble and evaluate. I met American educators and sundry other "visiting firemen" who were being whisked from place to place by the Russians as though they were on wires. There were other foreign visitors—none of them remaining for more than a day or two, a week or two at the very most. There were less than two hundred "permanent" Americans in the whole Soviet Union. There is not a single American student studying in a Russian university. On the other hand, there are two thousand five hundred Russians in America and not just any old Russians, either. They are very special Russians, here for a very special purpose, or they wouldn't have been permitted to go out of the country.

When a visitor from abroad comes to America and spends his time either in Washington or New York, Americans always laughingly assure him that he has not seen the real America. Both Washington and New York are cosmopolitan cities where you can hear almost any language spoken on the streets and

where you are likely to pass people from every country in the world in the course of a morning's walk. But when you have been to Moscow, you have been to Russia. Moscow is solidly Russian. You hear nothing but Russian spoken. Although the dialects may vary, the people are all Soviet citizens. Here is a quotation from a Russian book written for the guidance of foreign visitors:

> *He who has seen Moscow has seen in miniature what is taking place throughout the entire Soviet Union.... What is Moscow? It is a city which is, first of all, the center of political events so important that they make an epoch in the history of mankind; a city which is an immense laboratory of scientific and technical thought; a city with a rapidly developing industry striving to surpass the foremost, instantly experimenting with new ideas, and at the same time, a city of ancient monuments, a living museum of eight centuries of history, and finally a city where a new life and a new social structure are being forged. This, briefly sketched, is Moscow.*

Moscow is the heart and center of the U.S.S.R. No American citizen thinks about Washington the way the Russian thinks about Moscow. All through Russian literature Moscow is the symbol of the loyalty and the devotion of every Russian. Once a Russian girl said to me, "It is very touching to me how deeply Americans love their country. Whenever an American says 'America,' it is in the tone of voice one uses to say 'Beloved.'" But it is *America* that means that to us—not just Washington. When a Russian says "Moskva," it is in the tone of voice one uses to say "Mother."

So ten months in Moscow does give you a knowledge of Russia. Ten months of intensive discussion of Russian politics, of varied excursions around and about the city, ten months' association with people who speak only Russian, ten months' exposure to the atmosphere and customs and manners of Moscow do give you some idea what goes on just outside the Kremlin wall. I don't think I can be blamed for not understanding what goes on *inside* it, because all the rest of the world, and for the most part smarter people than I am, are cracking their heads over that problem every day.

Life in the "foreign colony" of Moscow has a distinctly Kiplingesque atmosphere. For Americans and British, Moscow is an "outpost of empire" and the handful of Americans and Britishers there make up a close little social circle that has some of the aspects of a merry-go-round. The little revolving group constantly whirls from dinner party to dinner party and cocktail party to cocktail party. This is less because the Americans and Britishers prefer American and British company to any other than because the Russians are not allowed to play with us. Americans who have been in Moscow for a very long time, or whose jobs take them into contact with Russians in a business way, do get to know a few natives. But the great majority just has to associate with one another and let it go at that.

I got to know about a dozen Russians intimately—a high average for an American who can speak only a little of their language. I knew a few others pretty well. And we learned that if we let politics alone, we could find quite a number of subjects about which we could converse with pleasure and understanding. But on the subject of politics there was no meeting ground. They never gave in and neither did I. They could not understand what I meant when I stated flatly that they were living under a totalitarian regime; and I didn't know what they were talking about when they told me blandly that my idea of "democracy" was ill-founded and absurd. Any conversation that involved politics was sure to end in mutual recriminations, no matter how fond you might be of your companion.

I remember one such conversation I had with a Russian girl who was as gentle and amiable a creature as you would be likely to find in a month of Sundays. We were talking about poetry, a subject safely removed from the dangerous one we both were glad to avoid. From somewhere and for some reason, some lines of Emma Lazarus' poem which is on the base of the Statue of Liberty came to my mind and I quoted it sonorously with deep emotion:

> "...Give me your tired, your poor,
> Your huddled masses yearning to breathe free,
> The wretched refuse of your teeming shore,
> Send these, the homeless, tempest-tossed, to me:
> I lift my lamp beside the golden door."

My friend had never heard of the Statue of Liberty and inquired eagerly about it. Unable to believe that anybody in the whole world did not know about Miss Liberty, I explained about it in detail. My friend smiled winningly. "Just imagine," she cooed, "you have no room for Liberty in your whole broad land, you have to put her on an island outside the boundaries. If we had such a statue, it would be erected in the Kremlin itself in the heart of the capital city." My husband, with the suppleness brought about by long experience, flung himself between the Russian and me and said through clenched teeth as he held my arms, "Nuh, nuh, nuh, act like a little lady now." I shrieked with rage. The Russian girl scuttled away. I spent the rest of the day thinking up sarcastic answers to her nasty remark and my husband, who already knew all the answers, had to listen to me. "Sure, sure, sure," he murmured soothingly, which only made me madder than ever.

"If they had a Statue of Liberty, it would have Stalin's face on it," I yammered. "If they had a Statue of Liberty and it was erected inside the Kremlin, they'd never be permitted to *look* at it even—except a few who had passes."

My husband said, "Be calm, if possible. You and I know— we understand. They don't and they can't. Let the matter drop."

I subsided, muttering, "That's the kind of thing that went on if you didn't watch out every minute."

But there were grounds for amity. I found that if you kept close to the following subjects, you were likely to have an enjoyable time with your Russian acquaintances:

God; religion; love. Families; children. Food and cooking; the cost of living, housekeeping, living standards; literature; the theatre, the ballet, the cinema; fortunetelling and superstitions generally; gardening, with the accent on flowers; travel, in America and Russia; architecture, fashions, cosmetics and beauty culture; house furnishings; art; music; antiques. All of these subjects lead to dangerous comparisons, but a middle ground can be found. There were probably other subjects, too, including woman's place in the scheme of things and, of course, the United Nations. Here, at least, we were solidly agreed. There was one word we both used in cementing on that important matter. That word was "Hope." We hoped earnestly and sincerely that the United Nations would work. We agreed that "Our Leaders" must make it do so.

Once you get away from politics, the Russians make a real effort to smooth life out as much as possible for the foreigner. When you consider that their own life is pretty rough going, you can't help being grateful for small and gracious favors. It makes you shudder to consider what some of the privileges granted to you mean in sacrifice to a Russian. As an illustration, I remember one incident that astonished me. We had been able to arrange the purchase of a Swedish car through friends in Sweden. It was to be shipped by boat from

Sweden to Leningrad where the Russians had to take over and send it by flatcar to Moscow. An automobile is precious cargo and thanks to tales we had heard, we had visions of a car minus tires, lights, wheels, upholstery and anything else removable. Americans laughed gaily and assured us lightheartedly that we would be lucky to get even a small assortment of nuts and bolts after a car had been shipped overland through car-hungry Russia.

When we received the notice that the car was awaiting us in the railway yards, we scurried down at once, although it was already night and snow was falling. The car was there, its paint gleaming impressively. A quick count assured us that there were still four wheels. As we stood there breathless before this astonishing thing, one of the rear doors of the car opened and out tottered a frail little gnome of a man. He was pale with fatigue, but his face was radiant with relief. He had been put in the back seat by the railway authorities in Leningrad and told to stay there and see that not one predatory hand was laid upon that car. They told him that he would be held responsible for every part of that car until it was delivered to its rightful owners. He waited wearily but watchfully until the checking over was done and then he wandered away into the snowy night. We thought that this was carrying personal service out to a pretty fine degree.

I feel deeply that there are many common interests between the countries, but the rock upon which the ship of understanding is shattered is *totalitarianism*.

The atmosphere of crushing paternalism smothers an American. What we consider the breath of life, individual freedom, individual enterprise, individual dignity, are elements missing from the Russian scene. Many people will tell you that this is all for the greater good when you take the long view. Others, the very young and the very old, wonder what they are to be given which will take the place of bitter years. Americans, viewing the tangled state of Russo-American affairs, wonder why our many gestures of friendship have been so coldly rebuffed. They wonder why, if the Russian people themselves believe in the friendliness of America, they do not bring public opinion to bear and force their leaders to change the present pigheaded policy and permit a solid relationship to become established. Americans forget—or cannot understand—that there is no public opinion as far as foreign affairs are concerned. Behind the Iron Curtain, the iron hands of the Politburo hold the reins tightly.

9

Chapter 3

The Russianness of the Russians

IT WAS SURPRISING how often I could see eye to eye with people whose viewpoint and psychology are so different from ours. America is the direct product of our minds and hands. This country of ours is young and vigorous and flexible and strong and we are always kicking it out of shape and molding it nearer to our heart's desire.

On the other hand, Russia makes the Russians. The Soviets speak of Russia as "a new country, a young country." What they have is a thin skin of new soil spread over a wild tangle of very strong old roots. Russia is very old, very wise, very deep, very solid, fundamentally changeless. Russians love Russia as they love God. They revere and adore her as a great eternal core of truth. It really seems to me as though this snarling tide which washes across her today is tolerated as a necessary cleansing wave which will bring out, ultimately, the fundamental beauty and strength of that wonderful old country. Old Czar—new master—what does it matter? Somehow, some day, under whatever leadership, Old Mother Russia will emerge, shining and glorious. Every Russian believes this with every drop of blood in his veins.

I have always been slightly unbalanced on the subject of America. All my life long my friends have said wearily, "Oh, there goes Oriana, making the eagle scream again." So when I got to Moscow and found myself surrounded by people who knew almost nothing about America and who blandly assumed that Russia was the greatest country in the world, I felt as Alice must have felt when she stepped through the looking glass. The Russians assume quite simply that Russia won the wars—the war against Germany and the war against Japan. They assume that Russia will dictate the peace, and find that assumption completely reasonable. They believe that the whole world of science, art, agriculture, philosophy and literature should be led and guided by Russia, since she already is preeminent in all these fields. To a chauvinistic American these views naturally presented some difficulties.

Many of the most interesting things I saw and some of the most interesting things I heard I cannot bring myself to write about for fear of getting people "into trouble." Everybody who comes home from Russia says the same thing and it is completely true but nobody here believes it. Nevertheless, everybody who tries to write about Russia remembers the faces of the Russians who gave him any information and the expression in their eyes when they said, "Don't say I said so." Maybe they are only being coy. Maybe there's nothing to be afraid of. Maybe nothing would happen to them if you gave their names and gave them credit for telling you. But as H. I. Phillips, of the *New York Sun*, often says: "Wanna bet?"

I don't know precisely what "getting into trouble" means, but I know that no Soviet citizen wants any part of it. There is not a moment you spend with a Russian when the fear of punishment does not hang over his head and slow his tongue. The Soviet government does not smile on associating with foreigners. If it becomes known (and it *always* becomes known at once) that a Russian in Moscow is consorting with foreigners for any except the most businesslike of reasons, "trouble" is likely to follow.

The purges of 1936 are still vivid in everybody's mind and nobody wants a repetition of them. In 1936 the search for antigovernment activity went wide and deep and terror stalked abroad in the land. Anybody who had been known to associate with foreigners was suspect and the investigation went beyond the person involved; it included all his family and all his friends and sometimes took in the most casual of acquaintances. People went around shaking with terror. They went to bed at night with a small package of clothing and food beside their beds, not knowing when "the knock would come at the door," not knowing when they might be pulled from their beds and marched off, without explanation, to some undisclosed destination. If an automobile stopped outside the house and feet were heard on the stairway, hearts within that house skipped a beat or two. Everybody—anybody—was suspect, and still is. The result is a permanent fog of fear.

You may be whisked away like *that*. You may lose your job and every member of your family may lose his. When your job goes, your food card goes with it, and he who does not work does not eat. In a country of stringently rationed food, this is definitely not funny.

An example of this omnipresent fear occurs to me. One day the Russian secretary of a foreign correspondent did not come to work. Since she was an extremely faithful employee and took her job very seriously, it was considered strange that she did not telephone or send an excuse. When noon came and she had not yet communicated with her employer, he became anxious and sent a messenger to her home to make inquiries. The girl's family said that she had started for work as usual. Of course by that time the news was all over the Metropole Hotel. The correspondent got into his car and went to the Emergency Hospital to find out whether she had had an accident. She was not there. Further inquiry along the same lines failed to find her and by three o'clock everybody who knew the girl was really in a tizzy. I don't know what we thought; I only know that everybody was extremely alarmed and that the Russians looked scared and would not discuss it at all. The Americans looked scared and discussed it at the top of their lungs. At four o'clock the girl arrived, safe and sound; pale, very nervous but intact. She made a feeble excuse which nobody believed, but nobody pressed her for details. She may have had a date with a boy friend, perhaps it was nothing more desperate than that. The fact remains that everybody was automatically afraid something very unpleasant had happened to her and the chances are very good that it had.

The Russians I knew were kind and courteous, for the most part but not over communicative nor at all revealing. Everybody I met was friendly but nobody wanted to tell me anything that had not already been printed in a Russian newspaper or otherwise officially released. After a while I felt as though I were living in jail, in a crowded place surrounded by impenetrable walls. You never draw a free breath while you are in Moscow and if you are an American, you never get used to that or like it, either.

I never heard an American say he didn't like the Russian people. Americans find the individual Russians friendly, generous, honest, thoughtful, fair and full of amusing curiosity. Their brand of humor is like our own—or at least their sense of what's funny is much like our own. Their humorous magazine *Krokodil* is always sniping away at bureaucracy and at human frailties and the cartoons that appear in it are excellent examples of the satirical humor that appeals to Moscovites.

You hear plenty of grapevine stories about the low standard of living and the lack of creature comforts in present-day Moscow. For instance, there was the story about the workman who was listening to an impassioned speech—what we would call a "pep talk"—in factory. "Overtake and surpass," cried the orator. "We must over take the Western capitalistic countries and surpass them!" "Good," said the weary Soviet workman, "and when we overtake, just let me off!" And another story about an even more pessimistic citizen who was listening to somebody extol the grand progress which the U.S.S.R. had made under the Soviets. "Yes, yes," muttered the listener, "after a quarter century of backbreaking labor, we are now where we were a hundred years ago."

People have said to me, "In one sentence you say the Russian are generous, yet in another you say that they are rapacious. One place you say that they have great dignity and in another place you say they are abject in a way no American can tolerate. You contradict yourself." I can only join with Walt Whitman and say, "Do I contradict myself? Very well, then, I contradict myself." Because all these things are true about the Russians.

I know some things about the Russians, and knowing these things I accept them as existing facts, but I don't attempt to explain them. After you get to realize the existence of these facts and govern yourself accordingly, you will find that you can get along all right with them. If I had to (which God forbid), I could live in Moscow and get along with the Moscovites quite pleasantly as far as human relationship go. But it means more than just learning another language. It means another tempo; it means accepting some things as self-evident truth and going on from there.

Concerning the tempo: you can't just bust up to a Russian in a train or a plane and say, "Hello, old pal, old pal, old pal. I'm an American and I think probably you're a good scout. Come on and have a drink." The Russian would freeze you in your tracks, excuse himself from having a drink with you—even though his tongue were hanging out—and he would get away from you as soon as he could. Tempo. If you sneak up on him and smile, tentatively once and then look away

quickly, then sit for ten minutes and don't say anything—that's better. Slowly and carefully he will begin to consider the possibility that you may be harmless. He turns over in his mind what the chances are that anybody is watching him. If slowly and gently you produce an American cigarette and slowly and timidly offer him one, he will probably take it. If you offer a light, he may relax a little more. If, after five minutes more, you make a remark about the weather (and say that it's *good*), he will probably answer you politely. If he still sticks around, smoking your cigarette, you may make another remark, but keep it simple. By and by if you are still determined to break down his resistance, you may slowly, slowly, sneak a bottle of vodka out of your luggage and set it where he can see it. Wait a minute. Then if you fill a glass (and fill it *full*, brother) and hold it out timidly as though you understand very well that he wouldn't *think* of taking a drink with a stranger—he may take it. But the tempo is everything. You may go on from there.

But on the other hand, if a Russian approaches *you* (it sometimes happens) and offers *you* a cigarette or a drink, you'd better take it at once and smile like the sun and make out that he's your best friend. Because if you don't, he will consider that he has been snubbed and he will go away and tell everybody that Americans are, without the slightest doubt in God's green world, pigs.

Another thing I know for a fact and can state only as such is the way they keep appointments. If you have an appointment with a Russian for, say, two o'clock in the afternoon, it is more than likely that the appointed time will find you cooling your heels alone, at the meeting place. And if you are durable, so will two-thirty and sometimes even three o'clock. An hour is considered not too long to wait for a friend. And when—and if—your Russian appears, he will be smiling and cheerful and with scarcely an apology for being late. He will not expect you to be annoyed and he will be bewildered if you are. If, on the other hand, you finally come to the conclusion that no Russian ever keeps an appointment on time and you make a date for two o'clock and go about other affairs and don't show up until three, you are more than likely to find your Russian friend there with a look of hurt incredulity on his face. He may not tax you with being late, but he will be pink with annoyance and it will be dear that he feels that you have given him cause for offense. It has happened thus to me. I don't understand it.

One more illustration may succeed in confusing you even further. This is their attitude toward criticism. Now there's no use saying that anybody likes adverse criticism. Adverse criticism hurts, even if you ask for it. But the Russians never want to leave well enough alone. They ask your opinion, urge you to criticize and then pout when they get what they ask for. "What did you think of the ballet tonight?" a Russian may say. Since you would like peace at any price, you say brightly, "I thought it was very interesting." "Oh, come now," the Russian will say, "you didn't like it at all, you know you didn't." But you think you're smart, so you continue to smile and say, "I really enjoyed it very much." The Russian will sneer and say, "Why do you lie about it? Do you think *we* think it is so wonderful?" Then you like a fool, say, "Well, perhaps the ensemble dancing wasn't so good as it should have been," and then he has you where he wants you. He says, "No doubt the American ballet is better?" in a sarcastic and incredulous tone—and then of course you're off.

They pick at you until you say something nasty; and even if you don't say it, they accuse you of thinking it. I once met the editor of one of the leading magazines of Moscow, and a very sightly magazine it is. The drawings and the colored photographs are really super and since I can't read much Russian, naturally I based my opinion on the pictures. He asked me whether I had seen his magazine and I said heartily and with complete honesty that I thought it was an excellent job. "You are making fun of it," he said crossly. I let it lie. If you tell them the truth, they think you're lying and get mad. If you lie to them, they know you are lying and resent it. You can't win.

One of the most annoying habits that the Russians have and another of their little ways which I accepted without understanding is their determination to get foreigners drunk.

I have heard a good many analyses of this, but since none of them would tend to add to the sum total of international good will, I omit them. They work at it with never-ending determination. Any foreigner who has visited Moscow in an official capacity or who has been a guest of a Russian committee, or any foreigner who has had Russian guests at an official dinner, will tell you that it is a well defined program. The vodka begins to circulate as soon as the introductions are cold and the playful business of "bottoms up" is started without delay. Glass after glass is poured out and tossed off, with the general idea prevailing that the Russians can consume endless quantities, while without doubt the guests will succumb in very short order. This serves a double purpose. A drunken man is in no condition to get into discussions of politics, or if he still insists, can be ignored as under the weather. You must either take the stand at once that you will not enter into this stupid contest, or drink as much as they want you to and get very sick and foolish.

However, sometimes the brave Russian drinkers get pretty glassy-eyed themselves and the fable that Russians can hold their liquor better than anybody else is just a fable. We have some two-fisted drinkers of our own nationality over there and though I never heard anybody say he enjoyed the Russian drinking game, I know of at least one case where an American came out on top of the table.

A mild-mannered friend of ours who shall here be nameless, except to remark that he is a captain in the Navy and has been in Moscow for almost five years, had a commission to perform in Archangel. He took the train and found that he had to share his seat with a member of the Russian Army, a husky young officer who spoke halting English. Our friend speaks a fluent Russian and is well acquainted with the customs and habits of the Russian people. He was therefore not surprised when a bottle of vodka was produced and the old business got under way. Now the captain looks like the mildest of men; he is a Bostonian; his smile is gentle and his voice is low. He is a slender man, tall, good-looking, with a very quiet manner. But strangely enough, he is very good at games and is always willing to play any game anyone suggests. Any game. So they were off, although he wanted very much to have a quiet snooze or perhaps dip his beak into a bit of Emerson. They finished the first bottle and still that captain wanted to read Emerson. Other bottles of vodka were produced. The captain listened to the Russian lad's story or stories and the train slogged along through the night. The Russian was still on his feet, and getting pretty mad about the whole thing. Other bottles of vodka were obtained. Finally, the Russian passed out. Our friend then pushed him over on his side and proceeded to do what he had wanted to do all along. He read Emerson. My friends, it is not always thus.

Vodka, let me tell you, is White Mule, Jersey Lightning, Bathtub Gin and Old Cawn combined. Except that it doesn't taste quite so good as any of them. It is raw and quick-acting and produces an ill tempered and melancholy bun.

The Russians have no patience with the American habit of drinking for pleasure and sociability. They drink to get drunk as quickly and as soddenly as they can. They also hold no brief for the American habit of drinking without eating, but insist on having a bit of bread with every drink they take. This is supposed to enable them to drink without getting drunk. Much good it does! This is called "a drink and a bite." So when a Russian invites you to have "a drink and a bite," it does not mean that he is inviting you to cocktails and dinner. It merely means that a hooker of vodka is indicated. He will often issue this invitation without saying a word. If he puts the tip of his forefinger against his thumb and snaps at his tonsil with it, it means "Let's have a quick one, pal." Or, in the case of Andrei, our chauffeur, it means "How about your giving *me* a quick one, pal?"

The Russians have a story that they tell on themselves that really needs a Russian to tell it, but it goes like this. It is the three stages of Russian drunkenness: 1—The Russian leans his head on one hand, his elbow on the table, holding his vodka glass in his other hand. He has been drinking, but he is not drunk. He looks at his friend and he says, with deep sincerity, "You are my friend. You are the best friend that I have. I love you and trust you with all my heart. Yes, you are my best friend." And they have a couple of drinks on this. 2—Then the Russian continues, still leaning his head on his hand, his elbow on the table: "True, you are my best friend and I love you deeply. Although it is well known that you are a rascal, still I love you. I do not trust you, you and your sneaky friends. Everybody knows what a dastard you are, but I love you. Yes; I love you, anyhow." And they have a half-dozen drinks on that. 3—Then the speaker continues, his head still leaning on his hand, a little more heavily now: "My best friend!" he cries in scorn. "A fine friend you are! I am surrounded by enemies! Every man's hand is against me! Why do I not die?" And his head slips off his hand, his elbow slips off the table, he slips off his chair and falls on the floor. His friend regards him silently for a moment, and then carefully lies down beside him. They sleep.

Chapter 4

Problems and Pigeonholes

IF YOU EVER enter into a discussion with a Russian about the comparative goodness of our ways of life, and if for the moment you seem to have the edge on him, the Russian will usually say, "Oh yes, but what about the Negro problem in America?"

It became a byword among the Americans. We used it for a wisecrack among ourselves. But we were thoroughly aware that it was no laughing matter, and we were pretty well perplexed when we tried to justify ourselves to the Russians (or to one another, either, as far as that goes).

Russians have no such national problem to justify and Negroes in Russia go about their business happily free from race prejudice. I asked an American Negro in Moscow if he found life pleasanter there than at home. He said he did. I asked him if he would like to return to the United States. He said he would—for a vacation. Russians intermarry with Negroes when they feel like it and no color line is drawn against them anywhere. Yet many American Negroes who went to Russia just after the Soviets came into power and others who migrated there later, feeling that the Soviet way had more to offer them than the American, have returned to the United States. This, in spite of the greater racial freedom enjoyed in the U.S.S.R. I have no explanation for this, since here is one situation where surely a man is offered greater opportunities than in the U.S.A. It is about the only one I can honestly say I ever encountered.

Yet another problem which vexes America is present in Moscow to a marked degree and that is anti-Semitism. There is no discrimination in the government against Jews, and some of the highest positions in the government are held by Jews. But I have often heard Jews spoken of in a derogatory manner and have heard them blamed for many things the Soviet citizens find irritating—for one thing, the fact that "Jews often have better living quarters than others" and for another they are somehow blamed for the lack of civilian goods. I don't see how either statement can be true, but I heard both of them.

There is no organized persecution of Jews in Moscow, but Red Army men who have returned home from countries where anti-Semitism had reached fanatical proportions will need a good deal of good Soviet indoctrination and re-education before they get rid of the taint they have brought home with them. Of course, among the Old Russians anti-Semitism was deep-rooted. Old Russia had a pretty bad reputation for that kind of thing, and some of the most dreadful pogroms the world has ever known were held in Russia. Anti-Semitism is dying out but there is plenty of life in it yet.

One thing which I know to be true and yet which I do not cite as an illustration of anti-Semitism is the fact that a Jew in Russia, no matter where he may have been born, must have "Jew" on his passport. A Ukrainian has "Ukrainian," a Georgian has "Georgian." But if a Jew was born in Georgia, he has "Jew" on his passport, not "Georgian"; a Ukrainian-born Jew has "Jew" on his passport, not "Ukrainian." No Jew I knew ever thought this strange, or resented it. The fact remains that "Jew" appears on his papers.

Bureaucracy in Moscow flourishes everywhere. It operates in a finicky, stubborn, timorous and thoroughly ineffectual way. Thousands of little men and women in key jobs are afraid of their shadows and their major ambition seems to be to evade ever making a decision and thus to avoid responsibility. These petty officials make life indescribably irritating both to Soviet citizens and to foreigners. Even in Moscow it is not considered dangerous or political bad taste to criticize their pettiness. The satirical magazine *Krokodil* uses these people for targets continually, and barbed cartoons fill its pages, sniping at their activities. Washington, during its palmiest days of red tape, was a well-oiled, well-functioning machine compared with what goes on constantly in the Soviet capital.

I could give many illustrations of this bureaucratic song and dance.

Any foreigner who attempts to get information about anything is sure to be a bundle of nerves before he finds out what he wants to know or, what is more likely, gives up with a scream of despair. My own attempts to get any kind of information about statistics, or even the most innocuous data of any kind were like taking part in a Lobster Quadrille. There was a great deal of shaking of hands and a great deal of amiability. But when the bowing and the smiling were all over and the figures of the dance had dissolved and I got back to the side lines, I discovered that I had met some pleasant people and that I was in a friendly glow, but all that I had achieved was a spirited session of gentle exercise. Everybody I got to see was serious and sympathetic, but nobody ever dared to tell me anything that had not been officially released. Many of the things I wanted to write about would have gone a long way toward helping Americans to a better understanding of how Russia operates. But when I asked anybody, each little bureaucrat had his own personal Iron Curtain which he pulled down in front of him and I was left staring at a blank wall. (Always excepting the doughty Mme. Petrova, who was generous, kind, open-minded and, apparently, fearless.)

When I sought some explanation of the fact that nobody would give out any information except that which had been officially released, I was told that invariably foreigners went home and wrote lies about Russia. But Russians won't let you find out the truth! It is also a fact that Russians hate like poison to admit that they are not first in everything. Unless they can show you beyond doubt that they are super-duper, they won't tell you anything at all, however trifling the matter may be.

My attempt to get an interview with the head of the "Cosmetic Trust" is a case in point. I wanted to write an article about Russian cosmetics and some of the ideas I wanted clarified by a person in authority were these: Did the Soviet Union have plans for entering world trade with Russian cosmetics? Had they any new ideas about cosmetics, any items that Americans do not have? How about Russian perfumes? (Since American women are always interested in anything labeled "Russian," I wondered whether the Soviets had any hope of getting us even more interested by sending us new perfumes or cosmetics.) Who decided on the names for their perfumes? Who had thought of "Red Moscow," "In Flight" and "Wait for Me"? What were their perfumes made of? Where did their essences come from? Whence "Red Poppy" and "Crimean Violet"? I thought perhaps American women would like to know.

And what went on? Our poor secretary nearly came unhinged, trying to get to anyone who would speak for the Cosmetic Trust. Finally, without further ado I descended upon the office with a translator in tow. They sent out a curt message to the effect that they had nothing whatever to tell Americans. (The impression I got was that the entire office force would like me to go jump in the Moscow River.) Now there was nothing about an interview on the subject of cosmetics which could endanger the security of the Soviet Union. But evidently such an interview would have endangered the security of the Cosmetic Trust, because they patently did not wish to be quoted at all.

The result was that I had to go to the Teje stores and buy samples of everything I wanted to describe (at very high prices), and not knowing the origin of the items, or whether or not they planned to make them better or different, I had to go ahead without any guidance from the people who knew. I could not help pondering on the reception that a Soviet newspaper reporter would have received at the hands of any of the cosmetic manufacturers of America. Such an inquirer would have been sent away with her ears ringing with miscellaneous information and bowlegged with samples into the bargain. Not in Moscow.

The Russians feel about bureaucracy just about the way we Americans do—frustrated, annoyed, hopeless and helpless. But the way Russians feel about their government and the way we Americans feel about ours are almost diametrically different. We Americans scream either, "There ought to be a law!" or "They can't do that to us! This is a democracy!" depending on whether we need a law to help us achieve our desires or have a law which prevents our getting them. We admit, reluctantly, that we have to have a government, but we want it to be flexible and adjustable and amenable. But not so in Russia.

Imagine a bowl into which has been dropped a large lump of magnetized metal. Imagine a handful of iron filings dropped into that bowl. That's Russia—the government and the people. The government has the power and the people cling to the government as naturally and inevitably as iron filings cling to a magnet.

Russians have explained to me that in Russia the government is regarded as the head of the national family. When the Czar was in power, he was the Little White Father and now they have just exchanged one father for another, who has their interests more at heart. (They hope!) The country at large used to be an enormous, ignorant, meek, underprivileged mass of serfs. In the old days they lived community lives, close-huddled and interdependent. Each serf looked to his own master for all decisions, including the most personal ones of his life: the right to work, the right to marry, almost the right to die. Each landowner had the power of life and death over his serfs, who regarded him as their father and the Czar as father of all. In this way life went on for thousands of years in a country whose antiquity and traditions make our young America look like a little yellow gosling peeping and cheeping around in the spring of the year.

The phrase you hear the oftenest from Russians to describe their lives under the Czars is "We were a dark people," meaning "We were lost in the darkness of ignorance." Doctor-Professor Paul Haensel, a gentleman of pre-Revolutionary days, has denied all the above flatly. He gave me the following information to refute it—I don't know who is right. All I know is that most Soviets now feel they are getting a better break than their parents did. But my friend of the old days says this:

"Do you know that in Czarist universities about half of all students belonged to the peasant and artisan class and that numerous scholarships existed?

"Do you know that for two hundred years a Russian married woman was independent in her property rights?

"Do you know that at the time of the military draft of 1913 only twenty-seven percent were illiterate?

"Do you know that no country in the world gave so much opportunity for women's education in higher learning as Czarist Russia? You say there was an 'enormous mass of ignorant serfs' [I said it, but the Russians in Moscow told me so]. The number of high-school students in Russia in 1910 was not substantially smaller than in the United States." Thus Doctor-Professor Paul Haensel, now of Williamsburg, Virginia, born in Moscow in 1878, graduate of Moscow Academy of Commerce (Gold Medal), Moscow Classical Gymnasium, Moscow University. Professor Haensel's other qualifications to comment correctly on conditions in Russia in Czarist days are far too long to list here. It is enough to say that he flings many of the Soviet statements back into the Soviet teeth and yields to no man in stating flatly that things were better under the Czars than they are at present under Mr. Stalin.

Chapter 5

The Beginning and the Belief

IT WAS A HANDFUL of intellectuals who planned and engineered the Russian Revolution. Intellectuals burning with the knowledge of the wrongs and sufferings of the people had made revolution an exact study, a science, a lifetime's work. The hope rose and fell, almost died out and revived again, until finally the light became concentrated in the eyes of the main leaders of the Revolution of 1905. Plans were drawn, decisions were made, schemes perfected and pigeonholed for future use by a small group of men whose lives were dedicated to the Revolution and the future of their country under the direction of the Revolutionaries. Only when the plans were finished and the staff work precisely and exquisitely completed was the mass of the people brought into the picture. Theirs was the final business of providing the strength and the force to overthrow the monarchy, as it is always the final business of the foot soldier to carry out the generals' plans. The Revolution came out of a book and came from above, not from below, although, of course, the time was ripe and the ground had been prepared. There were the Leaders and the Leaders led; and when the objective had been gained, the tyrants vanquished at great cost to the ragged, ill-armed, furiously determined people, the Leaders were right there with their planned organization to guide and direct the great, unleashed torrent of the masses.

There were few moments of indecision and bewilderment. True, there was a tumultuous interval when the idea of a coalition governmental between the Revolutionaries and the Liberals was entertained, hut the Leaders did not really waver.

Their iron hands never loosed their grip nor their cold brains the clear line of action. The people turned to these strong men with reliance and hope. Trotsky, furiously unwilling to cooperate along a new line of action, was swept ruthlessly aside and had to flee abroad where he was murdered. But Lenin, stately and cold in his tomb of red granite, still has his hands firm on the reins of government. Stalin—well, you know about Stalin, without my telling you, I guess. A few of the other original leaders are still at the helm. In the quarter century since the final victory, they have brought Russia, with bleeding feet, over a stony and thorny path into the place she holds today in world affairs.

Heads and hearts have been broken along the way. Dreadful purges have taken place and millions of innocent people have been (and are being) crushed beneath the giant machine as it passed along. Mistakes have been made, if you can use so mild a word for such terrible occurrences. Some of the original plans have been set aside for the moment and others less drastic and more expedient have been substituted. But by and large, the exact center of the original position has never shifted nor deviated much from the first blueprint. Let nobody think, comfortably, that the plan for world conquest has been abandoned. It flourishes, ever green and strong. During the period of mourning for Lenin, at the Second Congress of Soviets, Stalin made a solemn vow. He said, in part, "...Departing from us, Comrade Lenin adjured us to remain faithful to the principles of the Communist International. We vow to you, Comrade Lenin, that we will not spare our lives to strengthen and extend the union of the toilers of the whole world—the Communist International." And the people, bred for generations to the acceptance of paternalism and faced with the plain evidence of the success of much of the program, have bowed to the decisions from above and have marched along quietly under the iron yoke of the new authority.

Russia today is a country of the most abysmal kind of isolationism. It is blandly imperialistic, a cold-eyed giant, with possibilities for future greatness which would make your hair stand on end. Of course this has all been attained by the most dreadful kind of totalitarianism. Whether the results will be worth it is for the Russian people to judge. "What shall it profit a man if he gain the whole world and lose his own soul?" The people of the United States, I believe, would not wish to achieve *any* goal by such means.

The standard Party Line admonishes the people to beware of the ring of enemies around the Soviet Union. Russian newspapers, radio, magazine articles, lecturers constantly insist that the democratic or capitalistic world is solid against the Soviet Union. Eternal vigilance, they say, is the price the U.S.S.R. must pay for freedom. One of the members of the Politburo (the committee of fourteen who are the supreme leaders) said during the elections of 1946: "One must never forget that the weak are always attacked and insulted while the strong are feared and respected...One must remember that the U.S.S.R. is the center of capitalistic encirclement."

I got sick and tired of this never-ending campaign of warning and I said crossly to a Russian friend, "For heaven's sake, who's going to encircle you? Who could? Can't you people get it into your heads [I'm afraid I said *thick* heads] that other nations have plenty to do besides encircle you? America, for instance, has lots of things to do at home and all we want is just to be let alone to do them. Encirclement, indeed!" And I pointed to the map with its enormous expanse of Soviet territory—territory, I may add, that seems just a *little* bit bigger every day.

But even patriotic Russians get a little tired of being solemn. Sometimes flippancy will creep in. It was so just then. My friend's eyes twinkled. "Maybe so," said my friend, "but don't forget that not so long ago Finland encircled us. We distinctly heard her say *woof.*

"Yes," my friend continued more seriously, "what you say may be true. Perhaps there is no real desire on the part of America, at least, to attack us. But," with a sigh, "*our chief* is a stubborn old man."

Let me say here that I never heard a Russian call Stalin by name. Molotov, Kalinin, Malenkov, any of the others are called by name. But Stalin is always "The Chief," "A Certain Party," "The Big Boy," "The Old Man," or one of many other indirections. A funny thing, too, foreigners get the habit and come to do the same thing, speaking in a hushed tone. Foreigners call Stalin many things, among which are "Uncle Joe" and "Mr. Big."

The Russians don't seem to mind the lack of freedom of speech at all. "It will come," they say comfortably. "It is too early to relax restrictions. We Russians like to argue too well. We'd all be busy quarreling. Our way has been successful so far—centralization of power and no criticism of the government. Now, with the building half finished, is no time to begin to argue about the plans of the architects."

A visiting Englishman who was an honored guest at Mrs. Atkinson's Hot Plate Grill made a remark which I have considered thoughtfully many times since. This gentleman has had many opportunities to observe and study the Russians. He has made many long, extended visits to the country, some of them before the present government was in power and many times since. He is a deep student of Russian history and speaks the language fluently. He said, "The basis for all this is simple. The Russians are not a freedom-loving people."

One of the favorite slogans of the government is "Overtake and surpass!" Meaning overtake and surpass America, of course, since no other country has so high a standard of living or flings such a challenge to the Soviet leaders in matters of art, science and plumbing. People are exhorted daily to overtake and surpass and at the same time they are being assured that they are already preeminent in all fields of endeavor. So nobody looks at the holes in his socks—if he has any socks. He raises his eyes to the brilliant red banners flying overhead and feels ashamed for being momentarily sidetracked by petty grievances.

I never met a Russian who really doubted the wisdom of the men at the head of their government nor their purity of motive nor their ultimate success. I never met an American with any knowledge of Russian politics who thought that the headmen of the Russian government were crooked. Whatever they may feel about the Soviet system, I think that informed Americans believe that the Politburo is doing whatever it *is* doing for the ultimate good of all the people. If it doesn't kill them all off first, they are going to feel fine after it's all over. True, I have heard some Russians remark rather wistfully that life could be easier, and wish that some of the luxuries of the outside world could somehow find their way into Russian everyday living. But most of these remarks have been made apologetically as if the speaker realized that he was a frivolous weakling.

Every Russian I met lived in the future. A leaking pipe, a hole in the roof, failure of the gas or electricity supply, shortage of fuel, lack of a varied diet or any of the thousand irritations of everyday living were blamed squarely on the war and endured cheerfully because everybody was convinced that these irritations were only temporary.

Russia fought and sacrificed and suffered in a way that few Americans can even begin to imagine. She never wavered and her boundless courage and determination not only overcame her enemies but also welded her together with bonds of steel. Yet once again I must remind you that it was all achieved by methods which no American could long endure. A totalitarianism that would cause Americans to rise en masse and pull the tyrants from their thrones.

If I were asked to suggest a theme song for Soviet Russia, I could not think of a better one than a few lines from "Old Man River":

> *"Bend your knees an' bow yo' head,*
> *an' pull dat rope until yo're dead."**

Most of the Russians accept this state of affairs with very good grace. "They are a toff people."

Chapter 6

The Printed Word

RUSSIANS THINK many things about Americans are funny. Not only our insistence on freedom of speech, put our definition of "freedom of the press" strikes them as rather comic. The definition of "free press" means to an American that any newspaper or magazine may print anything it chooses, with no governmental control at all. "Free press" in Russia means that the press "belongs to the people." The people own the paper and the machinery the way we own the Capitol at Washington or the art galleries. But the Russian government and Communist Party edit and publish the magazines and newspapers and this makes the Soviet press the most rigidly controlled press in the world.

When reading an item in a Russian newspaper, you learn to get a double image. One, what is printed; two, *why* it has been printed. For example, if a tiny item appears that a certain apartment-house manager is remiss in his duties, everybody smiles, and says, "It has already gone hard with him," or "He is moving toward the back of the sleigh," meaning that he will soon be thrown to the wolves. The newspapers never criticize government policy, only the way the policy is *carried out by the bureaucrats*. The real leaders of the government, the Politburo, are never the subject of "personality" stories, which lends them a certain unassailable dignity and remoteness even if removing them from the healthy curiosity of the masses. Through their newspapers the Russians get no timely information at all. After a situation is clarified, settled and finished, they get a nice, cold, government-sponsored statement which, however biased and slanted, is easy to digest and remember. They are without doubt the worst informed great nation.

We Americans not only get a blow-by-blow account by radio and newspapers of everything that is happening anywhere in the world; we often get a good snootful *before* it happens. And we go into hysterics and say, "If such-and-such happens, we are doomed as sure as God makes little apples." And when it doesn't happen, we are off on some other hysterical chase up another alley. The American radio pounds away with its commentators and the American papers print and print, until a body doesn't know where he is half the time. I don't mean for a moment to say that I do not believe that we should be well informed. I just mean we don't need to be so well informed so *often*. The Russians, on the other hand, never hear about anything until it is all over and the Boys have had a chance to sift it and screen it and serve it to them in a nice, government-digested slab several days after whatever it was happened. But we Americans go very fast and the Russians go very slow. Americans believe everything and Russians don't believe anything. It reminds me of trying to get along with a small child. You either shriek at him, "Hurry up, can't you?" or you say, "For goodness' sake, keep still, will you?"

Americans get a lot of fun out of the editorial style of the Moscow papers. They adopt some of the more telling phrases and work them into their everyday conversation with colorful effect. A newcomer to the little journalistic circle in the Metropole Hotel might easily be somewhat startled to hear the conversation between two American newspapermen who meet casually in the hall. These men are known to be friends and yet the conversation might be like this:

"Hello, you Fascist beast, what revolting vomit of lies are you planning to spew out to the capitalist-controlled press today?" To which the other might reply mildly, "Your filthy mind seems to be possessed by crawling rodents. These pass for ideas but are implanted there by the slimy monsters whose chief interest in life is deception of the masses." They salute and pass on smiling. And it's no exaggeration. These very words appear nearly every day in editorials in Moscow newspapers. It's supposed to be forceful. But an experienced reader can pick his way among the more odorous adjectives skillfully and can emerge with a nugget of news which he carefully analyzes. And you would be surprised how often he comes to a conclusion not intended by the rampant editors. Sometimes the reader *really* smells a rat.

However, if there are labor disturbances in the United States, unemployment or bad housing conditions, the Soviet press does not think it necessary to withhold these tidbits from the Russian readers. Such items are always printed with relish in full. There was one item about the statement that a New York bank had made. The bank was alleged to have said that monopoly capital was making the workers of the United States pay for reconversion from war production to peacetime industry. Upon investigation in this country, that bank issued a flat statement to the effect that no such comment had ever gone out from it and it was at a loss to understand where such a news item had its source. One seldom sees a friendly news item about the United States. The unfriendly ones are too numerous to mention.

As an example of how blandly the news can be guided, take the instance of the way Russia and Argentina relations were reported. Russia, you will remember, stood out against the admittance of Argentina into the United Nations at the San Francisco Conference. We, on the other hand, insisted upon her admittance. Russia finally reluctantly agreed. But for a long time the Russian newspapers continued to foam and froth about Argentina. Eventually, they began to drop Argentina and the emphasis was put on Franco Spain. Conditions in Argentina did not change and when the United States began to object to the Nazi activities there as Russia had been doing a few months before, nothing ever appeared in the Russian newspapers about the strained relations between the United States and Argentina. Finally, agreements were made between Russia and Argentina, and Argentina was accorded full diplomatic and economic standing with the U.S.S.R.

I was discussing this about-face with a Russian and he looked at me in surprise. "Have you forgotten," he asked, "that *we* were the ones who objected to Argentina's membership in U.N.? *You* insisted on it. Since she is now a member, naturally we trade with her."

Two days after the first atom bomb was dropped, an accurate statement appeared in *Pravda* (Truth), one of the leading Moscow newspapers. But before *Pravda* burst into print the news flashed around Moscow like wildfire. Everybody was fascinated, incredulous and alarmed. People were torn between the wild hope that it would put an end to the war and uneasy conjectures as to what else might be done with so fearful a weapon. For a long time after the original statement in *Pravda*, there was no other mention of the bomb, only guarded references to the effect that it was Russia's entry into the war that cracked Japan—not the atom bomb.

The magazine *Krokodil* appeared with a cover representing a Red Army soldier with his foot planted on the writhing and decapitated body of the Japanese dragon. The next stage was reached when the term "Atomic Diplomacy" came to be applied by the newspapers to Byrnes's attitude on the First London Conference. Meaning, of course, that America, now feeling that she had the whip hand in world affairs because of the bomb, was pushing her advantage to the full. On November 5, 1945, in a "state of the union" speech, Molotov said to high-ranking Party members that among other things Russia was going to have in the near future was "atomic energy"! This statement was greeted with prolonged and spontaneous applause.

News items appeared in the winter of 1946 to the effect that "Stalin" prizes had been awarded to two scientists for work in uranium fission. In August 1945 one of the papers published a statement by another Russian scientist that he was much surprised to learn of America's use of the bomb since he had always supposed that the Russians were farther advanced in the knowledge of atomic energy than anybody else.

Of course nobody but the people immediately involved can know how much the Russians know about uranium fission or atomic energy. Russians would not permit outsiders to inspect their progress in that connection any more than we would. But foreigners who understand the Russian way of doing business feel that the Russians would cheerfully receive any information we would give them along those lines and what they would give back you could put in your eye.

Most informed foreigners think that it is extremely doubtful whether the Russians have either the number of skilled technicians or the factories and the mechanical equipment necessary for the manufacture of the atomic bomb. It is here that German scientists and technicians will be of rare use to the Soviet Union. Among the thousands of German prisoners now detained by the Russians, there are undoubtedly many highly skilled men. Surely they are not going to be put at manual labor.

I heard some amusing comments on the atomic bomb as well as serious ones. A young Russian messenger who had been sent to my room with a note, when bidden to enter, came in with mock timidity and said with a grimace, "No atom bombs, please!" But in general the news made a terrific impression, scarcely less, I think, than it must have made here at home.

It was during this period that an American officer in Moscow asked a Red Army officer whether he knew about the atom bomb. The Red Army officer said that there had been lectures in the Red Army on the subject and much discussion. "But," he added definitely, "even so, even if you have such a bomb, we will never get out of Manchuria."

When General Eisenhower was in Moscow, he gave a press conference for Russian and foreign press correspondents. He said, among other things, that we have no censorship of the press in the U.S.A. The conference was reported in full to the Russian newspapers but the statement about the free press was not mentioned. (Incidentally, when General Eisenhower appeared on the grandstand in the Red Square on the day of the Sports parade, the only applause he got was from Americans and other foreigners. None of the Russians seemed to know who he was.)

One notable exception to censorship, the only one I heard of there, a Russian-language newspaper published weekly by the British. It is called *British Ally*. This never goes to the censor at all. But it might just as well. The Britishers are so nervous over what goes into the paper, and so jealous of its reputation of being above reproach as far as censorship goes, that they nearly get heart attacks over their own copy and probably are just as severe with it as the censor would be. They have a Russian "editor" who is responsible, in the last analysis, to the censor, so perhaps it all amounts to the same thing.

On the other hand, the Russian-language magazine *Amerika*, published by the Americans, must be submitted to the censor. This magazine is a beautiful job, got out by the United States Information Service in Moscow and published in the U.S.A. It is a super *Fortune* with marvelous colored photographs of many different aspects of American life. The sky line of New York at night; the Grand Canyon at sunset; ranches of the West under the brilliant light of the afternoon sun are some of the subjects they have used for the colored pictures. And the colored photographs they have of the interior of factories would make you want to move out of your comfortable apartment and eat right straight off the floor of those glorious places. They sure put an edge on things and, of course, it's all true as gospel, but somehow Hollywood-true. Nevertheless, the magazine *Amerika* is considered more precious than much fine gold by many of the people of Moscow. It has only recently been allowed on a newsstand—that of the National Hotel. Heretofore, it was not for sale to Russians, but members of the American colony handed it out freely to all Russian servants and acquaintances. At first a circulation of twenty thousand was permitted but this has recently been increased to fifty thousand.

Unavoidable hindrances in its production and delivery have prevented the magazine from being as effective as it should have been, but even so its spasmodic appearance was always eagerly awaited by Russians who knew about it. The staff of waiters and chambermaids in the Metropole, to say nothing of clerks, couriers and secretaries, used to simply drool over the magazine and use every wile and smile to get one of them. I have heard it said that once they had read it themselves, they had no trouble getting one hundred rubles for it in the bazaar. It is an extremely attractive piece of propaganda and long may it wave.

There is immense curiosity about everything American. American movies (the few carefully selected ones that are shown) are always a sellout. American books (also preinspected and passed upon) are eagerly read. American magazines (obtainable only from American residents) are passed from hand to hand until they fall apart. While I was in Moscow, a Russian girl who worked in the American Embassy got hold of a copy of *Life* magazine and took it home with her on the subway. She was arrested for having it but let off with a reprimand. She was told not to take such literature home again. If it was part of her *duty* to read it in the Embassy, she should do so *in* the Embassy and never carry it away from the premises.

Winston Churchill's son Randolph visited Moscow during the winter of 1946 and the Moscovites were not pleased with him, nor his subsequently published articles based on his visit. The magazine *Krokodil* published the following article on his departure:

Schredin' s stories about famous travelers who studied our country has now been augmented by a new work. But before presenting this new work, let us remind our readers of the previous works by Schredin, called "Pompadours and Pompadouresses."

1——"Travellers and Art Impressions," by Count de la Cassonaaade, formerly Master of the Hounds to His Majesty Saluk I, but now, to the vicissitudes of fortune, Chief Garcon in the Cafe Riche, Paris.

2——"A Sad Story," Reminiscences of Travels in Northern Countris, written by Onisim Shepanan, former political detective who served under Monsiegnier Mop, Prefet of Police.

3——"How We Took Yamutski, Prinse Izdelin-Musafer-Mirza Rusha." Wrote down from reel facts by Habibull Naumatollovici, teecher of Prinses and former servant in the Bellevue Hotel (In Petersburk, on the Nevski, opposite the theyater. Dinners from 2 to o'clock at 1 and 2 rubles also a la carte. Suppers, Breakfasts) Published by the Society for Prevention of Cruelty to Animals."

To these wonderful works of art, solving the riddle of the Soul, must now be added the notes of a certain Englishman famous traveller in our country.

"I drank, I nibbled a bit on hors d'ouvres and canapes and I studied" by John Alcoholic, Member of the Respectable Tetotalers, London.

We will limit ourselves to a few excerpts from this diary of talented writer. They demonstrate his powers of observation, also his remarkable ability to swallow spirits.

"Nov. 2, 1945—Uncle said: 'Enough of your idling around here. Do something. Fly to Russia and study the manners of the Russians.' Well, if it's fly, we'll fly, as my pal Willie says when the lackies haul him out of the club by the arms.

"Nov. 3—What a warm send-off my pals gave me! We sang, 'There is a tavern in the town,' and 'Good-bye Dolly, I must leave you.' Don't remember how I got in the plane. Don't remember how we flew. Everything was in a fog.

"Nov. 5—Woke up in my old friend Mr. P's flat (secret!). Wanted to take a look at Moscow, but I couldn't refuse the invitation of American friends. Wonderful iced Martinis! We then went for drive around the Moscow streets—everything was in a fog. I said 'Just like dear old London.' All they did was laugh. Fogs bring allies nearer. (That's a good line.)

"Nov. 6—Cocktail party at Mons. Chas. G's. (diplomatic secret). Heard that things are miserable in Russia. No night clubs, no gambling dens—what a backward country!

"Nov. 10—Have been studying a drink called 'Vodka' for the last three days. Found out there are two ways of taking it. First—a bite of bread) ; drink; bite, drink. Second—drink, bite, drink, bite.... Discovered a remarkable phenomenon in

Russian scenery. It swings. It heaves. Everything heaves, houses, streets, people. I heaved myself, being unused to this state of affairs. Yes, the Russian character lacks firmness. It heaves and that is a threat to Europe.

"Nov. 12—Studied Russian fishing methods in the house of my old friend, the Attache (secret, secret, secret). He is an expert on customs of the country. We had some salmon and after eating it, he said, 'Fish like to swim.' So we had a drink. Then he made me acquainted with the ruff (a small fish of the perch family, he said). Amazing! We call a drink a cocktail, and the Russians call it 'Hersh' (Little Fish).... After this, I went home and I finally solved the Russian problems: The Russians double everything! For instance, a man walks along the street and suddenly there are two of him! In view of such ability on the part of the Russians to double, the Russians present a profound danger to Western civilization.

Nov. 13—After a wonderful reception at Mr. N's (now just guess who!) I decided to take a walk and make closer acquaintance with the Russian people. Although the streets were heaving and enveloped in dense fog, I managed to reach the crossing. I was very pleased with myself and started to sing 'It's a Long Way to Tipperary.' But a policeman said to me, 'Mister, you're not allowed to disturb the peace in our country, so just stop it.' Oh, poor Russians! My heart contracted with pain. How on earth can one live in such a country! Where there are no night clubs, no freedom to engage in street rows by distinguished young men! Poor Russia! Now I know Russia!

"Nov. 16—I remember how in Russia in the cozy drawing room of Miss——let's call her Miss T——we exchanged our impressions of Russia! How, after this I came to myself in London, I really cannot remember. All fog! To work! To work! The British public must know what the Russians are!"

Pyetr Zudoteshin

Chapter 7

A Lifesaving Engineer

WHEN WE WERE FLYING to Russia, we met an American engineer who was also "going in" to Moscow. His name was Gilbert Formel, and he had been over in the Soviet Union working for the American firm of Badger and Company on some kind of oil-refinery business for more than three years. He was over six feet tall, broad and self-possessed, and he knew the ropes of Russia and could speak the language.

He was a rock in a weary land and, to scramble a figure of speech, he took us in tow; and even after we got to Moscow and were settled in the Metropole, he was guide, mentor and friend. Our first meeting with him was typical of our future relationship. The plane had come down for refueling in Astrakhan. The broad, flat, muddy field was about as cheerless a place as you can imagine, and at the far end stood an unlovely, shoddy, shack-like building which was pointed out as the rest house. We were feeling pretty low anyhow. We had no Russian money yet, nor any knowledge of the language, nor ideas of how things were organized in Russia. We certainly were strangers in a strange land and hungry and tired besides.

We plodded across the field grumpily and entered a tiny room in which were two shaky, lopsided tables and a crowd of assorted Russians. Nobody paid any attention to us. Everybody was wolfing tomatoes. We couldn't imagine why everybody had ordered tomatoes to eat, but evidently everybody had, and they were all eating them out of their hands with the greatest enthusiasm. (We found out later that tomatoes were a great rarity in that land.)

One table was occupied by a Russian officer who sat grandly alone, viewing the scene with what dignity he could, considering the fact that tomato juice was trickling down his chin. At the other table sat a great, big, clean man, with a Stetson hat, a white shirt open at the neck, a pair of spotless khaki breeches, an enormous pair of well-shined tan shoes, and a look of amiability and boredom on his face.

When he saw us, rumpled, bewildered, fatigued and annoyed as we were, he rose to his enormous height, put out a hand like a ham and said with a gentle boom, "I am Gilbert Formel."

At that moment the sun came from behind a cloud.

With my usual delicacy, I opened the conversation. (My husband had already grasped the outstretched hand as though it were a floating spar on an angry sea.) "*If* you are an American," I said. Wasn't that silly? What else could he have been? "*If* you are an American," I repeated, "lend us some money."

Mr. Formel detached his hand from my husband's with some difficulty, reached into his pocket and brought forth a roll of strange looking money almost as big as his great big hand. He started peeling off bills and throwing them on the table. "How much you want?" he said without surprise.

And that wasn't all. Without asking a single question, he sat us down at his table and got hot tea for us from the Russian biddy who was scurrying around with mad haste. She had been running in and out of what was probably a kitchen at the rate of one round trip every thirty seconds, and yet nobody seemed to get waited on. Mr. Formel put a stop to all that. Gently, strongly, he suggested that she put on the brakes and listen to him. She did. And she emerged smiling with two glasses of hot, colored water no more than half an hour later. It was a miracle.

Mr. Formel shepherded us back to the plane, after paying for our tea and stuffing some money into my husband's pocket. He still didn't know our names. He settled us there and, after we took off, he opened a duffel bag and took out a bundle wrapped in a clean white cloth. He also took out a bottle which contained water, and a clean tin cup. "The water has been boiled and there are tablets in it," he said. (I never can remember to do things like that.)

He then unrolled the bundle and produced a fine big bologna, loaf of white bread, some butter and a number of other toothsome things the exact nature of which I have now forgotten. He served us as honored guests and we sat in the plane and munched with tearful enjoyment. After neatly stowing away the remains, he engaged my husband in conversation and I went to sleep. I slept like a newborn babe. Mr. Gilbert Formel, American, sent by God, was in control.

When I awakened, I was able to look around with some degree of enthusiasm. It was short-lived. True, the planeful of Russians was of engrossing interest. The plane was stuffed to the gunwales, or whatever the sides of a plane are called. The baggage, of which there were mountains, was thrown helter-skelter in the center, wherever a human being did not need the room. There were Russia officers and Russian privates, sitting on the bucket seats. There was one old, old peasant couple, great-great-grandparents by the looks of them, who could never have been in a plane before, probably never even on a train. They sat mouse-still, huddled closely together, giving no evidence of pleasure or of pain. They just sat.

There was a young mother feeding her child. It was the first time I had ever seen a Russian bosom and my introduction to it startled me. I could hardly believe the evidence of my eyes, but the evidence was there for all to see. That child would never starve. And forward, just behind the pilot's enclosure, were four snappy young Russian Air Force men.

The gasoline tanks in that plane were inside the open cabin, just behind the pilot's compartment. They were separated by a plank walk for the pilot's use. These snappy young men were sitting between the gas tanks on the plank. The tanks were leaking slightly, and the youths were airily smoking cigarettes to pass the time away.

When my horrified eyes fell upon this sight, my mouth went open and my eyes popped and my heart skipped several beats. The loading of the plane had caused me enough alarm—people piled in anyhow, luggage not tied down, smoking permitted before the plane got into the air—but this was a little too much. I could feel myself turning green. I looked at my husband. He was as green as I was. I looked at Mr. Formel. He was a healthy pink. I looked again at the smokers, who, seeing my frightened eyes, began to show off. They flicked their ashes and sparks over the gas tanks, with a swashbuckling air. They smiled at one another and then simultaneously burst into a roar of laughter. I wanted down—and out.

Mr. Formel smiled like a cherub. "It is always like that," he said and reached into his pocket and brought out a package of American cigarettes. "We might as well all go to hell together," he said quietly. So, with shaking hands, I lighted up, my husband produced his seldom-absent pipe, Mr. Formel exhaled a great cloud of smoke and on we went toward Moscow.

Nothing happened. It was good for me, I suppose, to get my introduction into Russian methods so soon. It more or less prepared my mind for anything that might happen thereafter. Mr. Formel attended to our getting transportation to the hotel, and although he was there for less than a week after our arrival, he introduced me to many of the stony roads my poor feet had to tread.

For one thing, he took me to the bazaar. Many times afterward when I was in the vortex of the milling mobs in that bazaar, I remembered with a sigh my first trip there with Gilbert Formel running interference for me. When we emerged, that first time, with my suit almost torn off my back, my hair streaming over my forehead and my feet throbbing from the pounding they had received at the soles of other people, he roared a great bellow of laughter. He didn't look so hot himself. He was pretty beat up, and he was carrying a small newspaper cornucopia of raspberries which had already begun to drip a small determined stream of red juice.

"By golly," he roared, "you can take it! If my wife ever got even one whiff of this place, she'd have to be taken home in the ambulance. She wouldn't stand for it for a minute."

I never could make up my mind whether I had been complimented or insulted, but at that moment I was in no condition to argue.

These things I mention are only a few of the kindnesses which Mr. Formel did for us. His crowning effort was the day he left. He came to our room with a small newspaper-wrapped package and handed it to me gravely. "You may not feel that you wish to accept precious gifts from a comparative stranger," he said, "but nevertheless, I want you to have this as a slight token of my esteem. You will understand the value of this long after I am gone from here."

I opened the package in some wonder. Perhaps it was a necklace from the hinterland where he had been, or a piece of the Russian sable that everybody in the world has heard about. But no. It was an empty pint glass jar with a tight brass screw top. And it was no joke, either. They are as scarce as auk's teeth, those jars, and this one was a blessing for many a long month.

Hail, Mr. Gilbert Formel! A man who knows his onions, a gentleman and, from all I hear, an engineer.

P.S. We paid him back the money as soon as we got rubles.

Chapter 8

The Metropole Hotel

THERE ARE THREE HOTELS where foreigners may stay in Moscow: the National, the Savoy and the Metropole. There is a pretty bitter feud on among the foreign residents of these hostelries as to which is the worst, each group claiming the palm for the one they reside in. Many and marvelous are the tales of the quaint goings-on in these places, but since I lived ten months in the Metropole, I feel fully competent to state that so far I have received no proof that our hotel was not the most peculiar in the capital city. Now this may seem to some people a very broad statement. But anyone who has ever lived in the Metropole will agree that its atmosphere is unique. This atmosphere is composed in about equal parts of stale air, old plumbing smells, assorted whiffs of cooking and ancient dampness, to which is added a strange and rather spooky emanation that comes out from the walls like ectoplasm. No. I stand firm. The Metropole should be given the booby prize without further quibbling.

I have been told that fifty years ago the Metropole Hotel was one of the finest in Europe, and if you stand back and look the old wreck over, and are fair-minded about what you see, you will be able to understand how this might have been so. I would like very much to be able to describe the plan of the Metropole to you, for I found it fascinating. Unfortunately, I was never able to figure it out. After ten months in the place, with daily excursions into the rooms of friends situated on various floors, I still felt that I needed a Seeing Eye dog to get me to my destination and back again. Just when you think you are at the end of a corridor, another hall juts off at an

angle and disappears in shadows a long distance off. At the
end of this passage, if you persist and try to continue on your
misguided way, you may find a door opening on a little iron
bridge which spans a yawning chasm and comes up against
a blank brick wall. This may startle you—but it shouldn't and
it won't after a while. Just try to retrace your steps now. You
will have forgotten whence you came and may continue to
wander shakily around for half an hour before you arrive at
familiar landmarks again. The strange old building stretches
its tentacles in all directions like a dying octopus, and the
story goes that there are many forgotten rooms in the place
where members of the Czar's court still sit playing bezique,
with their crowns on their heads, completely unaware that
there has been a change in government.

To begin at the front door. Go in the revolving door and
up the broad marble steps into the lobby. Pay no attention
to the two bronze dogs which flank this stairway—although
they are as big as cows, and look like a cross between
snarling lion's and tortured apes, they are only the first of
many things which may surprise you. The lobby itself is dimly
lighted, furnished with rubbery-looking old black furniture
and floored with dingy white marble. The odd assortment of
gentlemen in caps who sit brooding around this lobby all day
and all night are not sinister characters out of a Hitchcock
movie. They only look sinister—in fact, that is probably what
they are paid to do—look sinister. I don't know what they do
other than that, but you can safely ignore them.

To the far right of the lobby as you enter, past the
newsstand where you can buy picture post cards, pamphlets
of political significance in English, French, German and
Russian, Russian newspapers and magazines, you come to
the Intourist Bureau. I wish I might honestly tell you that
you need never come to the Intourist Bureau, but it goes with
being a foreigner in Moscow. When you open the plateglass
door to enter this long and mournful room, do not start back
thinking you have entered an old-fashioned funeral parlor by
mistake. The atmosphere of gloom and shadow is what the
Russians consider refinement. Go on in. Nobody will pay any
attention to you. Each person in the place is hoping against
hope that somebody else will take the responsibility of finding
out what the devil you want there.

The Intourist Bureau has been established by the
government to welcome visitors and to help them arrange
their affairs. That's what you will be told. My personal

opinion is that Intourist has been established to harass and embarrass foreigners and to inspire them to go home as soon as possible. It is a bemused and befuddled organization. I think that the manager, at least, had to take a long stiff course in Harassment and Embarrassment of Foreigners. I consider him worthy of a master's degree.

When we were in Moscow, the man in charge of Intourist in the Metropole was a small, sad man like Caspar Milquetoast and the White Rabbit combined. When you enter the office, you will see his desk at the far end of the shadowy room, well flanked and guarded by the desks of the other Intourist people. Nobody greets you. Nobody advances, smiling, and asks you to sit down. You can fairly hear the atmosphere sag with despair as though everybody present were saying to himself: "O God, *another* one!" Everybody immediately engages himself in a telephone conversation, in Russian naturally, that leaves you standing miserably first on one foot and then on the other in bewildered embarrassment.

Now in any organization it is perfectly natural that the personality of the headman be reflected down through the rest of the group, and in Russia this is trebly so. Nobody in Intourist dares to be cheerful or cordial. The young girls in the office are very pretty and they speak English, not fluently but well enough. After I got to know them, they were amiability itself, and when I met them off duty in the halls, we laughed and chatted together without restraint. Once one of them even helped me to play a practical joke on a friend—but not while she was on duty in the office. No, they take their pattern from the boss, who, if given an American aptitude test, would be found eminently qualified to be bookkeeper in a monastery. He should not be required to speak to strangers. He's not geared for it.

We squabbled with him daily over his having rented to somebody else rooms that had been reserved for us and paid for in advance. It wasn't really his fault, I suppose, what with the pressure of the housing shortage, but he was supposed to be responsible, and there was nobody else to go to. I feared for his heart whenever we approached him and I really suffered with him when he tried to think up a new excuse about not giving us a decent room. Still we were living in something equivalent to a coalhole and we felt justified complaining.

The service you will get from the Intourist will leave you puzzled and frustrated. As a rule, they know very little about anything you ask them and they make no effort to find out. They will get you a guide, usually an excellent one, and arrange tours of the city and under extreme pressure they may produce a car for a private excursion, but other than that. don't hope for much. (There are no taxis or conveyances to be hired on the streets.)

I called Intourist on the phone one day and asked them to tell me the name of the movie that was showing at the Metropole Theatre—a movie theatre in the same building. They told me that they didn't know. I asked them whether they would find out and let me know. They said they would call me back. I'm still waiting. I asked one of the girls to tell me how to go about having a blouse made at a State Atelier. She said the best thing to do was to ask an American friend. I did and found out that there was a dressmaking shop within two blocks of the hotel. I had heard about an old seventeenth-century house called the House of the Boyar, which has been preserved as a perfect example of the home of a Russian nobleman of that time. Intourist showed it to me on the map and I made my way through the strange streets to that location. The little museum had been closed for many months and was still not open to the public.

These are a few examples of Intourist Service and although I could continue indefinitely, I think the three will serve.

The little rickety elevators are located at the rear of the lobby, with the stairs winding around them, but before you go upstairs, take a look at the old dining room at the left of the lobby. It is easy to see how once this might have been the setting for much gaiety and elaborate entertaining. But now it has the atmosphere of an aquarium. The room is of noble proportions, rising three or four stories and roofed over with a great glass dome. The light that filters down has a shimmering aquamarine quality that makes you think somehow of fish. It must have had the same effect on the architect, because he had a little fountain made in the middle of the floor and the basin of it was formerly used as a fishpool.

When we were there in 1936, it was so used, and you could go to the pool and pick out a fish and the waiter would catch it with a net and the chef would cook it for you and it was all very special. At least that was the theory. In practice it did not work flawlessly. Albert Hirschfeld, our friend and fellow sufferer, was there at the same time we were and, being an incurable romantic, he decided that this fish business was for him. So he picked out a likely-looking specimen and the waiter netted it and disappeared into the kitchen with his wriggling prey. Al settled back expansively to await a tasty tidbit of fresh fish while we more benighted and less imaginative folks nibbled black bread and bologna. He waited and nothing happened. He began on the black bread and bologna himself. He inquired from hour to hour what had become of his fish or, indeed, of the waiter, but nobody paid any attention. He began to get wild.

"The hell with that particular fish!" he screamed. "Any fish will do—any food will do. Just give me something to eat and let me out of here." By this time we had cracked down on him and refused to share any more food with him. It's every man for himself in Moscow.

Al began running around the fountain, hysterically trying to catch himself another fish with another net. But he must have been weak from hunger because he couldn't get the slippery creatures, and by and by the management put him out for being uncultured and abusive.

The next night we saw the same fish that Al had chosen back in the pool. We decided that the fish was the Charter Member of the fountain gang and the Russians never had any intention of having Charter Member fried for anybody.

The dining room was not open to the public except on a few rare occasions when we were there in 1945, but I peeked in several times whenever I wanted to feel even more melancholy than I did at the moment. It always had the desired effect. But once when I was there, I was with an elderly Russian who remembered the palmy days. He waved his hand at the roof, at the chandeliers, at the rows of windows that line the side walls. "In the old days the merchant princes used to entertain here," he said, "and there was music and light and much laughter and gaiety...."

"And food," he added sadly.

"And all those windows that seem from upstairs to be just windows opening into a court—ah, Madame, those were the windows of little private dining rooms. One could see out, could hear the music—but one had privacy, you understand?" He sighed. "Ballerinas," he said, "beautiful women in Paris gowns—perfume, furs, lackies in velvet costumes.... And food."

Decidedly, they had been the Good Old Days. I never felt quite so bitter about the nasty old dining room again. And whenever I went into one of the small dark little bedrooms that opened on that court, I remembered what I had been

told. Nowadays they are inhabited almost exclusively by Russians—and very glad they are to get those tiny, grim little rooms. One such room that I was in several times, and which is about as big as a "hall bedroom," was the residence of a man, his wife and three children. It had two beds, a crib, a table, dishes and pots and pans, two chairs, a stove, a sewing machine, a wardrobe, a screen and two or three trunks in it. The window opened on the old dining room and if you looked down you could see the quiet and dusty little fountain below on the grimy marble floor.

I told an elderly Russian lady what I had heard about the Metropole's better days and she denied the whole thing. "It was a good hotel, I suppose," she said, "but no member of the aristocracy would have patronized it. It was used entirely by commercial people—merchants, traveling salesmen—such people. And it was always full of questionable women and outrageous parties! No lady would have been seen here!"

Nowadays the best rooms upstairs vary from one another in glory. Some are airy and spacious and have wonderful views out over Sverdlov Square and to the Kremlin beyond. From many of the rooms you can get a good view of the old "Chinese wall," part of which still stands. I have heard various explanations for the existence of this wall. It was, some say, the second of the circular walls which were built around the expanding bulk of ancient Moscow and surrounded the camping place of the merchants and traders who came from afar to buy and sell in the city. I have been told that this settlement was known as "Chinatown" because so many foreigners, including some Chinese, were huddled there in makeshift shacks which finally became solid residences. But other people have told me that the word "Chinatown" is a mistake in translation and should be taken to mean "fortress" since the word in Russian is "*Kitai-Gorod*." "*Kitai*" can mean either "China" or "bastion," so take your choice as to where the truth lies. Everybody calls it the Chinese wall anyhow, and nobody denies for a moment that it is as old as the hills. And nearly anybody who has a view of the old brick wall from the windows of the Metropole will be set to dreaming about its probable significance and its ancient story.

Some of the other rooms allotted to foreigners face on an inner court. (These rooms are not the darkest ones—*they* open on the old dining hall.) They are midway between the stuffy little hall bedrooms assigned to the Russians and the good rooms that important foreigners manage to get by screaming like wounded tigers. The back rooms are grimy in outlook and gloomy in atmosphere, but they have their attractive features just the same. You never get to know the intimate life of the hotel so well from the front rooms. The court has a life of its own. In the evenings, for instance, it is in the court that solicitous friends or bored waiters take the drunken Red Army officers to run off their jags. Of course there are only one or two things that any human being can do to relieve himself of a jag, and naturally, these gentlemen have to do all of them. But it would be boorish to begrudge a merrymaker a breath of fresh air and space enough to regain his composure, so after a while you don't pay attention any more.

In the daytime, if your room faces on the court, you have ample opportunity to study labor conditions in Moscow. It took me straight back to the W.P.A. days, when America was howling about a "generation of shovel-leaners." The average manual laborer in Moscow makes our "shovel-leaner" look like a busy little bee.

There was one "work" gang that came there for several days when we were unhappily sojourning on the court, and it was a soporific to watch them. The gang consisted of two workmen and a workwoman and the men arranged everything neatly so the woman did all the work. But don't feel sorry for her. She had plenty of rest periods. For three-quarters of an hour at a time she sat with her hands hanging out of her sleeves, gazing at the ground between her knees, silent and perhaps in meditation. The men had more animation. They smoked and talked and whammed each other on the back and relaxed nicely. But they never spoke to the woman except when work became imminent. Then they gave her the big smile and kindly tied knots arranged ropes and sat back to observe critically whether she was really putting her back into the job. Sometimes they stopped her as she was lifting a heavy load of bricks or lumber and pointed out to her kindly how stupidly she was handling the affair. They rearranged her load for her and slapped her playfully on the haunches as they started her on her way. They were very cheerful and pleasant to her, as far as I could see, and let her understand that although there was no use denying that she was a complete fool, still they really had no hard feelings about her helping them.

The last time I watched their cooperative efforts nearly sent me screaming to the madhouse. There were three or four large sheets of galvanized metal on the ground in the court. The project was to send this metal up to the roof, five stories above. From the roof projected a rickety plank, attached, I don't know how, to the roof itself. From this plank, by pulley arrangement, two frayed and knotted ropes descended to the court. Here they were wound around a tiny drum by means of a small iron handle. One of the men gave the free rope a turn or two around the bundle of metal sheets, tying it with a nonchalant knot.

The woman was given the task of drawing the burden to the roof. Bending nearly double to reach the low handle on the little drum, she began winding away, slowly and laboriously. Slowly and laboriously the metal began its upward way. One of the men, seeing that all was apparently under control, flung himself down on a pile of boards and began to smoke a cigarette. The other man stood looking at the load, and just as it was about to leave the ground, he sprang aboard it and balancing himself nicely, one foot on each side of the rope, he began to ascend.

The woman never looked up. She bent more strongly to her work, putting every bit of her vigor into winding the rope. The smoker waved his cigarette in jaunty salute. One hand on hip, other arm outstretched in theatrical gesture, head high, a broad and happy smile on his stupid face, the acrobat went his upward way. I looked up. The shaky board at the top was bending sickeningly. The frayed rope was taunt, and the doubtful-looking knot on the bundle of metal slipped an inch or two now and then. But up and up the clown went, swaying and swinging. At the third floor he burst into song. The woman ground away.

I tried to tell myself that one less fool in the world would only be a blessing, but I was unable to tear my eyes from the scene and my heart was in my mouth. And, of course, nothing happened. When they reached the roof, the gallant young man stepped off and drew the tin, or whatever it was, to the roof top. The smoker flipped his cigarette tube into the mud. When the woman got the signal from the roof that all was well and that she was permitted to cease hoisting, she sank down, breathing heavily, and took her kerchief from her head and mopped her face. Now you never would be able to see things like that from the front of the hotel.

We were inducted into one of these twilit caves with a court view upon our arrival in Moscow last year. As I have already indicated, the rooms that had been reserved for us had been given to somebody else with a strong mind and a loud voice. He was over there about some oil business or other and he was a smooth worker. Also, he promised me, when he met me in the hall, and I attacked him for sneakily grabbing our rooms—he promised me a lush dinner and a party to make amends and he never even did that.

Well, this cave that they gave us was a room about ten by twelve, with an alcove just big enough to accommodate twin beds. The room had a big desk in it, a big round table, a big wardrobe with double mirror doors, a small divan and a couple of chairs. It also had a lamp about five feet high, on the desk, with a tipsy orange silk shade about as big as a washtub.

There was a bathroom, too, with the three indispensable appliances and running water, which ran. In fact it gushed, all the time, and never stopped. It was a small Niagara. Hot and weary from our plane trip, I went to the bathroom before I had even taken off my hat and was about to wash my face. The faucet looked queer. It had a round perforated nub on its end, but I was too tired to investigate. I turned on the water and got a swift cold jet slam in the face. It poured *up*, not down, and it drenched me to the skin before I could turn it off.

Dripping and furious, I emerged to find that the plump and jolly manager on the floor had come in to see that we were comfortable. The lamp was not lighted—and we needed the lamp. She took the wire and plunged it into the floor socket. The wire was just a wire—two projecting ends of copper wire which she stuffed into the floor plug. "Hey, don't do that," I hollered. "You'll be electrocuted. Where's the black thing supposed to be on the end of the wire?"

"What black thing?" said the lady through a shower of blue sparks. The lamp lighted, and the lady, smiling amiably, looked at me in surprise.

"We have black things on the ends of wires," I said feebly. "We wouldn't be *allowed* to poke around into the walls with live wires!"

She laughed merrily. "Oh, Madame," she said, "we are a toff people." I was to hear that phrase often during my sojourn in that town and never was truer word spoken.

This gloomy room on the court was to be our home away from home for many weeks. Here in the beginning we had combination bedroom, living room, dining room and office. On the big desk, which at first glimpse had seemed to provide ample working space, my husband now composed articles of political significance, while I cooked a stew on an electric hot plate. He is the mildest of men, but after a while he began to find that my culinary efforts, plus the presence of a secretary, a courier and a chauffeur, were somewhat cramping. The Russians, however, never find crowded quarters upsetting. The courier and the chauffeur would sit for long hours doing nothing, completely happy. The fact that the chambermaid was weeping, making beds or dusting, never seemed to distract the secretary. I had to climb over their assorted legs to get to the culinary department. Both my husband and I were delighted when finally the hotel management was able to provide him with a separate office. I bade the office staff good-by without regret. I was having trouble enough trying to assemble three meals a day on my little electric stove.

We had been promised better quarters and we found that unless we waged a never-ceasing warfare with the hotel management, we could not hope to see the realization of that promise. So we nagged them. We did not like to do it, but Americans and Russians alike assured us that nagging was the only method to employ.

One day, as I was stirring my usual stew, the telephone rang and voice said impatiently, "How soon can you move into Room 467? It is ready and waiting for you," the implication being that I had kept the hotel management waiting until its patience was exhausted. I unplugged the hot plate and with a towel to keep my hands from being burned, I lifted it and the stew and rushed out into the hall.

Without slackening speed, I ran with the stew still bubbling up two flights of stairs to our new room. I got the hot plate plugged in the outlet in 467 before the steam had stopped coming out of the stew. Then I picked up the telephone. By great good luck, I was able to locate the lady who had asked me the question. "This is to tell you I am *in*," I said . "And thank you very much for your kindness."

When a foreigner first gets to Moscow, he is issued a ration book. This book entitles him to three meals a day (plus "tea" which is tea and cookies). If, after eating a few of the hotel meals, you decide that you can do better for yourself, you will have to come to an understanding with the hotel management who will take your hotel meal tickets and reissue you ration tickets good for food products in the Diplomatic Store. You can work out all kinds of complicated arrangements, part hotel food and part food from the store, but you can't just walk in and order a meal any time you like without forking over your ration tickets. Also, when I was there, there was no service in the main dining room at the hotel. You got your food served in your room. The correspondents had a big luncheon table where they all met at noon in a semiprivate dining room to eat and catch up on the day's gossip. But aside from that there was no dining-room service for foreigners.

There is no excuse for the quality of the hotel cooking, however. There they seem to think that you're lucky to get anything to eat at all. It can't be blamed on food shortages, because there was always plenty of food—not fresh vegetables and fruit, to be sure, but meat and bread and butter and pastry and potatoes were always abundant. They just didn't care. We got pale soup, flabby meat, in little variety—as though the cook were always muttering, "Ah, what the hell?" No other hotel was trying to get the foreign guests away from the Metropole—there is no competition in that or any other field. So the dreary grind went on. But after a few weeks it became unendurable, so we joined the ranks of the other rebels and bought our own food which I cooked on the hot plate. It was definitely nothing fancy, but it was edible and that helped a little.

Room 467 was a palace compared with the coalhole where we had been living. It consisted of a large, sunny room with an alcove for the beds. There was a private bath in which the plumbing seemed to be in good order. We had a little private balcony, and a magnificent view out over Sverdlov Square, and in the distance we could see the golden towers and the ruby stars of the Kremlin. There were the usual dusty, shabby, bottle-green velvet curtains at the windows, hanging full-length from ceiling to floor. There were the usual lace curtains darned and frail. But they were clean.

The furniture, as always in the Russian hotels, was fearful and wonderful. The prize piece was a tidbit set diagonally across one corner. This consisted chiefly of a mirror, which must have been eight feet tall. Its top was lost in the shadows of the high room, and what was the purpose of that piece of furniture I shall never know. I got real pleasure from it, for I was constantly reminded of Alice when she discovered the tiny door that led into the magic garden. There were two tiny doors at the base of this important mirror, each a foot high, enclosing a small cabinet about big enough to hold a box of face powder and a toothbrush.

There was a wonderful table in the room too. This was of heavy wood with a moth-eaten felt top. It was fastened to a cabinet about five feet high ornamented with brass cherubs. This cabinet contained several drawers, very small and shallow, but nevertheless providing some storage space. Immediately on my entering the room, the floor manager, Bella Markovna, came in. She was to become my good friend later, but in the first few months we regarded each other with suspicion. "Madame," said Bella, "this table is broken. Please, do not put anything on it, because tomorrow morning at ten o'clock the man will come to move it away and repair it." I believed her. Ten months later when I was bidding Bella tearful and affectionate farewell, I could not resist reminding her that the table had not yet been fixed.

There was a large wardrobe in the room with a full-length mirror into which I carefully avoided looking. Some things are better when not inspected too closely, and my personal appearance in Moscow was one of them. We had twin beds in the alcove and since I had the opportunity to inspect them first, I chose the one nearest the wall. My husband's bed was between my bed and the wardrobe. This proved to be very lucky. I will explain why. My bed turned out to be shaped like a hammock. It was deeply concave, and I fitted into it snugly and comfortably. My husband's, however·, was like a hummock, convex, and when he would lie upon it his body described a tense arc. It was very handy to have the wardrobe there beside the bed because he got so he could hang on to the wardrobe even when he was asleep; it kept him from falling out.

We were provided with clean bed linen occasionally, and I really mean linen. The sheets were very old and frail, much darned, sometimes full of holes. But they were linen. We also had a quilt apiece, feathery-soft, filled with down and covered with red satin. These were the most delightful quilts I had ever used in my life. It never got so cold but that we, snuggled under them, were toasty warm.

I had some shelves made on which to range my housekeeping equipment. Here I stored my few pots and pans, and all the food. Since the shelves were open shelves, and since there were no closed cabinets in which to store anything, I had a horrified vision of rats, mice, roaches and other assorted creatures being attracted to my stores. In all fairness I must say here, that never once while I was in the Metropole in Room 467 did I see a rat, a mouse, a roach or a bedbug. But there were houseflies and mosquitoes.

It is perhaps no more than the honest truth to say that there is probably not a window screen in the U.S.S.R. At any rate, there are none in the Metropole. In the beginning of spring, when first the weather stripping is removed and the windows can be opened, the houseflies appear. One size smaller than barn swallows, they zoom and swoop all day and then the mosquitoes take over and zoom and bite all night. American insect sprays are powerless against them. For if you kill off one crop and then open the windows, there they are again. If you don't just ignore them, you go crazy. But since there are so many other things which require your energy and attention, you soon get so that you are only mildly annoyed by them.

My statement to the effect that I never saw bugs or vermin in my room used to cause other Americans to gape at me in disbelief. But the effect it had on my friend, Dixie, Mrs. Craig Thompson, went far beyond disbelief. It enraged Dixie and no wonder. Her room on the third floor was always full of cleaning women, squirting kerosene under the beds and into the cracks of the walls. She waged unremitting warfare against mice. Roaches were not unknown to Mrs. Thompson. So, when she would come to my room, exhausted from her battles and half-smothered by the mists from the various insect sprays she had been using, and I would say blandly that I had no such trouble, Dixie nearly came unhinged. She finally analyzed the situation, at least to her own satisfaction. "You are probably such a sloppy housekeeper,"she said to me bitterly, "that no self-respecting vermin would come into your room. Also you probably wouldn't know a bedbug if you saw one." One must make allowances for taut nerves in Moscow.

Above our beds in the alcove of 467, near the ceiling, was a small register. At first we thought that it was ventilation for our bathroom. This proved not to be the case. All day and far into the night embarrassing sounds would come out of this register, and we finally discovered that it was indeed a ventilator but leading to the public toilet in the hall. We called our room "Our Cottage Small by a Waterfall." After we had lived in the room about six months, with the embarrassing sounds going on without cessation day and night, my husband said mildly to me one evening, "Do you know, I am getting a little bored by this?" It seemed to me the very acme of understatement.

The old plumbing in the Metropole Hotel in Moscow was always reluctant. In the bathroom the bowl of the lavatory was always sluggish and the feeble seeping away of the water drove me mad. I would implore Bella Markovna, our buxom, cheerful and efficient floor manager, to get somebody to do something about it. Bella always obliged and eventually a little wizened old man, about two days this side of ninety, would arrive, weighted down by plumbers' tools and a small suction plunger. The plunger I knew of old, the cure-all for balky sinks. He would put it over the narrow mouth of the drain, give a few hearty plunges and the water would flow away like a charm. But in three minutes the grease-clogged pipe, which hadn't been properly cleaned out since Ivan the Terrible, would fill up again.

"Bella," I said, "for heaven's sake make somebody clean this pipe out right!"

Bella regarded the trouble thoughtfully. "Madame," she said quietly, "this is all due to fatness."

I felt beaten. Probably she meant it was the grease, but you never can tell. "Keep my shape out of this," I told her sternly, "and try to get a plumber in here that knows his business. This man's so old he can't even stand up without leaning against something." I knew the gnome didn't understand English, so there was no chance of my wounding his sensibilities.

I made one more try. "Bella," I said, "tell him that he will only have to come back again tomorrow and do it all over again." Bella translated and the gnome smiled winningly. He looked at me fondly.

"He says," Bella translated, "that he will be glad to come back tomorrow." And he did, too.

The knob on the bathroom door was loose. If you handled it just so, you could close the door and sometimes even get it open again. But nearly always you had to stay in the bathroom emitting plaintive cries until somebody showed up outside who knew the cranky combination and could persuade the knob to work. It was hard on the nerves and gave me an incipient case of claustrophobia.

Again I implored Bella to send for a repairman. One day a cocky youth appeared with a battered hammer and two nails each about a foot long. He pushed the knob into place, inserted the nails in the holes left by long-absent screws, gave each nail a couple of smart licks with the hammer, and promptly disappeared. The nails projected about three inches from the surface of the door, although I must admit the doorknob worked. But they caught my clothes every time I passed and since my supply of clothes was strictly limited, I could ill afford a T-shaped tear in every garment I possessed.

I pointed out the state of affairs to the weary Bella. She wiggled the doorknob pointedly. That was what I had complained about and that was what had been fixed. Clearly I was hard to please. She drifted away in the direction of other urgent calls. I bent the nails over by whacking them down with the heel of a shoe and covered the savage projecting heads with adhesive tape. They're probably there to this day.

But the point of the story is this: Russians generally have little pride in personal workmanship—neither the gnome nor the youth cared a bit whether he did a good job. The water drained slowly away, the doorknob worked if treated tenderly, but according to American standards both jobs were slovenly.

There is no unemployment in the Soviet Union, they say with pride. That's easy to believe because no job is ever finished. It always has to be done over again.

Many examples of slovenly workmanship can be seen around Moscow. Some of the fine new buildings already are shabby and worn. A beautiful mural of inlaid stone in the Stalin Station of the subway is falling to pieces and its mosaic is loose and shaky. New sidewalks sag in a few weeks' time. New paint jobs look grimy and flaky almost before they are dry. Some say the explanation is that there is no competition, no incentive for good workmanship. Others say that slipshod workmanship has always prevailed in Russia and that education alone will change it. Anyhow, even the newspapers conduct campaigns to instill pride of workmanship and craft, but so far without visible results.

The chambermaids in the Metropole Hotel are husky, cheerful, energetic and capable. Bella Markovna asked me, when I first went to live on the fourth floor, at what time in the morning I wanted the maids to come. After we had decided what time would be the most convenient, they always arrived on the dot, armed with the tools of their trade. They work in pairs and while they are never able to make much impression on the dingy old furnishings, nobody can deny that they do try. Their brooms consist of bundles of twigs tied around a heavy stick. The first thing one maid does is to dip this broom in the toilet to get it thoroughly wet and then attack the shabby old rug. When I discovered this, I protested vigorously, and suggested that there might be some other way to do the sweeping. There was. She filled a large glass with water and poured it heartily in all directions over the old carpet. The rug scarcely dried out from one day to the next. But since I had already gained one victory, I did not believe in pushing my luck too far.

Every day I had long, involved conversations with the chambermaids. I found out all about their families, their

health, their hopes and their dreams. And they found out all about mine. You understand that I could speak only the simplest Russian, and they spoke no English at all. But these long conversations took place just the same. It was fascinating to me to learn what interested these girls.

One of them had been to Yalta at the time of the Conference. She had seen President Roosevelt and told about it again and again. The high point of interest to her was not that she had seen the President of the United States, but the fact that he had had a Negro servant to help him. I learned that another one of the girls had studied to be an electrician, and that she was longing for the time to come when she would get a job at that trade. A third woman used to tell me with great pride about her daughter who was enrolled in the Circus School. "Madame," she would say to me, beaming, "I have told the girl a thousand times that she will kill herself. But she wants to be an acrobat, and what can I do?"

It was during my conversations with the Metropole maids that I became aware of the Russian affection for the word "interesting." Where Americans have come to use and misuse and overuse the word "amusing," the Russians say things are "interesting." A new dress, a news item, a painting, a box of face powder or almost anything that pleases a Russian is "interesting."

The chambermaids, like all other workers in U.S.S.R., got one month's vacation with pay.

The laundry service in the hotel was not particularly expensive, but it was very slow. In the case of people who, like us, were poorly supplied with clothing, it was awkward to have to wait almost two weeks to have the laundry delivered.

You could get a dress or suit pressed within an hour or two, but dry cleaning took longer. In fact, it was well to approach dry cleaning in Moscow very, very cautiously indeed. I had only one civilian suit there, a sage-green flannel that showed every spot and stain. I sent it lightheartedly away to be dry-cleaned. I waited for its return and when, at the end of two weeks, it had not reappeared, I sent the courier to inquire about it.

She came back looking pale and distressed. "Madame," she told me, "they have spilled a pot of red paint on the skirt."

I received the news calmly. By that time I had been long enough in the Soviet Union to know that one must hoard one's energy and strength. I put the matter out of mind. But in day or two a smiling girl appeared with the suit which looked as good as new. She displayed the skirt with great pride, and even my critical eye could find no fault in it at all. The next day I decided to wear the suit to a cocktail party. Something seemed to be wrong. The skirt reached about four inches above my knees and the waistband would not meet. I looked like an obese ballet dancer complete with tutu, and that was no way to look at an Embassy cocktail party. I had to go back to my greasy old uniform.

What they had done, of course, was to wash the skirt of my green suit, and it had shrunk so that it was too small for even a kewpie. I finally gave the suit away, but to two different people. A little thin girl got the skirt, and a big fat girl got the coat, and they were both delighted. So what was an ill wind for me blew some good to them.

One other thing which I will never forget is the absolute honesty of the employees who worked in the hotel. In spite of the fact that every one of them would have been very happy indeed to have any of the things which were always left lying around our room, and in spite of the fact that several chambermaids had free access, never once during my Moscow life was anything stolen from me. Once a pair of rubbers disappeared, but I may have left them somewhere—I could never be sure. But there were other things of greater value than a pair of rubbers to be had for the taking. I had the warmest and friendliest feeling toward all the fourth-floor personnel. It seemed to me that some of them showed almost superhuman restraint in the matter of not pinching off a trinket or two. But they were very good girls indeed and I hope some all-seeing Soviet commissar will reward them. Of course, Bella Markovna would have skinned any miscreant alive. But that would not have helped me out if anything had disappeared. But nothing ever did.

Chapter 9

I Kill Mr. Bevin

THERE WAS a certain high-nosed English girl who lived on the same floor with us in the Metropole Hotel. She worked for the British Russian-language newspaper called *British Ally*. I never knew her very well; in fact, I stood in some awe of her, for a number of reasons. One reason was that her accent absolutely floored me and I seldom knew what she was talking about, and the second reason was that she always used to be floating around in a cloud of British Navy. You could see the top of her blonde head above the blue uniforms that surrounded her, but seldom got a glimpse of her entire person. She was long-legged and slim; I knew that, and she used to greet me in an absent-minded but very tolerant manner. So, as I say we seldom had much to do with each other.

I can't honestly say that I *liked* the girl because, after all, it's hard to work up a warm feeling of affection for anybody who has the faculty of making you feel as though your legs look like beanbags. When I used to see her and her satellites sailing through the hall toward the elevators, filling the air with incomprehensible chatter, I would hide behind one of the spare white pillars until they had passed. It saved so much trouble for everybody. But one day, during the Foreign Ministers' Council in Moscow, I met her face to face in the corridor. She was alone, and I was alone, and we both saw that we were in for it. I measured the distance between where we were and my door and it didn't seem *too* long. We greeted each other toothily, and proceeded down the hall together. She bent her head and murmured something that sounded polite, but since I was about two feet nearer to the floor than she was, I caught only a beelike hum.

I hated to be such a fool, but honestly my thoughts stopped dead and my voice stuck in my throat. She looked very grave and somehow worried, so I thought I'd give *that* a try, instead of mentioning the weather. "You look worried," I said in good clear New Yorkese and louder than I generally speak, hoping against hope that it would inspire her to speak so I could hear her.

"I am a bit upset," she replied, "and the office is like a madhouse."

"More so than usual?" I inquired brightly, noting with some satisfaction that we were almost at my door. She murmured like a bee. I couldn't make out a syllable. I murmured back and tried to throw a sympathetic note into the sound.

She raised her head and looked me in the eye. "And so," she said clearly "we are naturally distressed, and we are waiting for Mr. Bevin's doctor now!"

If she had pierced me with a pin I couldn't have been more galvanized. "Mr. Bevin's doctor!" I shouted. "Is he *ill*?" (None of the correspondents had mentioned such a thing. My husband hadn't had an *inkling*. Bevin ill, at the Conference? Holy smoke!) I stopped dead in my tracks and bugged out my eyes.

"A heart attack, we think," said the English girl coolly.

These English! I thought to myself. My God, the world could come to an end and they would make some stupid understatement about it! I left her in the hall staring at me and flew back downstairs to my husband's office. He was telephoning when I burst in, and I snatched the phone from his hands. He regarded me with what, even in that feverish moment, I considered less than husbandly affection.

"Hey," I hollered, or words to that effect, "do you know that Bevin has had a heart attack?" My husband's eyes, I regret to inform you, lighted up. But *he's* from Boston, which is darn near the same as being English. He put his pipe into his mouth and looked at me coolly.

"Where'd you hear *that*?" he said calmly.

"Well, don't just sit there," I howled, and I told him how I had come by the morsel of news. He couldn't help it—he got excited, too. Even I was satisfied with the speed with which he whizzed past me out the door. I sank back, exhausted. By golly, there was a day's work for you, and I was the one who had touched it off! I couldn't stay put. I had to see the way the story would be handled. My husband was already down in the A.P. office and nobody there knew a *thing* about it. They already had Eddie Gilmore on the phone and he said *he* hadn't heard it. They put me on the phone and I screamed at Eddie.

"It's *true*," I yelled and I told him where I had got the information. I could just see Eddie turning pinker and pinker at the other end of the wire.

"My God!" he said in a whisper.

I'd show those guys that I had the makings of a spot-news reporter! They thought I could write about women and children maybe, and cooking and stuff. I'd show 'em. In fact, I *had* shown 'em.

I departed. I went back to my room and sank down shivering. But you can't stampede a lot of hard-boiled foreign correspondents. When I went to my husband's office a few minutes later, being absolutely unable to stay out of the affair, he was quietly telephoning the British Embassy about it. He hung up, baffled.

"They say he's right there this minute eating quite a hearty lunch," he said.

"They're lying," I roared. "They're keeping it dark!" And I flounced out and went down to Farny Fowle's office—he was the C.B.S. correspondent. *He* had sense—he'd listen to me.

When I stormed in, Farny's Lily, a seasoned Russian girl who has been his secretary for years, was telephoning. "Dead?" she was saying in a hushed voice.

I hurtled out again. Back to my husband. "*There*, you see," I bellowed. "He's *dead!* Farny's Lily was just phoning and she said 'Dead.'"

My husband whizzed out again. Well, I couldn't do more. If the stupid fools wouldn't believe the evidence of my own ears, let them just get their own news, that's all. I went back upstairs and started stirring my chicken stew, which, by this time, was burned a deep black.

I didn't see my husband again until dinnertime. He came in quietly and stood looking down at me with a very strange expression indeed.

I began to have a cold feeling around the feet. "What about Bevin?" I stammered.

"It seems," he said gently, "that what the English lady *told* you was that a gentleman named *Smith*, who works in her office, had had a heart attack, and that they had sent for Mr. Bevin's doctor to come and attend to him. Mr. Bevin, dear, is and has been in perfect health."

I didn't eat much dinner.

We were to go to a party later to which all the correspondents had been invited. I knew that by this time the news had gone like a jet bomb all over the foreign colony. Those who were not puzzled would be in stitches. I was in for a ribbing such as hadn't happened since Adam. But I knew I had to take it. It had been an honest mistake—but even honest mistakes of that magnitude do not insulate you against derision.

My husband never mentioned the matter again. But *he's* from Boston. I cringed into the party. Although I held my chin high, that chin was certainly wobbling. And here let me pay tribute to my countrymen. *Nobody*, not a single soul, said a word about my fiasco. It was as if it had never been. I murmured to my husband, "I think I ought to try to explain." But he muttered around his pipe, "Leave it lay." To this day none of the Boys has ever brought the subject up. Aside from their innate kindness and generosity, and aside from any good will any of them may have felt for me, I always thought that maybe, in the depth of every heart present, was a tiny voice "There, but for the grace of God, go I."

Later I tried to apologize to the English girl. Naturally it caused her untold trouble and she had been called out on the carpet for that which was not, in the slightest degree, her fault. I told her that I would do anything I could to repair the damage and I must say she was extremely courteous about it. Whenever I see a picture of Mr. Bevin, broad, beaming and bumptious, I remember how I did my best to kill him in Moscow and how he robustly resisted the attack. You've got to hand it to the British. They're so durable.

Chapter 10

The Mother of Cities

THE RUSSIANS CALL MOSCOW "the mother of cities." Be that as it may, Moscow is only a pin point on the Union of Socialist Soviet Republics. It is not a beautiful city, but it certainly is a solid big one. There are plenty of ambitious plans afoot to make Moscow "the most beautiful city in the world." Already several broad boulevards have been plowed through the town, paved and lined with impressive buildings. Many of the finest of the old buildings have been retained, remodeled and refurbished and made into museums, shops, libraries and hospitals. As yet, the effect of this is still raw and new and there is a crowding background of the past looming dark behind it. But the beginning has been made, the plans are clear and the future will probably be pretty near what the planners dream.

Under a socialist system of government, private ownership is no obstacle to city planning, and the bulldozer of the construction crews under the guiding finger of the architect can snarl and buzz in any direction he may indicate, if his plans are approved by the Politburo. Some day Moscow may be a beautiful, modern Mecca, but today it is a sulky, stubborn, rather gloomy big place, resisting with every stone in its walls the glittering ambitions of the new leaders.

You realize how strong are the old roots, and how defiant the resistance remains when snow falls on the old city and all the past slowly evolves in every outline of dome and turret. It is then that Moscow comes into its own; then, under the soft, flattering touches of the sympathetic snowflakes, that the real town comes to life. Brooding, solemn, dignified, aristocratic and immovable, this snowy spirit was to me a never-ceasing wonder. Coming from America, where progress is so ordinary a part of everyday life, where a twenty-year-old building hangs its head in shame, I felt that in Moscow I was living in a fairy tale. I do not mean that I thought I was in fairyland. I mean that Moscow made me feel as if I were where many old fairy tales and folk tales had their origins. For instance, I remember once when I was crossing a small bridge somewhere on the outskirts of the city, that I said to myself, "This is the kind of bridge a troll might live under."

The vast antiquity of the city, eight centuries of being lived in, eight centuries of being trodden upon by the feet of men, has resulted in a strange, knowing emanation which seems to creep up from the stones of the streets and hang like a cloud over the onion-shaped domes and the tall spires of the churches. The alleys, the courtyards, the high walls, the hundreds of wrought-iron gates set into the high walls, the bundled-up people with shawled heads and felt boots, made me think that many of the old tales which children the world over listen to with shining eyes, here really had their beginnings.

I never had much of a head for dates. About the only two I'm really sure of are the date of my birthday and the date Columbus discovered America. (They are nearer together than I wish they were, too.) However, what I'm getting at is this: When Columbus discovered America, presumably in 1492, Moscow had been in existence almost four hundred years. A prince whose difficult and unpronounceable name was Yuri Dolgoruki had an estate on the present site of the city. The serfs who served this master and the peasants who came to depend on the estate for a livelihood grew in numbers until there was enough of a settlement to require the protection of a wall. Around this nucleus of humanity a wooden wall was built in 1156. That's a long time ago; but that's the beginning of Moscow, mother of cities.

Perched high on the banks above the Moscow River, this little stockade dug in its toes and became the important center of an important trade route. In that vast land of uncharted spaces, what roads that were led to Moscow. By land or by water it was easy to reach and the Tartars soon had their eyes on its riches and treasure. One day in the fourteenth century they rode down upon Moscow, scaled the stout wall and laid the city low. They pillaged and burned and left the small town a smoking ruin. But the hardy

Moscovites scraped around in the ashes, gathered what they could of their village together again and began anew. The Tartars made them pay tribute for a hundred and fifty years. The Moscovites paid because they had to, but finally they got tired of appeasement. At the beginning of the sixteenth century they rose up and kicked the barbarians out of the city, built new ramparts and fortifications and settled down to become the capital of the new State of Moscovy. This is the first we hear of the Kremlin.

The Kremlin was the strongest fortress of the city, the center and the heart. It combined fortress, church and palace of royalty. The great Kremlin wall, which stands there to this very day, was begun in 1485. Columbus hadn't discovered America even yet! Inside the Kremlin wall in 1475 they began to build the darling little Cathedral of the Assumption. This has an arched roof and five golden, onion-shaped domes. Its architecture combines Byzantine, Italian, Gothic and antique Russian and it's worth going miles to see. The Czars were crowned in this little church. The second cathedral is the Cathedral of the Archangel, built in 1505. This little church has five domes too, and it was inside this church that the Czars and their families were buried. Some of the caskets are enclosed in solid casings of crystal. Ivan the Terrible is buried here, and the son he murdered, and the second son, Fydor. The third of the cathedral group is the Church of the Annunciation, begun in 1484, and in this are housed many holy paintings by Andrei Rublev, the greatest icon painter of the time. All these cathedrals are toy-sized as far as cathedrals go, but are so steeped in history and antiquity that the imagination is stirred by even a glimpse of their golden domes.

You will see the old Bell Tower, too, called the Bell ·Tower of Ivan the Great, which he had built to hold what was intended to be the greatest bell in the whole world. The tower was built in 1600's, but they didn't get around to the bell itself until a hundred years later. What's a century or so to the Russians? They worked on the bell, father and son, for many a long year and finally they fabricated a monster of a bell, chased and patterned with a sprawling bas-relief of men, animals and cannon. And then one day they erected a scaffold and arranged their ropes and a mob of eager workmen hauled away to lift their wonder bell to its place in the wonderful tower. And the crowds stood around in amazement and excited delight while the dark bell rose and rose against the white beauty of the slender tower. And the rope broke and the bell smashed down amid a ruin of splintered wood; fell to the rocks and the mud below with a great crash that cracked the bronze from rim to top. And the only sound the great bell ever made was that one scream of its death.

Can you imagine the misery of the makers? Can you picture the wrath of the Czar? Can you even begin to think about the disappointment of the people when they heard about it? Or the sneaking delight of those who saw such a spectacle and were made into heroes forever after by the telling of the tale?

Anyhow, everybody was good and disgusted and they left the bell right where it was, half-buried in the mud, a miserable and irritating object. Some say the bell stayed there for more than a hundred years. Nobody had the heart to do anything about it. It got to have a very bad reputation, that bell, and they let it strictly alone. But after a long time, somebody or other with a progressive attitude and maybe a neat mind decided that great bronze lump was an untidy mess, lying in the mud, so he had a fine stone platform built, and raised the bell up out of the muck and washed it off and set it up in style, crack and all. And, with real Russian sense of the superlative, he called it the "Great Bell That Never Rang." And it's still there.

In the 1500's the town began to put on airs. Little self-governed centers, neighborhoods really, established themselves and got connected with one another by narrow, crooked streets. It wasn't more than a hundred years or so after that before a slatternly picturesque sprawling, dirty city really was in the making. Around a few grand houses of the nobility was a super-slum, slippery with mud, noisy with the cries of the peddlers, smelly with markets and bazaars, teeming with all the business that man in his folly stirs up around himself.

Peter the Great got sick of the whole mess of uncontrollable activity and moved himself and the court, bag and baggage, to St. Petersburg in 1703. There he settled down to making a dream city which would fill the eyes of his European neighbors with envy. But Moscow didn't care. Moscow, ancient and proud, kept the allegiance of many of the nobility who refused to remain permanently away from their familiar and beloved surroundings and trickled back from St. Petersburg to their plush estates that stood up like

stone flowers in the midst of the mire. Trade remained in Moscow; art and culture flourished there. If Peter the Great didn't like it, there were plenty who did, and Moscow, though by Czarist decree no longer the capital, continued her way without the blessing of the court.

Along came Napoleon in 1812, and in his invasion and siege nearly the whole city was destroyed by fire. But the durable Moscovite crawled out of the smoking ruins, shook the sparks from his whiskers, brushed the ashes from his boots and began all over again.

By the middle of the nineteenth century, when Queen Victoria was just smoothing her pudgy hands over the ruffled feathers of England, Moscow, seven hundred years of age, was hitting on all sixteen and getting along good. New railroads were being built, new factories were springing up, and Moscow once again was a great trading center. Culture flourished too, and many famous foreign actors and musicians came to the city and scored tremendous successes in the theatres and music halls. Moscow, in those days, was a cosmopolitan place, brilliant, experimental, vigorous. Her great palaces and mansions stood arrogantly at the edges of the crawling, crowded slums, and her fur-bearing aristocrats rode roughshod over the abject peasants who served them.

Only a few wise people heard, beginning rumbles of discontent. Only a few sharp-eyed observers noticed the muddy mobs drifting to the underground rendezvous. Only a few dreamed of the roaring torrent which was soon to burst the dam. But all Moscow shuddered when finally the dam broke and in 1917 the Kremlin itself, long the stronghold of royalty, from ancient times the center and secret heart of the dreaded ruling power, was stormed and taken by the Red troops. The next year Moscow again became the capital of the land, this time under the new Soviet regime.

The years that followed were years of chaos. Disorganized, devastated and bewildered, but hopeful and determined, Moscow struggled for life under the steely hands of the new state. Moscow endured hardships and survived purges and terror by night from the Secret Police. It quivered under the pitiless lash that was driving it on to a far but hoped-for goal. It starved; it toiled long bitter hours; it sacrificed; but because it believed, it survived.

Then, just as the country and the city were beginning slowly to find a new pattern of life, World War II crashed down upon it and swept its pitiful gains away. The very stones in the streets must have sighed in despair. How wearily the city must have girded itself for more warfare!

In the olden time the Tartars scaled the walls that had seemed invulnerable, and now the airplane rendered all the defenses useless. Moscow cowered under the bombs that rained down upon it. The golden domes of the churches were painted black, so that the lovely gleam would not be landmarks for the enemy. The city lived in darkness and horror. Finally, when the enemy was only a few miles from the gates, old men and old women and even the littlest children streamed out into the streets and once more there were barricades. But the stubborn, proud old city was victorious. The enemy was repulsed by the Army before reaching the defenses. Battered and ruined in many parts, still the city stood. And the citizens looked red-eyed and weary at the unscathed Kremlin wall and rejoiced that the barbarians had been driven away one more time.

And today the bulldozer is blazing broad boulevards through the heart of the town. Glittering, glass and shining steel are slowly taking the place of the muddy slums, and the blind alleys are being opened to the sun. A lot has happened to the mother of cities since Prince Yuri Dolgoruki strode across his riverside acres in 1156. Maybe, after all, the first thousand years are the hardest.

Looking back over the history of Moscow, one finds it easier to understand the suspicious and standoffish attitude of the Russians. Through the centuries they have been bedeviled by enemies. They have been beaten like a gong, as Noel Coward says. So, when a big, strong country with an atom bomb in its hip pocket greets them smilingly and roars good naturedly, "Come on out! What're you scared of? You haven't got anything we want!" why shouldn't the battered Russians reply sourly, "Sez you!"?

Although in the old days foreigners traveled freely throughout Russia, and Russians toured Europe whenever they wanted to (and had money enough), for the past quarter century the new leaders have clamped down and the old Iron Curtain has become a well-known reality.

Many of the top-bracket men of the Soviet government have never been outside the Soviet Union, and their knowledge of the world beyond their own borders consists entirely of what they have been told by suspicious and partisan teachers. No one who has not been in Russia can imagine the dark isolation in which most of these people live. The press is guided; the radio is guided. All information is carefully screened, sifted and slanted. They really don't know very much about Outside. And the dark, tricky, morose attitude the Russians maintain about other countries is an old, deep-rooted, hard-taught lesson from time immemorial. Still, even though you can understand and sympathize with this attitude, it remains an irritating and annoying one and everybody wishes they would try to believe that such a thing as friendly co-operation can—indeed, must—exist between modern neighbors.

Chapter 11

The Kremlin

WHEN YOU LIVE just outside the Kremlin wall, you get to feel as though the mystery of the ages must be within. The great brick wall must be more than forty feet high. It has a kind of crenellated brick border along the top, and there are high towers at intervals, nineteen in all, breaking the surface of the great triangular wall that protects and hides the buildings within. Each tower differs from the others—at least I never was able to find two that seemed just alike. There is a tremendous four-faced clock over the enormous square East Gate, and it chimes out the hours with a clang of bells that can be heard a long way.

In the old days the black, double-headed eagle of the Czars rose from the pointed tips of many of the towers, but now the Red Star has replaced them. And these red stars, mounted so that they turn with every variation of the wind, are made of rubies, they tell me; Russian rubies, mined in the Urals, so they say. At any rate, they are a brave sight, mounted in gold and turning, turning on the soaring towers. When the sun strikes them, they give off a rosy gleam, and when the moonlight falls upon them, it is easy to understand why they might be regarded by the people as stars of hope. Yes, the Kremlin seems a fascinating and mysterious place, and every foreigner tries hard to get inside it.

I was walking in the Kremlin Park one day, a park that runs the length of the Kremlin wall to the west, and I kept looking at the old wall in awe and wonder. That wall had been there for eight and a half centuries! At last I came to a door in the wall, a door of black iron, blank, bulky, frowning as the wall itself. But high up in the door was a pane of clear glass, gleaming and beckoning in the sunny air. It was too much for me. I went over to the wall, put my hands against the door, stood on tiptoe and peeked in. I got a good look, but it was a fast look, too. As soon as my nose was pressed against the glass, like a jack-in-the-box released by a spring the door was flung open and an armed soldier, frowning like Jove, sprang out at me, shouting imprecations. Of course, I fell away in horror although I had expected nothing less. He shouted questions at me and, though I attempted to be airy, I walked away very quickly indeed. My husband was in stitches. He roared with laughter and wiped his eyes. But it was only after the guard had returned to the stronghold and slammed the door furiously at my back that I was able to collect myself and arrange my thoughts.

I will tell you what I saw inside the iron door, through the clear glass pane: I saw several piles of quite new boards. I saw several short lengths of black pipe. I saw a small heap of dirty snow. And, too late, I saw the soldier! He was in full uniform and armed to the teeth. He seemed to be about seventeen years old, and when the sun touched his face, it showed a golden down like ripe baby wheat across his cheeks. His eyebrows, which were drawn together in quite the most ferocious frown I have ever seen, were like two streaks of gold paint above his fierce baby-blue eyes. His chest—quite a big chest, it seemed to me—heaved with indignation and menace. He indicated, with every quiver of his furious frame, that plenty of people had gone to Siberia for less than what I did. But, as I told my husband afterward, he really owed me quite a debt of gratitude, that soldier. I bet he had to stand behind that door for hours at a time, looking at that lumber and those pipes and that snow, and it was a godsend to have me peek in. It will probably be years before he gets a chance to scare the pants off anybody else.

Go all through the Kremlin, if they'll let you. Nowadays it's a touchy business, getting permission to go. The vast majority of ordinary Russian citizens never get their noses inside the gates. A favored few, with their passports and their passes, get by the armed sentries and the watchful guards, but it is as a reward for service rendered on battlefield or in factory or workshop, not because it is a place that belongs to the people. Foreigners can usually get permission, after asking in writing and being well considered.

I went one day with a group of newspaper correspondents, and that trip was for me a very rewarding affair. When I came away, I was dazed and fatigued and my eyes were glazed and my feet throbbed—museum feet, well known to all sight-seers. But as the days and the months passed, I remembered many things I saw and now I know that I shall never forget them. The Russians have not destroyed their historical relics. Instead, now that the war is over, they are refinishing and restoring them. One little cathedral in the Kremlin was already newly refinished, and it stood as proud and clean as a modern bungalow in a medium-priced suburban development. Its little outside was a glistening white and its fat little domes were an uncompromising fresh gold. The old lace ironwork which had been crocheted airily over the windows centuries ago was all painted a new and shiny red, and within, the smoky old icons had been cleaned and refinished with a glittering transparent varnish which made the saints look like figures on a feed-store calendar. Happy workmen were swarming all over the other churches, too, wielding the brush of progress, and before long not spot nor stain will remain on the fourteenth-century buildings.

All was pristine in the Old Palace, too. This is a doll's house of a place, designed by a Venetian architect. The rooms are minute, with painted, domed ceilings and mullioned windows in which bright new stained glass is set. All is so clean and so neat, so repaired and painted and fixed up, you have to keep pinching yourself to remember that it is no replica or stage setting but the real thing, built in the 1500's and once inhabited by Czars and their families. Even then the old boys were taking no chances, for you are shown a small window on the second floor in the Czar's apartment where the Czar used to stand and give audience to the people gathered below. If they got at him, they had to make a real try for it.

This baby palace is connected by a gallery with the newer and vaster palace built in 1800. Heaven alone knows how many rooms *that* one has; acres of gleaming floors seem to stretch in every direction, with hundreds of doors, millions of windows. All the furniture is newly reupholstered and has a never-in-this-world-sat-upon look. The rooms are full of stuff: heavy Victorian bric-a-brac, pianos in marquetry, tortured clocks, crystal chandeliers as big as hay wagons—goodness knows what all. Dizzy knickknacks and dopey whatnots, damask silk on the walls, priceless rugs on the floors—they didn't stint themselves in those days. It is easy to imagine how a Czarina, returning from a visit to Mrs. King Edward or Mme. Roi Henri, would say crossly, "Well, *she* has a velvet-lined soup tureen, and I certainly am going to have one, too!" And the edict went out and the palace workers got busy and another doodad was added to an already overstuffed domicile.

This palace is now used by the Soviets for meetings of the Supreme Soviet, and the marvelous St. George's Hall is big enough and impressive enough to house the United Nations Assembly. It might be a good thing, too. Whenever I hear about the Russians objecting to New York or San Francisco for the permanent home of the United Nations, I wish the rest of the delegates were smart enough to insist on Moscow. That would give the old Iron Curtain a slash that might prove its final undoing. If the United Nations Assembly could get in *there* and stay right there for a long time, the Russians would find a thing or two, and, make no mistake about it, so would the foreign crowd.

One wing of this big palace is called the Armoury, and although by this time I was almost in a state of coma, with my tongue hanging out, I insisted on going in there, too. I figured I might never be there again and I might as well see as much as I could.

The Armoury is now a museum where all the treasures of the former royal court and church are housed. A more tremendous assortment of infinitely precious junk is impossible to imagine. Mountains, simply mountains, of gold, silver and precious stones are displayed in glass cases. It reminded me of all the bridge prizes and carnival gifts in the entire world. True, *these* things are all made of real gold and real jewels, but they are as useless and foolish as bridge prizes ever were.

Here again I could almost hear what went on. The Queen of Sweden would say to the King of Sweden, "What in heaven's name can I give the Czarina to commemorate her sixth-and-a-half wedding anniversary?" And she would go to *her* royal treasure house and pick out a piece of precious absurdity and say, "Here's that two-foot gold platter the Shah of Persia gave us as a bread-and-butter gift two years ago. It certainly is a great big clumsy thing. What in the world he ever thought we could do with it I *don't* know. I'll send the Czarina that. Probably the Shah of Persia will never remember it anyhow. More than likely he never even *saw* it."

So the golden cartwheel would be wrapped in tissue paper and tied with an imperial ribbon and sent by messenger to the Czarina. She would receive it with a brilliant smile and an inward sigh and, without opening the package, have it stowed away in some bottom drawer with a hundred other useless, ugly things. I saw such a platter—set awkwardly on its side, taking up too much space and doomed to eternal banishment; pure gold, two feet in diameter, bumpy with pictures of cross-looking animals and foolish-looking hunters. It couldn't lie flat on a table. It couldn't hold food—gravy would trickle off in streams. And that is just one illustration of the treasures of the Czars.

One or two others I remember. One is a gift made by the Shah of Persia to Catherine the Great. It is a business in the shape of an ostrich plume—a thing about six inches long, designed with delicate grace, fashioned in gold. And the feather fronds are paved with diamonds—the whole affair priceless and really very beautiful. And nobody can say that *this* was useless. No, indeed! This diamond ostrich feather was for Catherine to pin on her horse's bridle!

The crown jewels of Russia are not on display. I don't know where they are and I couldn't find out. But enough treasure remains to make it crystal-clear that many of the causes for an uprising of the people are right here in plain sight. People who lived on that scale at the expense of others deserved what they got. The treasures of the church are staggering. Priests' robes stiff with gold and priests' crowns set with diamonds as big as twenty-five-cent pieces. Bibles, held in covers of solid gold, with rubies and emeralds sprinkled thick and fat. Even children's toys (toys!) so precious and so priceless that the value of them, turned into rubles, would buy food for many hundreds of undernourished peasants.

One toy is in the shape of an Easter egg. It is made of brilliant blue enamel with a band of diamonds around its middle. This egg is about three inches long, is hollow and comes apart in halves. The interior is gold, and cunningly designed to fit into the oval cavity is a tiny golden train, with locomotive and two or three cars. (The little train had been taken out so that the beauty of the craftsmanship could be appreciated. It seemed perfect in every detail.) They told me it was an exact replica of a famous train which had just been built at the time the toy was made. The minute engine, all its wheels and rods and spokes, is made of pure platinum with gold touches here and there. The cars are entirely gold, complete with wheels and windows. The train can be tightly coiled up and tucked away inside the egg box.

Can't you just imagine the delight of the child who got that toy? And the curiosity and pleasure of the Czar, his father? And how, after a few minutes, the Czarevitch ran crying to his mother saying, "Papa won't let me play with my train!" And how the Czarina, bristling with indignation, came bustling in and said sharply, "Give the child his toy! For heaven's sake, act your age!" And how the Czar sulkily and unwillingly handed over the plaything and went out muttering something about spoiled brats and nagging women? It probably happened, at that.

But the most wonderful display of all, for my money, was the exhibition of state coaches. Here was where I went right back into Hans Christian Andersen, head over heels. The coaches of the Czars and Czarinas, gold and gold-encrusted, upholstered in softest velvet, bejeweled and bedizened, are Cinderella coaches in very fact. One darling little golden sleigh, about four feet long, has pink and green jewels outlining its dainty curves and rose velvet covering its downy cushions. How the peasants must have stared when the Czarina rode in that, behind a white horse which also glittered with gold and gems! With a sable lap robe, or maybe ermine, she must have made almost as charming a picture as a modern moving-picture star.

Other coaches were much bigger, and their wheels covered with gold leaf and the bejeweled doorknobs dazzled me and left me breathless with wonder. I had to keep saying to myself, "This is not fake stuff. This is real—those hen's eggs are real rubies—that hunk of white glass is *not* glass, that's a diamond!" But it was hard to believe, even if I saw it with my own eyes. No matter how vivid your imagination may be, no matter what grandeur or sumptuousness you can dream up in the way of clothing, or house furnishings, or jewelry, one excursion around the treasure house of the Czars will convince you that you are a piker and that they must have been the pets of destiny and the darlings of the gods—until destiny turned sour and the gods got sick of them. For now the day of royalty is indeed done. And all the trappings and frippery of royalty belong to the people and are on display in the "people's museum"—in a museum surrounded by high walls which are patrolled by armed sentries and guards. The people are still outside looking in. Will the day ever come when the treasure will be freely visible to all?

Stalin lives in the Kremlin and has his offices there, too, but when we asked the guide, in all innocence, to point out his windows to us, the poor girl turned pale-blue and stammered that she didn't know. She was terrified at the mere question. Once, after Mr. Byrnes had been in Moscow and Mr. Harriman, the American ambassador, had taken him to call on Mr. Stalin, we asked Mr. Harriman where Stalin's office was located. Mr. Harriman looked very solemn indeed and said in a most stately and mysterious manner that he really felt he shouldn't give us that information. Did you ever hear such nonsense?

This secrecy and inaccessibility are accepted without question by most Russians, but there is a faint wonder stirring in the hearts of some, just the same. A Russian woman once said to me as we were walking along outside the Kremlin, "It is true, is it not, that any American citizen can walk into your White House and shake hands with your President?"

I was startled. I said, "Well, it's not quite *that* easy."

But the Russian woman persisted. She had a dream and it is not easy to undermine a dream. "I have been told," she said firmly, "that it is possible for any ordinary citizen in America to approach the President and to shake his hand. I have seen pictures of this."

I hedged. "Right now, during the war," I said, "it is not possible."

"I have seen pictures of long lines of people being received by the President," she said. "Not diplomats, you understand, quite ordinary people. Is this, or is this not, true?"

I said, "Not now, naturally. Roosevelt is too busy to stand around receiving long lines of people"

"Naturally," she agreed. "These are not normal times. But in the past, this has been done?"

Well, of course it has. It used to be quite the usual thing. I remembered back. Once President Taft had been at our little church in Greenwich Village, and after the services he had stood expansively in the front of the church and everybody had lined up and he had extended his big, firm hand and pulled back his big smiling face and with the utmost good humor had shaken hands with all the congregation, who had lined up and passed by him, one by one. We were all enchanted but nobody felt that it was a world-shaking event, although, naturally, we were all delighted. (I was the merest child at the time, of course.) "Well...." I said.

"Have you, personally, ever shaken the hand of the President?" said the eager Russian woman.

"Yes," I said, with complete truth.

"You see?" she cried in delight. "I told you so!"

Chapter 12

A Street Scene or Two

MOSCOW IS NOT a cosmopolitan city today. It is solidly Russian. When you are in New York or Chicago, or London or Paris, you can hear a medley of languages nearly always, and the people you pass are likely to be from the four corners of the world. In Moscow, Russian is spoken and the people you pass are people from the four corners of the Soviet Union. It is an old saying and a true one that if you have been only in New York City, you have not been in America. But if you have been only in Moscow, you have been in the heart of Russia. It is in Moscow that everything comes to the center, drawn to the hub of the capital of the land.

Life in Moscow is easier than anywhere else in Russia, they say; so besides the legal residents, other people keep sneaking in, without permission, and stowing away with relatives and friends until they can wangle jobs and then manage to get a food card. Before the war Moscow had a population of about three million. Now there are more than seven and a half million people, living, working and trying to get enough to eat where even half that number was crowded. But the lure of Moscow cannot be denied or resisted. It calls to every citizen of the Soviet Union and more and more of them are listening to the call and answering it. Once there, it is almost impossible to get them to leave again, unless it's a "direct order."

I knew one girl who had the opportunity to marry a fine young engineer and go with him to Gorki. She refused him. I asked her why. "And leave Moscow?" she said in horror. Not even true love could induce her to leave her beloved town.

A foreigner, especially a foreigner from America where the right of a citizen to grow up intact is pretty closely guarded, is usually surprised at the number of hazards to life and limb in any ordinary Moscow street. Holes in the sidewalk are common, and an unwary foot might ever so easily slip into one of these unmarked traps. Loose stones go unnoticed; iron gratings are broken and gape for the unwary. Pipes jut out viciously from walls and in the dark of the night constitute definite menace to the pedestrians.

Live wires break and dangle in the wind to electrocute you. The network of trolley wires that cross and recross overhead is another danger and is regarded nervously by people who walk below it,

Near the Metropole Hotel there is a tremendous junction of these wires. One day, just as I was walking underneath, one of the wires snapped with a snarl and the end whirled viciously into the street scarcely a yard from where I stood. My guardian angel was taking care of me that day, all right, for the force of that wire could have sliced me in two with no trouble at all. By great good luck nobody was hurt, although the street was crowded at the time. The wire snapped itself into a tangle and came to rest in a harmless heap in the gutter. Then the patient girl conductors on the busses climbed to the bus tops and did their best to adjust the trolleys, but traffic was held up for a long time until the trouble wagon came and repaired the break. Things like that happen all the time. Nobody seems to mind.

The streets and boulevards in the central part of the city are enormously wide, so wide that you have no chance in the world of getting across them before the traffic lights turn against you. And the Russian automobiles, driven by Russian chauffeurs, who are easily the maddest in the whole world, bear down upon you in a wide, sweeping torrent. If you can keep your head, or indeed your arms or legs, you are a cool, well-balanced person.

I am reminded of a story I heard which we Americans used to laugh at heartlessly. It seems that one of these reckless Russian chauffeurs, who was in the employ of a foreigner, was eager to make his getaway as soon as the lights turned green. This happened somewhere in the neighborhood of the British Embassy. The eager young man, in accomplishing his purpose, neglected to notice that an elderly gentleman was just in front of his car. Away he went, knocking the old gentleman down, naturally. As the old man disappeared

under the car, the horrified chauffeur slammed on his brakes and brought the car to a halt. He stared in terror at his employer sitting beside him on the front seat. While they sat there in silence, trying to decide what to do, up from under the car rose the battered old man. He stood wavering for a moment in front of the radiator of the car, trying to get his bearings. His appearance so startled the driver that he inadvertently stepped on the gas, the car started with a jerk and ran over the old man again.

I never found out what finally happened. But it only goes to illustrate that the Russians, like everybody else, are more interested in the traffic lights than they are in the pedestrians.

Moscow is a clean city. During the spring and the summer months the streets are forever being washed. The street cleaners, big husky women wielding hissing hoses, bring all their good-housekeeping instincts into play. They have, I regret to tell you, one-track minds. Their job is to keep the streets clean, to wash the streets, and this they do, solemnly, thoroughly, humorlessly. Let the passer-by beware! The darting stream of water may slosh over your feet, or wet you to the skin before you can leap out of the way. That's your fault. No apologies will be made nor the slightest consideration given to you as you pass.

The streets must be washed, so watch your step. It's a risky business. Sometimes the hose connection will be down in a basement and an innocent-looking hose may be projecting out of a basement window and lying on the sidewalk at your feet. The street cleaner is inside connecting the water. Run! She hasn't the slightest interest in the world as to what is going on upstairs. She will turn the water on and when she has it turned on, she will come up, take the nozzle of the hose and wash the street. Meanwhile, the hose, unattended, writhing like a mad thing, is squirting a jet of water this way and that, and irate pedestrians just have to go their soaking way without redress. The cleaning women don't mean any harm; it is doubtful whether they even know that they have outraged anybody. They have a job to do. They do it.

In the wintertime, as soon as the first snowflake comes drifting down out of the sullen Moscow sky, the husky street-cleaning girls are out with their scoops and their shovels, their picks and their brooms, and as long as the winter lasts, they fight their battle with frost and ice and snow. The ice freezes so hard and so thick on the city streets, in spite of never-ceasing efforts to keep them clear and clean, that the children don their ice skates and skate on the sidewalks.

It was always a surprise to me to see women cleaning the streets. It was hard, rough work very often—in winter especially so. It was certainly no easy task to stand for long hours in the middle of the bitterly cold, slippery street, chopping away at thick layers of stubborn ice with a heavy pickax. Yet the women attacked the work cheerfully and performed it well.

I asked a Russian woman how it came about that women were required to do such laborious tasks and she answered, "Why, they are glad to get the chance to do it!" Most of those women, she told me, are peasant girls from farms and this work is the first work they have ever done that was not farm labor. "They find it much easier than farm work," said the Russian lady. "They love to come to the city. They are given a food ration card and are housed in barracks, and after a while they are given something better to do. This is a kind of apprenticeship."

I asked about the pay for such work, but my informant said she did not know. It can't be much. I asked what the Committee for Labor Protection had to say about such work for women. This committee is supposed to watch out for the interests of the workers and prevent their performing any harmful labor. "Surely," I said, "such work must be bad for women."

"Oh, I don't think so," said the lady airily. "Anyhow, they don't keep at it more than a year or two."

But oftentimes among the crowd of busy peasant girls with their ragged, padded clothing and their worn-out felt boots, you would see a woman who looked like a white-collar worker or somebody in even higher brackets. It was not unusual to see a woman in a good fur coat shoveling away amid the other women, and very often a small child of eight or ten would be cheerily picking at the ice with a small shovel. I inquired about this, asking (1) why a woman with enough money to buy a decent fur coat should be shoveling snow, and (2) why, when presumably no child under fifteen is ever granted working papers, a child obviously far under that age was working in a street gang. The answers were (1) that the women in the fur coats did that work in order to get a Worker's ration card, entitling them to more and better food than they could get on a Dependent's ration, in case they had no other work, or a Clerk's ration, in case they were white-collar workers; (2) the children often wanted to help their mothers and did so as part of their social-service program in the school. Something like our Boy Scouts' "Good Deed for the Day," I suppose.

Never while I was in Moscow did I see a garbage-collection truck, and never did I see a garbage can or any trash standing around waiting for collection. They manage that smelly and unsavory task pretty neatly. Garbage must be collected, but I don't know when or how. Mrs. Craig Thompson was with me one day in the Diplomatic grocery when this brilliant thought occurred to me and I told her about it. "What do you suppose they do with the garbage?" I asked.

Mrs. Thompson looked thoughtfully at the soggy little apples and the doubtful beets which were on sale that day. "That's easy to answer," she said: "they eat it."

The cold of Moscow winter did not seem any more severe to me than that of a winter in New York. Moscow is not a windy city, and the cold crispness of the air, still and icy though it may be, has no more penetrating quality than the wintry air of New York. As a matter of fact, Moscow was a comfortable place compared to the arctic winds of Riverside Drive where our apartment in New York is located. When crossing the great open squares in winter in Moscow, like Sverdlov Square in front of the Metropole Hotel, I always braced myself and said, "Here it comes!" And I was always surprised to find that no bitter wind was cannonading through the square and that it was no colder there than it was anywhere else. The buildings in Moscow are not skyscrapers, and so do not constitute canyons for winds to howl through. It's cold, all right, in the winter, but it's far from being the "Russian Winter" celebrated in song and glory. The Moscow summer was bright, sunny and warm. But it is the winter that gives the city its real medieval character and mood. The sun seldom shines in the winter—the skies are usually a pearly and luminous gray. And it is then that all the old churches, old walls, old towers and low roofs, hold the twentieth century at bay.

During the ten months I lived in Moscow, I often felt sorry that I was not permitted to travel to other parts of the country. But at the time, although now the restrictions are more relaxed, I was not able to get permission to go anywhere outside the city. We applied for several different visas, and although the Foreign Office never said an outright "No," it very definitely never gave outright permission or sent through the necessary papers. So I had to make the best of things and concentrate on Moscow itself. I found it a fascinating place and I never tired of the vivid contrast between the modern buildings and the old ones. This is nowhere better illustrated than in the Red Square.

The Red Square is the sweeping, open section to the east of the Kremlin. It is not called "Red" because of the Soviets. "Red" and "beautiful" are the same word in Russian. At one time it was a market place where the buying and selling of all kinds of food and clothing took place—a huge bazaar. Now it has been cleared of all such commerce and is the center of the whole town.

The main Kremlin Gate is here, under the square tower with the four-faced clock and the deep-toned bell that clangs out the hours. With one of the high Kremlin walls as a background, here is the red granite tomb of their Leader of Leaders, Lenin. In this tomb of the most modern simplicity of design, lies the mysteriously embalmed body of the chief who died in 1924. Long lines of patriots stand before the tomb on specified days; and walk slowly and reverently past the armed guards of honor to view the remains of the great national hero. No day is too rainy, no day is too bitingly

cold, no day is too bakingly hot for the long lines to wait, respectfully and quietly, finally to file through the door into the dimly lighted coffin place.

Back of the tomb, behind the white marble seats which are permanently in place for the viewing of parades and "demonstrations," sealed within the wall itself are the urns with the ashes of many who died in the Revolutions that freed the people from the Czars. Here, among others, are the ashes of John Reed, the American who gave his life to the cause of the Russian people; Bill Hayward, the American leader of the I.W.W.; Charles Ruthenberg, leader of the Communist Party in America. I was not permitted to approach within several feet of the wall the day I wished to see the resting place of John Reed's ashes. The guard motioned me angrily away. I never could figure out why.

To the left of the modern tomb of Lenin and the Kremlin gate there is the finest example of medieval architecture in Moscow—the Cathedral of St. Basil. It is alone, on a small elevated place overlooking the square, and if you once see it, I do not think you will ever forget it. Nothing could be more unlike the austere tomb of Lenin. St Basil's is Byzantine and utterly fantastic. It was built at the order of Ivan the Terrible, and has at least five domed towers, each one different from the rest. And yet so cunningly has it been planned and so carefully have the colors been blended, that the effect is bizarre but strangely beautiful. Ivan gave the assignment for each tower to a different architect, so the story goes, and told him to design the loveliest tower he could. And as each tower was finished that particular architect's eyes were put out, so that he might never design another tower like the one he had done for St. Basil's.

Chapter 13

Moscow Goes Modern

I FOUND a good description of the architecture of Moscow in an Intourist book. This is the way the Russians themselves describe Moscow architecture:

> *Foreign architects, especially Italians, and Russians trained in Western schools, have designed most of the important buildings. The Italian influence is everywhere conspicuous, both Renaissance and the florid rococo. Perhaps the most satisfying of the Russian adaptations of Western architecture are the buildings in what are known as the classic style, especially the spacious eighteenth-century mansions with pillared porticoes and classic details around doors and windows, painted yellow with white trimmings and set among old-fashioned gardens and branching trees. Like the Georgian houses of the United States and England, they belong to a time of patriarchal families and retinues of servants. It was in these houses that the characters of Tolstoy's novels lived and of Chekhov's plays. Domestic life in Moscow, as in many European cities, had a tendency to turn its back to the street; to understand it one must penetrate to the deep, inner courtyards of the immense city blocks, or peep behind the walls of these older houses. Visitors to nineteenth-century Moscow were charmed by this easy,*

comfortable life. But this ruling class was, after all, only a minute fraction of the population; under their control Russia remained the poorest and most backward of all European countries, her per capita production the lowest. As administrators they were hopelessly inefficient, and when at last the disinherited ninety percent ·took the power into their own hands, the old social order inevitably came to an end. The new order has also developed a type of architecture suited to its needs, and the contrast with the old is as dramatic as the contrast between the two social orders. Sternly utilitarian, often painted a "battleship gray," and stripped, like a battleship, for action, these severe and sober structures reflect with an extraordinary precision the spirit of these difficult and self-denying transitional years. Certainly the enormous windows, flooding the interiors with sunshine, are eloquently symbolic of a generation seeking more light.

We have a phrase in America which we use so often that it finally became the name of a play. I mean the phrase "George Washington slept here." Goodness alone knows how many houses in America claim the distinction of having had George Washington as an overnight guest. In Moscow the comparable phrase is "Pushkin visited here." Whenever I asked a guide or an interpreter to tell me what had been the former use or ownership of one of the beautiful old mansions, I always got this answer: "This building was built by a merchant prince for his mistress who was a ballerina." Then always came the added information, "Pushkin visited here."

One of the most famous, or at least the most outstandingly noticeable of these old buildings, is one which is now used by the British for the publication of their Russian-language newspaper. I will try to describe this building to you, but it is nearly indescribable. It is built of stone, massive enough for a fortress. Towers rise, bay windows bulge, porticoes jut out. Magnificent iron gates open into courtyards and all over the building occur what at a slight distance appear to be stone carbuncles, polka-dotted generously over the towers and buttresses. On closer inspection, however, these pimples turn out to be rather pretty little stone shells. This building was built by a rich young man for his mistress, who was a ballerina. And the story goes that on its completion the young man's mother drove around one day to look it over. She did not bother to go inside, but drove back home in a rage. She sent a message to her son which read: "I always knew you were a fool, but now you have proved it to the world."

Two of the best examples of modern architecture that I saw were the Lenin Library and the Palace of Culture and Rest of the Stalin Automobile Works. There were many others, of course, but these two I remember best. The Lenin Library is an impressive granite building, certainly a block square, built on severe, modern lines, yet somehow combining with this severity something of the classical. It is about three stories high and along the front at the edge of the roof silhouetted against the sky there is a row of more than life-size statues of their best-known and best-loved authors. As the library itself was under repair during my visit to Moscow, I was unable to see the interior. But to judge from the outside, I would think that it was well planned and spacious. The library is said to contain over two million volumes. It is not a circulating library nor is it possible for the passerby to saunter in and read awhile. In order to be able to use the library a citizen must first get a certificate of residence from his concierge. He must then have a letter from his foreman or the manager of his place of work. He is then permitted to make use of the reading rooms, but the books may not be taken home.

The desire for books and the appetite for reading in Moscow are enormous. It is impossible for the state to keep the citizens supplied with enough literature. Every new book published goes into many editions and the seriousness with which the Moscovites regard literature can be observed any day in any bookshop in the city. Comparatively few citizens of Moscow speak or read a foreign language, although more and more interest is being shown in the study of languages. Nevertheless, the foreign-language bookshops are usually stuffed to the doors and foreign authors are eagerly sought and voraciously devoured. Do not forget that any foreign book which appears for sale or on the shelves of the library has been passed on by the board of censors and the decision made by them whether or not it is fit for consumption by a member of the Soviet citizenry.

The Palace of Culture and Rest of the Stalin Automobile Works is also built on the severest of modern lines. It is a concrete building three or four stories high and it has many big, wide windows. It is for the exclusive use of the people employed by the Stalin Automobile Works at the edge of the city, and it made clear to me why the Russian worker is willing to have his life center around his place of employment. This Palace of Culture and Rest houses all sorts of recreational activities. It is possible for a worker to join one of many clubs. There are a dramatic club, a singing class, a gymnasium. There are music clubs, dancing classes, language classes, literature and science classes, lectures on many subjects, a band made up of musicians who work in the plant, and all kinds of athletic activities. There in familiar surroundings, amid familiar people, the Russian worker may find rest and entertainment without having to battle for them. Buying a ticket at the box office of any of the theatres is a battle. If he wishes to study after work, it means a long, involved business of getting registered at some institute and traveling on the crowded subway when he is tired. Under the Culture and Rest system, he is easily capable of providing himself and his family with the needed change and happiness.

During elections the Palace was used as a polling place. I watched some of the workers vote, deeply impressed by the dignified setting and contrasting it with the barbershop polling places in American cities. But I also watched them take the paper ballot handed them, fold it carefully, walk across to a ballot box and drop it in. They did not read the ballot, nor make a choice of candidates—that had already been done. There was only one party, one candidate, and no choice at all. A voter could cross out the name of a candidate if he wanted to—no more. That was his "vote." Yet over the ballot boxes, above the potted plants, was a triumphant banner which read: The Soviet power is a million times more democratic than the most democratic bourgeois government on the face of the earth," a quotation from Lenin. The people believed it, too.

The best new modern apartment house which has been constructed in Moscow is the fourteen-story "Government House." Glass, steel and concrete, it is possibly the most impressive new building of all they have erected. Here the government employees live: members of the Communist Party and other "big shots" who have earned the prize of a decent dwelling place. This building is always regarded with envy and awe by other Soviet citizens who have to share one small room with another family, sometimes with two families. I have heard some bitter criticism about that "Government

House." But I have heard also that the housing shortage has not been abashed by the high-bracket folks, either, but has even penetrated within those severe walls. Some "doubling up" takes place even inside the vaunted Moscow "skyscraper."

Housing in Moscow is a problem, as indeed it is everywhere on this disorganized planet. Of course, no new buildings were erected during the war and bombings leveled many or made many others so unsafe they had to be demolished. Moscovites, gazing sadly at their teeming streets and crammed subways and busses, often say ruefully, "Why don't some of these people go home?" That would certainly make life in Moscow more agreeable.

I visited five or six of the apartment houses built just before the war near the center of Moscow. They were what we at home would call cold-water walk-ups. Great, gloomy, fireproof affairs, they had halls and stairs so dark that walking through was actually dangerous for anybody unfamiliar with the place. All the buildings had elevators or at least elevator shafts, but none of the elevators was working. All were rusting away into uselessness while the tenants puffed up the stairs. But the token was there and some day maybe the elevators will work.

The living quarters I saw were those of working people with no pretensions to riches or grandeur, just middle-class white-collar folks. The rooms were all cheerless, mostly small and arranged around a central foyer with one kitchen for all the tenants and sometimes one bathroom also. One seven-room apartment housed nine people. Another of four rooms housed nine, too. The kitchens were old-fashioned, according to our standards. In fact, all the equipment was what we would consider tenement-house quality. The kitchen sinks were wooden and there was only one water spigot—cold. There were gas stoves but the municipal gas supply was so erratic the tenants usually bought auxiliary kerosene stoves—a costly solution, since kerosene is scarce and expensive. Whole sections of the city were often without electricity for weeks at a time and people either went to bed early, used kerosene lamps or scoured the bazaars for candles.

But the tenants seemed to be living quite happily under these conditions and the rooms were clean, even if cheerless and bare. There was a kind of heavy concrete-like atmosphere over these apartments, as though the astonishing fact that they were fireproof was sufficient.

Those who were lucky enough to come through the siege of Moscow unscathed have a few precious heirlooms which they use carefully and display with pride. The hand of the English Queen Victoria is heavy on the *décor* of Russia and whatever furniture remains is a sorry mixture of heavy Victorian plus Russian ornamentation. Some women had house plants blooming gaily from tin cans or earthen pots. And I noticed that the tiniest scraps of gaily colored material had been made into cushions or bed coverlets. I saw a lot of handwork—embroideries and laces in tablecloths, tidies, pillows and bedspreads. The utter absence of luxuries in housefurnishing for a while past makes it easier to understand the savage battles in the commercial stores to buy sleazy, highly colored lamp shades of the most appalling design and garishness, and the happy payment of up to fourteen hundred rubles for the privilege.

The people I visited were well off according to Moscow standards of living. One woman I knew had been bombed out and at the time she was talking to me had neither a bed nor a table. She said meekly, "Life is hard and sometimes I get a little downhearted. But what can you do? Nothing but wait for better times." "They can't be worse than they have been," said another, "so naturally they will have to be better." Many articles in the Russian papers told about the consumer goods soon to be available in huge quantities—clothes, shoes, textiles and fabrics, furniture, household utensils, electrical equipment. Few of them are available yet. Overtaxed housing facilities are of course not unknown to Americans.

There are slums in Moscow, as there are—or used to be—in every unbombed city in the world. Moscow, like every other big city, has definite plans for the eradication of these sore spots. But they are still festering there. I have ridden and walked through many of the back streets and seen some of the dilapidated old buildings which still shelter the large part of the population. I have walked through some of the little ancient byways and have wandered through some of the old alleys and courtyards. It is easy to see that here the living standards are very low, but one surprising thing I discovered was that the side streets and the byways and the muddy courtyards look clean. It is true that the courtyards were usually full of clotheslines, and the clotheslines were usually full of clothes. It is true that the clothes on the clotheslines were usually as dingy as clothes must be if they are washed in cold water with no soap or soap of a distressingly poor quality. But the courtyards, though muddy, held no piles of rotting garbage or sodden masses of foul old rags or newspapers. Everything was picked up and as sanitary as the poor drainage system would allow. We could learn a lesson from the Moscow city government at least in the matter of city sanitation.

The theatre buildings are probably the best buildings of the kind in the world. They are built with the idea firmly in mind that there must be room enough for everything connected with a theatrical production. The Soviets even remember what everybody else in the world seems to have forgotten—that actors are people. Behind the scenes there is no grudging hodgepodge of narrow halls and cell-like cubicles for dressing rooms. The architects have made provision for the actors to dress and to rest. Pleasant, well-furnished dressing rooms and greenrooms are always provided. And even if it is true that in general Russian workmanship and craftsmanship are not of the best, behind the scenes in any of the theatres you will find a well-organized, well-ordered world of make-believe.

The comfort of the patrons of the art has also been well considered. The new theatres are all spacious, well planned and extremely comfortable. The seats are wide and soft, and you can see the stage from every single one. The excellent plan extends beyond this, even. For when a Moscovite goes to the theatre, he goes to spend an entire evening having a good time. All the theatres have big lounges, wide promenades with comfortable seats, smoking rooms and, wonder of wonders, buffets. It is to be admitted at once that these are rather cheerless places, but nevertheless they exist. There are good-sized tables with clean tablecloths at which you can sit during the ample intervals and sip hot tea, nibble a pastry, or drink some of the appalling red raspberry syrup, which is the Russian soda pop. The pastries are expensive and too sweet for the American taste, but the idea is sound. To be able to go out between the acts without being trampled to death in a tiny lobby not adequate for more than ten or twelve people would be something, but to be able to walk around a spacious hall or sit in a comfortable lounge or have a bite to eat, while panning the show in peace, is really the lap of luxury.

The most glorious example of the theatre of the old days is the Grand State Theatre of Opera and Ballet, the Bolshoi. It faces Sverdlov Square and on the pediment is a magnificent bronze of Apollo with horses. The theatre itself is what most people dream that a theatre should be. Tier upon tier of boxes rise, festooned with gilt and curtained with red velvet. Acres

of red velvet must have been used in the decoration of this magnificent place, and it is not rayon velvet either. It's the good old lush silk velvet, that hangs in heavy, gorgeous folds.

I don't know how many people the Bolshoi Theatre can seat. This was the favorite theatre of the Czars. You can still see the grand royal box—only instead of the imperial eagle, now the hammer and sickle is mounted above it. Here grand opera and the famous ballet come to fullest flower. Here still the aroma of olden days hangs like incense.

One night when my husband and I had attended the ballet, we were walking back to the Metropole Hotel. It was snowing. And the picture of the crowds coming out of the wonderful old theatre into the shadowy, snowy night was one I shall never forget. As we walked along, we met a young American sergeant from Syracuse, New York. He had never been out of Syracuse before he was inducted into the armed forces, and now he found himself in Moscow going to the ballet. He had never seen a ballet in his life in America, never even heard of it, knew nothing about it. But in Moscow he became a balletomane. He went every time he got a chance, which was often. As he said himself, he was nuts about it. So as we met him face to face in Sverdlov Square, he was smiling with the pleasure he had just had.

"Tell me," he said, "how does this Bolshoi Theatre stack up against the Metropolitan Opera House in New York?"

I replied, somewhat grudgingly I am afraid, that I thought the Bolshoi bigger, better and more beautiful.

The young sergeant's mouth fell open. "You mean to tell me," he said indignantly, "that this Bolshoi is better than the New York Metropolitan?"

I had to admit that I thought it was.

"You mean to tell me," he shouted, "that these bozos got something better than we got?"

I said that in this case I thought they had.

"Well, these guys better look out," he said; "they just better look out, that's all." And he stamped furiously away into the falling snow.

I haven't the slightest idea what he meant, but he was a very angry young man.

The Red Army Theatre is just about as different from the Bolshoi as it is possible for a building to be. This too is a vast building, but it is as modern as the day after tomorrow. It is built on the plan of a five-pointed star, the star being the symbol of the Army. You may think this sounds crazy and I admit that it does. But the fact remains that it does not look crazy at all. I have never been in a building better suited to its use, more functional or more beautifully adapted to housing the drama and its patrons comfortably. There is plenty of light, which is not always the case in the Soviet

buildings. There are plenty of good, wide doors, and plenty of lounges and resting rooms. Let me add that in this case the performance we saw came up to the standard set by the building. We saw Goldsmith's *She Stoops to Conquer* and it was the best performance of that play that I ever saw anywhere.

I am, however, at this point reminded of two performances I saw in Moscow of Lillian Hellman's plays. These were translations of *The Little Foxes* and *The Watch on the Rhine*. It is my sincere personal belief that if any American producer presented either of them in America as they are being presented to the trusting citizens of Moscow, Miss Hellman would shoot him in cold blood. And no American jury would find her guilty either. But this is beside the point.

The theatre buildings and the theatre performances are two different things. And although I do not admire Russian plays or acting as they appear under the Soviet system, I say flatly that I go all out for their theatre architects and am second to none in complete admiration of them.

In America the best effort ever made toward the establishment of a national theatre, the W.P.A., was brought to nothing by the monkey wrenches which the American Communists happily heaved into the works of that organization. The old central power in Moscow is getting the same results. They are determined to force the art of the theatre into the mold of propaganda and what is potentially the best theatre in the world is being squeezed and smothered. Anyone who remembers the Moscow Theatre when it came to America in 1922 or the Chauve-Souris a little earlier will probably be unable to believe that the present Russian theatre is a flabby, colorless and pretty futile thing.

In the main, only the classics remain; some of the plays have been performed in the same theatre by virtually the same actors for twenty years. No wonder the actors know their parts and are letter-perfect in every cue and piece of business! And no wonder they play like sleepwalkers, without sparkle and without life! There is not one new play on the boards in Moscow today which can be said to be an excellent modern play. They are nearly all patently propaganda without entertainment value. The genius for the theatre is still present: you feel its potential strength. There is something to be said for the lighting, the scenery, sometimes—only sometimes—the direction. But the spirit is dead. The blight is there, eating away at the plant. Freedom, the ultimate nourishment, is not in the soil. The Puppet Theatre and the Children's Theatre, which lean heavily on the innocuous fairy tale for their material, are really happy examples of what the Russian imagination and artistry in the theatre can do. But the adult theatre is a sad wreck.

There are several large, impressive-looking movie theatres in Moscow, but we only attended one of them. The American ambassador has a showing of American movies once or twice a week in Spaso House, where he lives, for Americans and their friends, and we saw movies there. If you invite a Russian friend to accompany you, he is usually delighted, because American movies are not widely shown in Moscow. I saw a couple of Deanna Durbin pictures advertised on the billboards in front of the movie houses. Evidently, Deanna is considered innocuous enough for the Russians to look at safely. Be that as it may, I know she is a prime favorite with the Russian men, who practically drool when they speak of her. The fact that she was slightly plumper than usual when the picture shown in Moscow was made was only added allurement.

Hollywood has its troubles with Moscow. Although I am slightly vague about the process involved, I know that Hollywood sends some films to the Russian capital. These films are shown first before a film committee consisting of people who are presumably best qualified to judge of the films' suitability for the Moscow masses.

But this does not mean that no Russians see the films. At the request of various high-bracket clubs, the Architects' Club, the Actors' Club, the Engineers' Club, etc., the amiable American State Department sends the film around for their entertainment. Thus it is kept from contaminating the masses, a goodly number of irreproachable Soviet citizens have some fun, and the Russian government pays nothing. The final decision is usually "Thank you very much, but no."

When we curiously inquired why so few American films were shown in Russian theatres, we were told by the patriotic Russians, "We cannot afford it. Hollywood wants too much money for them." This seems a strange way to figure, inasmuch as any American film shown in Moscow can play to packed theatres as long as the film holds together.

An American film could play for three or four years without exhausting public interest. But only a very few Russians, a very favored few, ever see the majority of Hollywood products.

The only time my husband and I ever went to a public movie theatre we rued the day. We decided to go to the Metropole Theatre to see a Russian film called something like *Hello, Moscow*. It was the most ambitious movie the Russians had attempted for many years, and we were anxious to see the results.

In order to get tickets an elaborate routine had to be gone through. My husband had to dictate a letter to his secretary on *New York Times* stationery. This he not only had to sign, but had to stamp with the *New York Times* stamp. The courier then took the letter down to the box office, about four o'clock in the afternoon, to ensure tickets being ready for us by eight o'clock that evening. (Nobody ever just walks up to the box office and buys a ticket. You have to sneak up to it.)

·After dinner that night, we went down to the theatre and fought our way through the crowded lobby to the ticket window. Our secretary had assured us that everything was in order, that they would be expecting us at the ticket window, and although we could not speak Russian, the ticket seller would understand who we were and give us our tickets. This proved to be slightly less than the truth. The woman at the window glared at us uncomprehendingly and, when we were unable to make her understand, motioned us impatiently aside.

We stood helplessly there, laughing a little, because it was no more than we had expected. But a Red Army officer (who spoke no English, incidentally) seemed to sense what our difficulty was and took us to another window in a smaller, side lobby. This window was closed; it had a wooden panel which slid down over the opening. Upon this panel our good Samaritan beat with a heavy fist. What ensued was like a Punch and Judy show. The window panel flew up, an angry woman's head popped out, she glared at the officer, and before he could speak she had snapped the panel down again. But he was a man of mettle. Unabashed, he beat upon the panel again. Immediately it flew up, and immediately the furious woman peered out. This time he was able to say half a sentence before she disappeared.

Now he was really mad. I think he had lost sight of his original plan to help us, and was only determined that the woman should hear all he had to say before she got away from him. He thundered at the portal, he beat upon it with both fists. It took a little longer, but finally the woman appeared. She fooled him. As soon as she caught a glimpse of his angry face, she vanished as if on a wire, and the little door snapped shut again.

My husband and I were convulsed with laughter. It became obvious that we were not to get in to see *Hello, Moscow* that night. So we thanked the soldier profusely and departed. But he remained. He was still beating on the little door as we left the theatre.

We approached the problem in a different manner the next time. We took our secretary and our courier with us and between them they finally got us in. *Hello, Moscow* proved an elaborate, disjointed propaganda picture whose story got lost early in the film and only reappeared for a smashing finale. As I remember it, in the final scene the hero and the heroine stood bravely shoulder to shoulder, reunited at last, under the wildly waving Red banner. This is the Russian equivalent of walking out into the sunset together.

The Film Trust has a small, luxuriously appointed projection room to which it occasionally invited accredited foreigners. We saw several Soviet films there, including a technicolor effort called *The Stone Flower*. The handling of the story was lethargic and childish, but the color effects were brilliant. Lest anyone be frightened at the prospect of the Russians overtaking and surpassing us in color photography, let me add that we were told that *The Stone Flower* had been made on "captured" German film, not Russian at all.

Chapter 14

The Metro and the Churches

ONE OF the very first questions a Moscovite asks you after you become acquainted with him is, "Have you seen our subways?" Most Americans smile and wonder why on earth anybody wants to take you down in the subway for a sight-seeing tour. A subway, in New York for instance, is a place where you go reluctantly and only when you want to get some place fast. We have had subways for so many years that it seems hilarious to be proud of one. But there is a reason for pride in Moscow.

Although the Moscow subway covers only a rather small circuit compared to New York subways, and although it is even more dreadfully crowded than ours, one brilliant difference exists. The Moscow Metro is beautiful. Every station has been regarded as a separate artistic project. Each station has been lovingly planned by a different architect and his imagination has been allowed free rein. No expense has been spared. And the results are stunning. The most modern lighting is employed. Colored marbles, sweeping murals, precious metals, infinite pains with detail and in the execution of the plans have been used. The upper stations are spacious and impressive; the lower ones, where the trains come in, have vast vaulted ceilings, pillars, marble benches and statues.

The subway is greatly admired, greatly appreciated. And why not? The mobs of tired people who throng through these stations daily cannot help but be momentarily uplifted and refreshed by the soothing atmosphere of such beauty and such promise. I have watched the faces of the people as they ride on the long escalators—all of the Moscow stations seem very deep to me. And it is a sight to remember. Nearly everybody who rides on the subway carries a bundle—sometimes the bundle is nearly as big as the person. And as these people stand on the escalators, being carried deep down or conveyed out of the depths, I have seen them, time and time again, raise their eyes to the illuminated ceilings or the fine paintings that adorn the walls, and they always relax a little, they always seem pleased and rested.

Many of the subway engineers are women, and all the conductors, cashiers, ticket takers and cleaners and porters that I saw were also women. The names of the subway stations are interesting. They don't just call a place "Twenty-third Street" or "Broadway." "Palace of the Soviets," "Park of Culture and Rest" are what they use.

The stories about the subway are not exaggerated. It was a wise man who first thought of the idea of bringing beauty to the masses in just that way. It was a quick and concrete showing of what the new Soviet government intended to do. Who could fail to be impressed by the power of a government that would build such magnificence for the use of the common people? The Czars themselves never lived in greater grandeur.

But when you ride on the Metro, it's hard to keep your mind so uplifted. It is a terrifying experience and one that I underwent as seldom as possible. During the rush hours people line up, three deep, in a queue a block long even to get into the doors. A loud-speaker system is utilized to keep the crowd moving efficiently and inform it how many more can be accommodated. The escalators, though swift, are, of course, narrow, and the throng must converge sharply before it can use them. Below, an even more vicious bottleneck exists. The doorways for entrance to and exit from the trains are extremely small, and the whole trampling, hurrying, bundle-laden mob must crush through those tight spaces. The moment when you are actually going through the door is one when you are almost squeezed unconscious. It is a thoroughly horrifying business and if you should have the bad luck to faint, you would be a bloody pulp in very short order.

The trains themselves are well designed, smooth-running and spacious, but jammed, like our own, to inhuman overcapacity. I tried to avoid taking the Metro during rush hours, but even in the middle of the day the crowds are enormous. Moscow has the same trouble as many other cities—no amount of transportation facilities seems adequate. The busses are always stuffed to the doors and people are hanging on outside, with arms and legs dangling. The trolley busses, too, are not numerous enough to accommodate the thousands who must use them. And, when I was there, there were no taxis, or even horse-drawn vehicles to be hired.

Most foreigners manage to get cars of their own, because to be dependent upon the subway and busses is to be practically hamstrung in severe weather. Summertime is bad enough, when everybody is going to market and coming home laden with sacks of potatoes and onions and crushing themselves onto the subway or busses with all that extra bulky load, but when the ice forms on the pavements and the snow piles up on the sidewalks and walking becomes a real hazard and everybody is swathed up with padded clothing and wearing heavy muddy boots and carrying enormous bundles into the bargain, life just isn't worth living if you don't have a car of your own.

Be warned. Don't go into the subways at rush hours in Moscow. Or in New York either, for that matter.

Churches

Before the Revolution, more than four hundred churches were holding services in Moscow and every church had its bell. There is a good firm foundation for the phrase, "the Bells of Moscow." When the Soviets came to power, religion was derided and Karl Marx's ringing statement, "Religion is the opium of the people," became one of the slogans of the new regime. Indeed, it has been cast in bronze on a tablet that is set into the wall of the Lenin Museum, and is still there for all to see. Most of the four hundred churches were seized by the government and changed into museums, cinemas, office buildings, libraries and even dwelling houses. But a few of the churches never closed their doors. They continued on, bravely holding Mass in the face of dangerous governmental opposition. Most of the bells were silenced, if not all. Earnest Soviet workers were deprived of much-needed sleep and rest by the ceaseless clanging of the bells, and so those of the bells that were not confiscated "for governmental necessity" hung silent in the bell towers.

The Roman Catholic Church in Moscow never closed its doors. This church was for many long years—twelve, I think—under the leadership of the American priest Father Braun, who came to know the people of Moscow like a father indeed. He never ceased to be the shepherd of his flock and to minister to their spiritual needs whenever they called on him. He said Mass every day during his entire tenure of office in Moscow and is justifiably proud of the record. He recently returned to America and his place has been taken by Father La Berge, another devout leader who is continuing along the lines Father Braun laid down.

There was a rumor that the church bells were going to be rung for the first time in ten years on Easter Day 1946. Not the old bells of Moscow, naturally, since most of these had disappeared down the maw of "national necessity." But the government, formerly of the opinion that "religion is the opium of the people," had decided, for some reason, that religion had to be tolerated, and had therefore supplied bells to many of the largest churches. One big cathedral had a series of small substitute bells, hung temporarily in the bell tower to bring out on Easter Day. Without doubt, the faithful worshipers will soon band together again to provide bells for their churches. They have always supplied them in the past, even going so far as to give silver money and golden trinkets to be melted down with other metals to lend a melodious tone. Meanwhile, the government is supplying the bells.

My husband, curious to know whether the Roman Catholic Church would have a bell ringing on that important Easter, called the new priest, Father La Berge, and asked him about it. The priest replied that he did not know whether his church had a bell but that he would inquire and let my husband know. He called back awhile later and said that his church was indeed the proud possessor of a bell; that the bell was rusty and dusty from disuse and needed oiling. But that it *would* be oiled and that, come Easter Day, the bell would ring out through the Easter morn. It did, too.

There are about twenty churches now which have been reopened and put to their original use. Nowadays freedom of worship is permitted in Russia. Anti-religious campaigns formerly in force and anti-religious museums which were set up in many revered and famous cathedrals have been abandoned. Some informed foreigners in Moscow think that the pressure of public opinion was so great the government considered it expedient to permit Russians to resume their worship. Others insist that the church has now become the servant of the state. Anyhow, the pendulum is swinging back.

A visit to any orthodox church will prove to anybody that the people are determined to worship. I attended several Masses in small churches in poor districts of Moscow and the way the people flocked there filled me with awe. I have never seen a drowning man gasp for breath, nor have I seen a starving man cram his mouth with food long denied. But now I can easily imagine how the lungs of one inhale as deeply as possible, how the other almost frantically stuffs himself when he is given a meal. That is the way the people worshiped in Moscow.

Many abased themselves on the floors over which hundreds of muddy boots had passed, pressing their lips against it in abject devotion. They formed in lines before the icons of their favorite saints and patiently waited their turn to kiss the paintings. The crowded church was still, the faces of the people turned to their priests as to a heaven-sent light. They listened to the chanting and seemed uplifted, comforted and transfixed. The priests, clad in robes stiff with gold thread and silks and jewels, passed among them, and the people touched their garments as they passed and kissed their hands and received their blessing with closed eyes. They stood there in their ragged, dirty clothes, in their ragged, battered shoes, drenched in belief, wonder, hope and love. Even though they themselves were poor and ragged and cold and hungry, they kept their church like a palace. They put their rubles and kopecks lovingly into the collection basket and breathed in the incense smoke and looked at the gold and color of the paintings, at the marble of the walls, at the icons and the bundles, all bought and maintained with their mites, as though they were seeing a preview of heaven. For a few elevated enchanted moments they could forget all the grimness of their daily lives.

The congregations included many older women. But there were lots of men—young men, Army men in uniform, sailors and working men—and also many children, standing wide-eyed and wondering in the smoky magnificence of the church. I saw one grandmother carrying a child of about three years, bowing his little head with her hand and guiding him in the motions of the Cross at the proper times during the service.

At any christening service of a Sunday morning, young mothers gather with their babies—fourteen of them the morning I went. Swathed in quilts and shawls, held in their mothers' arms, the babies form a big circle around the priest in the murky little chapel. There, with an enormous oval silver bowl as font, the mothers unwrap the wailing infants and present them, naked as they were born, one by one, to the old priest. He takes each little bare worm from its cocoon and, holding it by nape and ankles, dips it deeply into the water, while the choir chants and the incense smoke swirls high and the candles flicker in the cold drafts that sweep through the church. As each anxious mother receives back her dripping young, she hastily rewraps it into a clumsy bundle and hurries away, torn between fear lest the child sicken of exposure, and comfort that if he does, he dies in the faith. No, religion is not dead in Russia, nor even absent.

Although *Pravda*, one of the most influential newspapers, maintains a running feud with the Vatican, the Roman Catholic Church still flourishes in Moscow. The Russian Orthodox Church never lost its hold on the people and is gaining strength every day.

The Lutheran Church, a hundred years ago, was very strong in Russia. Many of the high government officials and cabinet members were Lutherans. But I was not able to find evidence that any Protestant church exists in Moscow now.

Chapter 15

Getting Museum Feet

AN OLD GUIDEBOOK states that there used to be a hundred and seventy museums in Moscow. Certainly many of these were closed during the war. Still, no small number remain. I did not visit all the museums though many times at the end of the day my feet felt as though I had. One museum I regret not to have been able to visit was the Museum of Modern Western Art. The Russians have there one of the finest collections of French paintings of the late nineteenth and early twentieth centuries. Only the Paris collection outranks it. Represented are canvases by Renoir, Cézanne, Picasso and Matisse. These paintings had all been taken away for safekeeping and had not yet been returned to the building provided for them.

I did, however, go to the Museum of the Revolution. This is situated in a beautiful old building of classical architecture which was formerly the British Club. I spent two successive days in it with an Intourist guide and a guide from the museum. We traced the Revolution from its beginning in 1905 through its successful termination in 1917. The Museum of the Revolution is an excellent sample of the Russian determination to put only the best foot forward. The tattered flags, made of scraps of material carried by the insurgents, are carefully washed, pressed, mended, and kept folded in glass cases. A striped jersey singlet, said to have been worn by one of their earliest and most ardent naval heroes, looks as fresh as the day it was woven. You'd hardly believe it had been worn by a warrior who sweated and fought through a bloody battle.

Whenever a hero falls from grace, as did the late Leon Trotsky, all mention of him is carefully expunged. When he must be mentioned (Trotsky is once), it is to point out he was a scoundrel from the start. No one can help being impressed by a successful revolution begun furtively in attics and cellars. To see their country today, founded upon the first precepts and now grown strong and vigorous through being nourished by the blood and lives of the believers, to be forced to the greatest respect for the original planners. A little blood and dirt on the trophies could hardly detract from their impressiveness.

I could not help reflecting how different is the American attitude. Our museums are full of peeks at the clay feet of our beloved great men. And nobody cares a bit. We do not care if there is evidence that our great ones were human. But a Russian great man must be as perfect as the saint on an icon. True, I have heard many sly stories about their present leaders, but I am sure that none of these stories will get into the folklore or the biography.

There is one picture in the Museum of the Revolution that I shall never forget. It is a vicious cartoon of Kerenski escaping from the Bolsheviks disguised as a nun. He is rushing down a flight of steps, holding his wide black skirts high, and his betrousered legs are showing as he runs. His face is twisted into a grimace of the most abject fear, and altogether the man is made out to be a cringing coward. I have never heard tones of such vitriolic contempt as were used by my guide to explain this picture to me. It seemed to be more than just a portrayal of somebody the Soviets considered a traitor. There seemed to be a personal scorn, bitterness and hatred about it that made my flesh crawl. The Soviets are good haters. And where they consider hate a weapon, they do everything they can to nourish it and keep it alive. A member of the Women's Anti-Fascist Committee once explained to me that the main object of that committee's work during the war was "to teach hatred of Fascism." I had the phrase repeated and had it translated twice so I cannot be mistaken. Teaching hatred must be a queer sort of career. I wonder how it affects the teacher?

I went to the Tolstoy Museum also. It contains a collection of articles belonging to this author, many of his manuscripts, books and personal things. It gives a keen insight into the life of his day and particularly into the life of his family. Tolstoy's study has been kept intact and it contains, besides his big desk with its pens and writing materials, a large assortment of bulging black leather furniture including one of the most tremendous couches I ever saw. It was very impressive, that study. Standing there among Tolstoy's own possessions gave me a deeper understanding of his outlook on life. The guide took me through the bedrooms and dressing rooms of the other members of the family. Each room had the imprint of the former inhabitant still clearly upon it.

In 1936 I visited the New Maiden's Monastery, which was one of the most popular museums for tourists. At that time it contained examples of the needlework and other handcrafts of the luckless ladies who had lived there. I say luckless because the convent was in reality a prison. When a Czar or other member of royalty got tired of his wife or indeed any female relative, he sent her to the New Maiden's Monastery. She was out of his way, but nobody could say she was in jail. Nobody but the lady. Now, because of the tremendous housing shortage in Moscow, the vast old building has been turned into dormitories and living apartments. The New Maiden's Monastery is so called because it is located in the New Maiden's Field. This in the ancient days was a field to which young girls were brought each year by Tartars who sold them as slaves or concubines to the Moscovites. Each year a new crop was brought in and thereby came the name New Maidens.

The New Maiden's *Monastery* was really a convent. It was originally built as a fort in the sixteenth century and years later was enlarged and partly reconstructed. A bell tower and several churches were ultimately added. The church of the Smolensk Mother of God is here. Within the walls are two old cemeteries. It is here that Anton Chekhov is buried and here is also the grave of Stalin's first wife. I wanted to see this grave and found it enclosed within a high hedge of evergreens. A simple white marble shaft marks the grave itself. The shaft is surmounted by a marble head of the lady which has been done in classic style and shows her as a handsome woman with clear features and gentle expression. One cheek is rested against one hand and this hand with its long fingers showing delicacy and strength is added proof that Mme. Stalin must have been a woman not only beautiful but with character and grace.

A little way from the stone bridge across the Moscow River is the Tretyakov Gallery. In 1856 a wealthy merchant in Russia, P. Tretyakov, established the museum for his own pleasure. In 1892 he gave it to the city of Moscow. It now houses the greatest collection of paintings and drawings in the Soviet Union. There is an impressive collection of ancient Russian church art, with many icons taken from the finest of the cathedrals. There is also a notable collection of political art—pictures showing Stalin in Napoleonic pose standing on bridges looking over his domain; pictures of all the great national heroes in various inspiring poses. But for the main part the museum consists of nineteenth-century art. If you like early McKinley pictures, the Tretyakov Gallery is for you.

There used to be several antireligious museums about the city. But since the Soviet .government has now decided to smile on the church, these museums no longer exist. At one time during my stay in Moscow there was a "Booty" exhibit, which consisted of tanks, guns and all kinds of war goods which had been taken from the Germans. There were huge piles of military decorations which had been stripped from the enemy; literally thousands of iron crosses and other orders to show how many of the hated Nazis had been brought low. This exhibit was extremely popular with soldiers and small boys who would hang entranced over the thrilling sight. Inasmuch as there was a brisk black-market trade in iron crosses in the streets in Moscow, it would seem that even more booty had found its way in than that which appeared in the governmental show.

Chapter 16

Parks and Flowers

THERE ARE PLENTY of little parks and green squares throughout the city, with trees, with benches to sit on and with walks for the children to play on. In the winter it is, of course, usually impossible to sit in the parks, because of the snow that falls nearly all the time. In the early spring they are so muddy they are usually closed, the Kremlin Park at any rate. But in the summer they are used by many people. The park scenes are like park scenes anywhere. Mothers and babies or grandmothers and babies or nurses and babies or little children make up the greatest part of the parks' population. There are the soldiers home on leave, with outstretched, booted legs and uniform collars loosened to let in the good air of the summertime; elderly, scholarly men with their noses deep in books; young couples; old women nodding to themselves over their memories or their sorrows. The parks welcome anybody who has a few minutes away from his work, and under the leafy shadows it is possible to sit and dream and forget for a while the pressing demands of a workaday world.

I was sitting in the Kremlin Park one day with my husband when a big Russian soldier approached and sat down beside us on the bench. He was an ugly customer, well over six feet tall, with an apelike face and great arms and hands. He stared at us coldly, his little eyes steely and brutal. Seldom an advocate of appeasement, I felt that this might be the moment to employ it. I smiled, rather weakly I am afraid, and offered him an American cigarette. He snatched it, popped it into his mouth, lighted it and puffed the smoke in our faces.

We waited. It seemed a rather pitiful way to die—in a foreign land, in a park, at the hands of an implacable savage. But after all, you can die only once. He continued to smoke and to stare without winking.

"Where are you from?" he asked us in a rasping voice.

We both were very thankful that we understood what he said. Not to have been able to understand would, we both felt, have only hastened what seemed our inevitable end. My husband said, very mildly indeed, that we were from America.

"Latvia?" shouted the soldier.

But we would not deny our land, even at our imminent peril. It would have been easy to nod. To our honor be it said that we did not. "The United States," said my husband bravely.

"Ah," said the brute, a vicious smile splitting his face and showing all his stained and broken teeth, "the Ukraine!"

Again we had just strength enough to shake our heads. But he had had enough of us. He rose and left us in disdain, striding over to a bench where a comely young Russian girl was sitting alone. He began to discuss us and our patent insanity with her, but she wouldn't talk to him at all. We went away from there about then, breathing a prayer of thanksgiving for deliverance. But the Russian girl was completely unaware of danger. By the cut of her jib we gathered that she was giving him the brush-off and by the cut of his we gathered that he had forgotten all about us. He had never heard of the United States or of America; and as far as he was concerned, it was evident that he had never felt better in his life.

The Lenin Hills on the outskirts of the city were one of my favorite places to go for a drive. They used to be called the "Sparrow Hills" before the wave of political nomenclature washed over Moscow. In the old days there used to be a fine restaurant there to which parties of merrymakers would drive after a night on the town. Here they would finish up the long Russian evening by watching the sunrise. The restaurant is not open now, and I never got ambitious enough to go there to watch the sunrise, but the view of Moscow, sprawling out at the foot of the ridge, is beautiful. In the summer the hillside is used by Moscovites for little gardens, and every day you can see dozens of industrious people bent double in the familiar pose of earnest gardeners the world over, weeding and tending these plots. In the winter ardent skiers go there to swoop down the steep hillsides, breaking their legs and twisting their ankles with enthusiasm. Some day, the Plan says, the pine-covered hills will be built solid with apartment buildings and workers' dwellings. Now, however, the wooded land is sparsely settled and mainly with small, delightful log houses which have painted and carved window frames, looking like illustrations from old fairy-tale books.

To the left of the road approaching the Hills turns the old Exile Road—now a paved boulevard. Over it the exiles used to start out for Siberia, many of them never to return. I always saw these ghost figures in my mind when we passed the road; it always seemed full of sorrowful, melancholy people, plodding their weary way to the dreaded Siberia. And since Siberia was easily thousands of miles away, the poor souls surely had a walk ahead of them. They probably go by car or train now. The Soviets in this connection also are progressive.

The Russians love flowers and will spend a good hunk of their hard-earned rubles to have a few fresh ones in their homes. During the spring and summer there are little flower stalls and pushcarts here and there throughout the town laden with colorful fresh blossoms, and the stalls are always well patronized. Flowers are never cheap. A good-sized bunch will cost a purchaser ninety rubles. Three hundred rubles is an average monthly wage. Early in the spring, mimosa is flown up from the Crimea and makes a golden glow in the gray of the gloomy Moscow streets. Not only women purchase this first spring flower. I have seen husky men striding along with fistfuls, smiling down at the frail and fragrant blossoms.

Potted plants are available in the spring and these, too, are expensive. A Russian girl I knew brought me a lovely one, with a note from the florist giving me explicit directions on how to care for it. I followed the rules carefully and as a result the plant flourished and blossomed for several months.

Later, one day, this friend came into my room for a moment and caught sight of her gift, still covered with flowers. "How wonderful!" she cried. "It is still living! How do you take care of it?"

I told her.

"Oh, no," she said, "that's not the way I do it at all!"

"And how is your plant getting along?" I asked.

Her face fell. "Unfortunately, mine perished," she said, and was astonished at my shout of laughter.

In the summertime you can buy fresh flowers in the bazaar. Dozens of peasants, women and girls, bring armfuls to sell to the flower-hungry people of the city. You can buy lovely

roses and all the familiar annuals, zinnias, snapdragons, gladioli, calendulas, poppies and such. But after the garden season is past and even the chrysanthemums have vanished from the scene, the Russians manage to keep the memory of summer in their hearts. Then the little booths blossom out with artificial flowers, made of paper or cloth. Although the flowers bloom in colors slightly more violent than the natural ones, still they are gay and vivid. The roses are very red or very pink, the nasturtiums are a gaudy orange, the violets are unrelenting and violent purple, but they are symbols just the same.

The Moscovites are fond of dyed grasses and you see long feathery plumes of grass dyed brilliant red, yellow, green or purple. They have straw flowers, too, and other dried flowers, and so they manage to keep the gloom of the long Moscow winter at bay.

Since flowers are expensive, the people of Moscow do whatever they can to make them last as long as possible. I have seen a Russian woman take a large bunch of roses which seemed to me faded beyond help and go through the following routine: First, she clipped off a few inches of the stems. Then she put a large pot of water on to boil. When the water was bubbling hard, she plunged the stems of the roses deep down into it and held them there for a few seconds. Then she put the roses into a vase filled with cold water. When I saw these carryings-on, I said that it looked to me as though she were planning to have boiled roses for dinner, but my friend only smiled gently and said, "Wait and see." Within an hour, the faded roses had taken a new lease on life and were as perky as you please. You can't do the boiling-water trick more than twice on the same flowers, but I'm here to state flatly that I've seen it work twice, myself.

Chapter 17

Vanity Fair

YOU CANNOT be so badly dressed in Moscow that anybody will look at you twice. You see everybody in hand-me-downs, threadbare and shapeless; and battered boots and tattered shoes are much more in evidence than whole garments or decent foot-gear. Particularly civilian men's clothing is in shockingly bad condition. At this point, I am, like the speakers at banquets, reminded of a story. There was a Russian who worked for Americans and he was an extremely handsome man. The fact that his clothing was shabby made him very much ashamed and upset. His pants, particularly, were literally in rags. So he did what all Russians working for foreigners do—he asked permission to use the employer's ration book in the employer's Diplomatic Store to get a suit for himself. Permission was granted, but no men's suits were available even in the Dipstore. The Russian therefore asked permission to buy woolen material instead. But there was not enough woolen material to make both coat and trousers of the same goods and the Russian was forced to buy blue serge for the coat and black woolen material for the pants.

Then came the long and dreary task of getting a tailor to make the suit and waiting for it to be done. During this trying period, an American friend of the employer's came into the office one day and foolishly let it be known that he was going on a trip to Sweden. The Russian immediately implored his employer's friend to bring him a suit back from Sweden and in spite of the annoyance involved—all the business of changing rubles into dollars (an illegal transaction) and then into Swedish kronen, and taking up precious time buying a suit for a comparative stranger—the American agreed. He set off for Sweden with the Russian's rubles and measurements in his pocket, promising to be back in eight or ten weeks with the coveted suit.

During this period, the Russian met another American who was going home. The Russian implored the American to sell him a suit, which the American did. Then for the first time in all these transactions the Russian really had a decent suit. Before you could say "scat" however, the tailor had the first suit finished and the American from Sweden came back with another suit. The Russian was in the seventh heaven of delight. "Just see," he said, his face beaming, "how much better conditions are today than they were even a year ago! Formerly, I was in rags, but now, as you can see, I have three good suits!"

And he wasn't kidding. He really meant it. To point out that he would have had nothing at all except several holes in the seat of his trousers if it had not been for illegal transactions with Americans, would only have annoyed and confused him. He preferred to think that this new status was due to the careful planning of his own government and so we all let him think so. It's grand to have stars in the eyes, even though they prevent your seeing what really is going on.

New clothes, good clothes, even decent clothes are readily noticeable. The day after my arrival I went to a tea at the American Embassy, wearing what I would have worn on a similar occasion at home—a green wool suit and a flowered hat with a crisp green veil. I was nearly mobbed. Pedestrian traffic stopped on the street as I went by. People goggled at me, jostled and pointed and laughed in my face. It was a shattering experience that taught me never to wear an American hat on the street again. Eventually, the suit was accepted on the street. Stared at, it is true, but with reluctant admiration. But the hat was too comic for them ever to accept. I gave it to a Russian girl who adored it. But she has probably had to use it for a wall decoration. I don't see how she'd dare wear it.

I brooded about the Russians' laughing at me. Once it became necessary for my husband's secretary to escort me somewhere and I said to him sarcastically, "Are you sure you are willing to be seen with me on the street? You know I was considered a kind of freak the other day." But Mr. Zellikoff was gallant. He bowed from the waist and reassured me. "Other people may consider you a freak," he said, "but I do not." Thus soothed, I was forced to be content.

It has been such a long time since the Moscovites have had new clothing that the appetite for anything new is enormous. They have mended and patched until the clothes will hardly hold together any more. Ready-made clothing is extremely scarce and what you can get of it is shoddy, poorly made and expensive. You can get things made to order in the state dressmaking shops if you furnish your own material. The workmanship is excellent. Russians are very proud of the tailoring and needlework of these shops and they have every right to be. American patterns are used almost exclusively. I saw *McCall* pattern catalogues, and copies of *Vogue* and *Harper's Bazaar* are in every shop. (This, incidentally, is the only place I ever saw foreign "literature" exhibited.) But most customers must be patient to the point of exhaustion, for many weeks will elapse before they get their garment.

My own experience in the state shop was far more fortunate than the experiences of Russian girls who almost wept with disappointment and impatience as again and again their coat or dress was not ready when promised. In my case, I took my material to the shop, chose my pattern, had my measurements taken and was given an appointment the following week for a fitting. When I arrived at the specified, the blouse was ready for the first try-on. It fitted so well that only a few minor changes had to be made and I was told I could have it the following week. When I went for it, it was ready. I was astonished and inquired why I got better service than the Russians themselves did and they looked at me in surprise and said gently, "But you are our guest!" I don't think the bars of soap and the lipstick I gave the fitter made much difference. The Russians have to make these little "gifts," too. They really were anxious that I should have a good impression of the state shop and I got it.

After many discussions with Russians and much observation and thought on the subject, I have come to the conclusion that the real Russian ideal of a woman is about what we in America know as a Bostonian lady. A well-educated lady, a little aloof, a little cold, and extremely dignified. Dressed with quiet elegance in clothes of classic cut, severely simple, of excellent quality. Well-groomed, with no cosmetics, or else cosmetics very sparingly applied. Neatly shod, beautifully gloved, restrained—"serious." Such a woman is the Russian ideal and would be received everywhere with heartfelt admiration and respect. All "high style," all bright paint jobs, all foreign fads and fancies, though they may be relished by teen-agers, "Gimme girls" and "May I?s," are for the most part regarded with contempt.

It is an interesting and amusing thing to stand for half an hour or so in front of the Metropole Hotel and watch the street scene in Sverdlov Square. In the spring of the year, when the weather is beginning to relent and the air blows warm, it will give you a pleasant interlude to observe the passing show.

Gradually and suspiciously, people have begun to shed their ragged, drab winter clothes, and the young girls, like young girls the world around, are the first harbingers of spring. In Moscow their clothes are neither fashionable nor new, but somehow, some way, the girls manage to inject into the springtime attire a note of freshness and gaiety and bright color. There are no fads or fashions in Moscow— each one wears what she has and makes the most of it. To have a fad it is necessary to be able to walk into a store and buy what "is being worn." What is being worn in Moscow is what a clever girl has been able to accumulate from her own wardrobe, her mother's probably and anyone else's who can be persuaded to swap or sell. A ribbon picked up for no small sum in the bazaar and woven into her braids; a baggy old sweater given a new lease of life by a bit of bright-colored hand embroidery around the neck and sleeves; a coat turned inside out and pepped up with a yard or two of braid donated by a sympathetic neighbor—that's the way costumes come into being in Moscow.

Few of the working girls can afford to buy anything in the big Mostorg—the prices are prohibitive. If a girl earns three hundred rubles a month—and many earn even less than that—she will have to save a long time before she can afford to spend nineteen hundred rubles for a coat, five hundred rubles for a pair of shoes, two hundred rubles for a sweater— or even thirty rubles for a small spool of thread. And what is available in her own ration store is usually nothing. She "makes do" and the result is oftentimes admirable.

I think the Russians really have excellent taste. They know what is good and what is bad instinctively, and completely without the influence of "fashion groups." When you realize that these women and girls have been cut off from the outside world for many years, that some of them have never seen a fashion magazine or a foreign style, it is amazing how instinctively right they are in the selection of color and line. Of course, I am not talking about "floozies." The Russian floozie chooses her clothes just as any other floozie chooses hers—for flooziness. But the steady working girl, the professional woman, knows what is excellent unfailingly.

Another place to watch the fashions is in the theatres. Here, again, the individuality of the people impresses you. And the dignity and grace of the women, decked out in shabby hand-me-downs, revived and restored and given a certain something, really make you feel that you are in the presence of people who certainly know the meaning of elegance.

One day when I was standing in front of the Metropole Hotel waiting for a friend, a very tiny, very frail, very shabby old woman came up to me. She asked me whether I understood Russian, and when I replied, "Not very well," she spoke to me in French. "Permit me to compliment you upon your dress, Madame," she said, touching the trimming at the neck of my frock with gentle fingers. "It must be in the latest mode. The color is certainly charming." And she bobbed her head, and smiled toothlessly and hobbled off happily.

There was a fashion show while I was in Moscow and all the foreign correspondents were invited. It was less a fashion show than an occasion for the material manufacturers and the designers to get together and compare notes and criticize one another's work. What they wanted to determine, as far as I could make out, was which materials and which designs were best suited for mass production. I think the U.N. meetings must be a little like that one. Criticism flew fast and furious. When a model—say, a woman's suit—appeared, there would be outspoken remarks like "The shoulders are too broad" or "The tucks at the waist make the coat too bulky," to which there would be rejoinders like "They are not, either!" and "The matter needs more thought!"

The show was held upstairs in a State Atelier, and a modernistic setting had been built. All across one side of the room a partition had been erected behind which the mannequins dressed. An entrance from each side was provided. A low platform, with shallow steps had been built, and the mannequins, entering slowly from one side would mount the steps and pose for a minute or two, turning gracefully, lifting their arms to show the lines of the garment, and descend the other side and exit.

As is ever the case with the Russians, the lighting was abominable—dim, and in all the wrong places. But it showed that somebody had been around, somewhere, and had brought back ideas from some foreign fashion shows, which, translated into Russian, had gone slightly askew. However, it was a sporting try.

The mannequins were very interesting. Most of them were tall and slim and they all wore the clothes with an air. It was not the sophisticated, hard-boiled, neuter manner of American models, but rather self-possessed, modest and ingratiating. Make-up was used sparingly, and the girls' hair was simply and neatly dressed. As for the men models, they had a slightly truculent air which hardly succeeded in covering up the fact that they felt slightly silly and wished they were dead. The young men were husky characters, scrubbed and shining, and they stalked out and held a belligerent pose for a second or two and got the hell out again. You could see from the set of their jaws that they thought that duty could sometimes get one into extremely uncomfortable spots.

There were two or three darling little girls in schoolgirl costume. They began by being shy but in about two seconds got perky and show-offish. The real pet of the show, however, and the girl who could have put over a remodeled potato sack, was a brown-haired miss whose eyes were slightly crossed. Her eyes were a tawny sort of yellow, and the fact that she was slightly cockeyed simply entranced everybody. "Piquant!" I heard on all sides. What is there about fashion that makes people into lunatics?

Well, it is my honest conviction that there is nothing so hopeless as trying to describe clothes. I have never read a review of a fashion show that didn't leave me bewildered. As I look over my notes on the various costumes, I am convinced that any account I might write of the event would be no better.

There were costumes for many occasions, ranging all the way from tailored suits for street wear through lounging pajamas to evening clothes. The suits were trig and well made of pleasant materials; the lounging and leisure clothes were imaginative, but most of them just missed the mark. The evening gowns were dreadful.

As for the men's clothes, they looked all right to me and certainly better than anything I saw on civilians in Moscow. None of the things had as yet been manufactured. After the designers and the fabric manufacturers had got together and decided on the best in both fabric and pattern, the goods were to be manufactured sometime in the future when the Five Year Plan gave the green light. So it was a vision of the future only.

Some of my notes read as follows:

> *Woman's suit; jacket black-and-white hound's-tooth pattern over slim black skirt, knee-length. Good shoulders and smart tailoring, Collarless. Worn with black bumper beret, black medium-heel oxfords, black gloves.*
> *Wine-colored wool "covercoat" for women. Fitted at waist, gathered into front yoke. High-necked. Worn with blue medium-brim sailor hat, wine-colored shoes.*
> *Loose coat for teen-agers. Blue wool wrap-around, trimmed with inexpensive gray fur at neck. Worn with blue beanie with bow on top. Black slip-on pumps. (Savage criticism greeted this one—"Cheap-looking material," "Pockets too high," "Bad lines" and "Cheap fur."*
> *Woman's green wool wrap-around coat worn with green beret. (Comments from audience— "Good, let's have more of this.")*

There were several men's suits and overcoats about which my notes say, "Look like 'heavy-duty' pictures in the Sears-Roebuck catalogues."

Then came an "ivory wool lightweight coat, with deep pleats over the shoulders and braid trimming at the cuffs." This was worn with a large wide-brimmed black hat, tilted at a provocative angle. Some of the audience said this was not good for mass production. Others said it was so. I have a note here which reads, "We insist on acceptance." I forget what happened.

A bright red-plaid material was presented in five different ways: 1—in a sports suit for women, 2—in a jumper dress worn with a long-sleeved white blouse, 3—as a shirtwaist dress, 4—in a separate blouse worn with a dark blue skirt, and 5—in a "mother and daughter ensemble," the child's dress accompanied by a dark blue cape.

There was a dress made entirely without seams—cut on the bias of wide material. I examined it closely, but I couldn't figure it out. It was a good trick and they'd done it. There was a man's work blouse made of blue denim, cut like an artist's smock and worn with a black Windsor tie. The big blond brute who modeled this glared at us all as if he dared us to snicker. We didn't. He looked cute. I don't think this job will go into mass production, however.

Well, there were dozens more, but I staggered out into the afternoon sun which dazzled me after the gloom of the showroom. And when I looked around at the shabby crowds scurrying along the muddy Moscow streets, I couldn't help wishing that the Five Year Plan would hurry up and give some of these threadbare folks a whack at even a heavy-duty number. They could certainly use it.

I went to an exhibit of decorative fabrics while I lived in Moscow. All the designs were by women artists, forty-three different exhibitors in all. There were designs for dresses, shawls, handkerchiefs, tablecloths, parasols, cushions, carpets, curtains and lamp shades. Excellent materials had been provided for their use and they had been given two years in which to work up the show.

There was nothing strikingly original about any of the designs; most of them stemmed from the antique Russian motifs but there were some based on French and even American Indian conceptions. But it was heartening to come in out of the drab out-of-doors world to the sunny gallery where these bright textiles were hung. They told me that the fabrics were to be used in the manufacture of consumers' goods in the near future, but I never saw anything of the kind while I was there.

Perhaps these things, like the styles for mass production, will go into the files and be used when the manufacture of war material and munitions seems less pressing than it does now.

Chapter 18

Gilding the Red Lily

THE MOSCOW WOMEN have a voracious appetite for foreign cosmetics and perfumes, as well as for foreign shoes and clothes. Some of the Russian girls I knew had obtained—heaven knows where, one doesn't ask too many questions—little bottles of authentic French perfume. One charmer went around reeking of "Peut-etre" and smiling wickedly because she knew very well she had used too much and she didn't care. She was so glad to have it that she soaked herself in it and let it go at that.

My husband's courier, Lydia Vyschinskaya, was one whose taste and elegance were undeniable, although she had hardly anything to show for either. She used to pore over the advertisements in the American magazines we had, her eyes wide with surprise and wonder. One advertisement she became enamored of was Hildegarde's trademark—the "ad," you know, with the little gloved hand holding a lace handkerchief. Lydia used to cut those ads out and take them home. She thought they were the most adorable things she had ever seen in her life. She spoke no English, Lydia, and I spoke very little Russian, so when she asked me to explain about the little ads I really was at a loss. Imagine, please, trying to explain in Russian what a little gloved hand holding a lace handkerchief means to a Russian who has never been out of Russia. I was stumped. I just said I didn't know and when I come to think about it, I guess I don't, either.

Comparatively few women in Soviet Russia use cosmetics. Peasants would be ashamed to be seen with make-up and many earnest professional workers feel that their personal efforts for the advancement of their country are more important than their personal adornment. I have seen hundreds of these women, meekly content with their drab lives—office workers, clerks in the post office, all kinds of government little women—with their hair pulled carelessly back into frowzy knots and their noses shining bright. But their eyes shine, too; they are radiant with a deep purpose. Their lives are dedicated to the future and they regard with honest contempt the superficial lures of the Cosmetic Trust.

Then I met some of the other girls. No less patriotic than their sterner sisters, these girls have grown pretty tired of the creed that life is real and life is earnest. They have lived for years in a country where life is one long monotone. I began to realize that love of cosmetics was deeply ingrained in them; that they felt a real need for glamour. These girls want cosmetics, and they buy them and use them and they don't see that any of it reflects on their integrity.

With the release of many ingredients from war priorities, more and more cosmetics are for sale in Moscow. All the standard stuff can be found: face powder, lipsticks, cold cream, mascara, rouge, perfume, bath oil, hair pomade, shampoo, scented soaps, hair dye, but I never saw any deodorants or depilatories. Many of the blondes in Moscow are natural blondes, but there must have been some chemical bleach available, because I saw many girls, who, whatever their natural pigmentation might have been, had decided to be forever amber.

I was told that the Georgian women use a kind of mud pack for the removal of superfluous hair. It's made of some ingredient found in Georgia, but it's called "Persian mud." They spread this on the area they wish to defuzz and let it dry. Then they pull it off and the unwanted hair comes with it.

Does it hurt?" I asked, and my informant looked at me scornfully. "Of *course* it hurts," she said, "but afterward you are like satin." I never saw anything like it for sale in Moscow. All the other things can be bought in the commercial shops and sometimes also in the closed shops (shops for workers only).

There are several big, luxurious shops—"Teje" is the trade name—all government-owned, of course, which deal exclusively in cosmetics. These are large, airy, modern shops with fine plate-glass showcases. The interior lighting fixtures are extremely modern, but utterly impossible to see by. The

atmosphere of the shops is dimly cathedral. The buxom saleswomen have a faintly disapproving air. "The stuff is here," they seem to imply. "If you want it, buy it." Nobody tries to break down your sales resistance. Nobody extols the virtues of the wares.

Ail Russian cosmetics are made by the government Cosmetic Trust; there is no competition. The prices are determined by the government and are the same in all Teje stores. One brand is called "Red Moscow," another "New Dawn," a third "Horizon." While American manufacturers lean heavily on sex and romance as inspiration for the names of their cosmetics, the Soviet Cosmetic Trust goes to nature— and I don't mean human nature. They have a "Snowflake" cold cream and a "Red Poppy," too. There is a line of floral perfumes of which Crimean Violet, Crimean Rose, Camellia and Hyacinth are a few.

The salesgirl does not assure you that the perfume is almost lethal in its potency and that any man who gets a sniff of you thus perfumed will fail flat on his face before you in adoration and surrender. No, Americans may go for that stuff, but the Russians don't get a chance to. They are told that it smells nice and that's all.

However, I did hear a couple of stories that tended to make me think that the Cosmetic Trust had got wind of some American monkeyshines and was trying them out. I heard that a committee on perfumes had been called to meet on a certain day and that the various scents, properly labeled, were on display. Each bottle was passed around for sniffing purposes and after all committee members had sniffed every brand an orchestra played soft, classical music and the committee was asked to vote on which perfume was brought to mind (or nose?) by which musical selection. I don't know what the purpose of the meeting was, nor what came of it after the sniffing and listening were all over, but that's the story as I heard it and had it translated from one of the newspapers. Sometimes you get a glimpse of a bit of cockeyed insanity like that that is very refreshing amid a sea of deadly serious affairs. Only they were all probably deadly serious about this sniffing business, too.

I read once that the U.S.S.R. People's Commissariat for Food Industry was conducting a competition for new brands of perfumes, soaps and creams and that the first prize was to be eight thousand rubles. But I never could find out who competed or who won or anything more about it. Nobody would tell me a thing.

All the Moscow perfumes are pleasant, but the lasting qualities are poor. Nail lacquer is in great demand and this is called sedately Light, Medium and Dark. There is a Pearl finish too, which is very pretty, but the lacquer chips easily. The polish remover is also of quality much inferior to the cheapest American product.

Whenever I see pearly polish I am reminded of a young saleswoman in one of the Commission stores in Moscow. It is a very busy store and she is a very busy girl and she spends a long day reaching for things on shelves and taking things out of showcases for eager customers. But she yearned for glamour and she always had her very large fingernails painted a very ugly, pearly red. I think she must have achieved the result by mixing "Dark" with "Pearl." At any rate, her nails glowed a deep and angry pearly crimson even though her hands were of necessity very dirty all day long. It used to set my teeth on edge, but from the way she lifted her fingers around daintily I think she got food for her soul out of the smeary-looking stuff.

Russian girls love the seductive glances that dark eyelashes help bestow. But they have found that Russian mascara often lets them down. If they laugh a lot or cry a little or unfortunately get caught out in the rain or snow with mascara on their lashes, they find themselves in a sad state. The mascara streaks and smudges and instead o making them look irresistible it makes them look like fugitives from a clown troupe. But some of the Russian girls have beaten that game. They have discovered that a certain dye used for coloring furs will color their eyelashes and so they use that. The dye is poisonous, "Your whole head can swell up like a pumpkin," I was told. "You may even go blind!" But never mind. It makes eyelashes black and that, of course, is wonderful. Eye shadow, however, is not in general use. It is used mainly by actors on the stage.

Permanent waves are close to the top on the list of desired beauty items. A permanent costs about forty rubles plus a tip of one hundred percent. Cold permanents are unknown. An American woman I knew had an American home-wave kit and took it to a Russian hairdresser to have him apply it for her. Entranced, he begged her for a bit of the lotion. He said he would have it analyzed and manufacture it and be awarded the Order of Lenin for his enterprise, without a doubt. The Russian permanent wave is wavy, all right, but to American eyes it looks like a specimen of contour plowing. So does Russian finger waving.

Nobody I met in the Soviet Union seemed to be a slave to the bathroom scale. Russia admires poundage. Why anybody should be ashamed of looking as though she had enough to eat is something no Russian can understand. So reducing treatments are rare. They say that some of the upper-bracket ladies, actresses, wives of diplomats, Red Army wives and so forth, sometimes indulge in this ungentle pastime, but I never knew anybody that did. Many of the artists of the stage and the screen have reached elephantine proportions and still play sprightly and youthful roles with impunity. Russians stand by their favorites even if they have to shut their eyes to do so.

This attitude of the Russians toward fat was a great relief to me. After living the life of a pariah in America because of irrepressible poundage, it was sweet relief to be surrounded by women who often outweighed me. I had not quite realized how my nerves had been rubbed raw for years by the never-ceasing American warfare against fat. I had not eaten a square meal in thirty years. I had spent hundreds of dollars and hundreds of hours being massaged and pounded into some semblance of the American ideal and still plumpness would keep creeping in. I had writhed under the withering glances of bored saleswomen who were trying to stuff me into a size-eighteen dress. I felt like a criminal every time I took over eight hundred or nine hundred calories a day.

When I went to Russia, I had managed by the simple expedient of eating between six hundred and six hundred fifty calories a day for six months to beat my weight down to one hundred twenty-eight pounds. In Russia meals consisting of fresh fruits and vegetables could not be arranged. My carefully and painfully obtained weight went zooming merrily upward and my new uniform burst at the seams and had to be let out again and again and again. I could not diet. I ate fat meat and starchy foods or I starved. And nobody noticed or cared whether I was fat or not. (I am not talking about the members of the American colony who watched my zooming with malicious American smiles.) The *Russians*, I repeat, didn't care. They made me feel as slim as a willow wand and extremely fascinating as well, and for this I shall always remember them and love them.

But to return to the cosmetics—Russian cold creams are terrible. I tried several that I bought in the Teje shop and they all made my face more like a nutmeg grater than usual. But the Russians know this and so there is a brisk trade among beauty-shop operators and other enterprising ladies in the manufacture of cold creams. Formulas are evolved and jealously guarded, though where the ingredients like "peach oil" and "olive oil" come from is hard to understand.

The serious Soviets have to admit grudgingly that women are interested in beauty culture. Even the plodding newspapers occasionally break away from their solemn political panegyrics and print a beauty hint or two. I had one such column translated. Inasmuch as soap of any description was almost impossible to find, it was not surprising to read that the doctors recommended the use of "cow's milk" and eggs instead. But these were scarce and expensive too. I had the feeling that if anyone could get either, they'd eat it, but maybe the serious seeker after beauty is just as dizzy in Moscow as anywhere else on this dizzy globe. The beauty column follows, just as it was translated for me:

DOCTOR'S ADVICE
The Care of the Face and of One's Hair

By Dr. Yakov Veniaminov, Cosmetician

"Wrinkles are appearing on my face. How can I get rid of them? Is it really old age?"

Such questions are often heard in the surgery of the face specialist.

As a matter of fact, a network of fine wrinkles often covers the faces of still young women. Of course, this is by no means premature old age, or fading, as our alarmed patients are inclined to think. But what then is the matter? Can these phenomena be controlled by medical cosmetics? And for how long can one preserve the skin in a blooming, healthy and elastic condition?

Though the skin and color of the face possess many individual features and peculiarities, by classifying them we can speak of greasy, dry, elastic, porous and other types of skins. I will dwell mainly on dry skin as this defect particularly frequently leads to wrinkles. Nevertheless, any woman, by following a correct regime, can easily get rid of dry skin, without even applying to a cosmetic medical cabinet.

A premature network of fine wrinkles, scaling, unpleasant skin irritations, are all results of dry skin. Dry skins are very sensitive to all kinds of climatic and meteorological changes. Cold, excessive winds or heat are particularly harmful for such skins. The skin of the face can even be spoiled by staying for a long time in a cold room or in a dry, hot room. Dry skin should be looked after and should be helped by external nourishment.

It should be above all remembered that dry skin should never be washed with soap, and water is very undesirable for it. Such faces should be washed with lotions which can be obtained in all drugstores. Instead of washing, it is recommended that very sensitive skins be swabbed with cotton wool lightly dipped in a vegetable oil—olive, peach, etc. In the absence of these oils, ordinary cow's milk is recommended. Before retiring, cover the forehead, cheeks, neck and temples with a thin layer of nutritious cream, which should not be rubbed—that only irritates the skin. The cream should be helped to penetrate the skin by lightly slapping with your fingers. In the morning, another, lighter and less greasy cream is used.

Women with dry skins should always remember that powder should be used after cream, for powder, applied directly to dry skins, harms it and frequently causes scaling. Plastic cosmetic massages accompanied by nutritious vitamin masks are useful for dry and flabby skins. But such massages should be prescribed only after consulting with a physician, for massages and other operations connected with definite treatment should be strictly individualized.

I shall now touch on another skin defect—excessive greasiness, which sometimes spoils even the prettiest face. Freckles, blackheads and wide, flabby pores frequently appear on greasy skins. It is recommended to rub soap lather with a shaving brush into greasy porous skins. We advise such faces to be washed in the following manner—first of all in hot water and then immediately with cold water to which has been added a few drops of ammonia.

In general, it is useful to rub such faces with various spirits and ethers. This cleans the skin from freckles and helps in closing the pores. But this should be done only on the advice of a doctor....

Hair treatment is an important field in the practice of medical cosmeticians. Both men and women apply for hair treatment, and the course is very long. It requires a great deal of patience and insistence on the part of the patient.

In essence, hair treatment can be boiled down to the treatment of the skin of the head and its blood vessels, the perspiratory and oleaginous glands, and the nervous apparatus. Both excessive and insufficient secretion of oil leads to scurf which in its turn weakens the hair and facilitates baldness.

Greasy hair should be washed not more than once in four or five days, with liquid soaps of the "shampoo" type. It is good to add a little mustard to the water. It is necessary to rub special spirits prescribed by the physician into the roots of the hair daily.

Dry hair should be washed less frequently, about once in six to eight days; very dry hair—once in ten days. In these cases, "children's soaps" are the best, and after washing, the hair should be lightly oiled with some oil or other—castor oil, peach oil, etc.—together with spirit alcohol.

Egg yolks give very good results in washing hair. One or two yolks should be mixed in cold water and added to the hot water during washing.

In addition to the above-mentioned methods of hair treatment, there are various physiotherapeutical treatments and skin massages which should be applied only on the prescription of a competent medical man....

Captions under accompanying photographs:

PATIENT (RED ARMY OFFICER) taking a steam-bath treatment for facial scars received at the front.

PATIENT·(ESS) taking a nutritious face mask.

Chapter 19

For the Stomach's Sake

AFTER READING the beauty column I began to get
hungry—all the business about olive oil and eggs brought my
thoughts back to what's for dinner. After long and arduous
shopping in all kinds of stores, with extremely meager results,
I wondered what kind of cooking recipes the Russians used.
It is a difficult task to prepare an appetizing and nourishing
meal from the things usually available in the food stores, and
I knew very well that I, with my "Diplomatic" ration card, had
access to foodstuffs that most Moscovites themselves were
unable to purchase.

I asked some Russian girls I knew what kind of food they
ate and how it was prepared. Most of them were "career girls"
and had little to do with the preparation of their family's food.
Their mothers were the housekeepers, as is so often the case
with our young women in America. But they were friendly
and affectionate kids and they got together and painfully
assembled a few recipes for me. I am going to present them
just as they were given to me—for several reasons. The first
reason is that these gay youngsters had plenty of fun with
me and my spoken Russian. They would listen to me kindly,
smile gently, and before they could help themselves they
would tip back their heads and shout with laughter. They
always excused themselves, mopping their eyes, and assured
me that even though they couldn't help laughing at me, I was
certainly making progress. I print these recipes in English—
(their English)—to show these scoffers that they aren't so hot
in *my* language. The fact that I could not write a recipe in
Russian *at all* does not enter into this discussion.

The second reason I present these recipes as written is to show how proud and gallant these people are. Most of the ingredients are completely unobtainable—or, if obtainable after long and patient search, would certainly be much too expensive for the average white-collar worker. The first recipe was written in Russian by Lydia Vyschinskaya. I had it translated by another Russian girl, who spoke English. It is a complete reflection of Lydia and her ideals of living. I painfully collected the necessary stuff, at some expense, and Lydia made such a cake for me. It was wonderful—very sweet, as are most Russian pastries and cakes and almost as big as a cart wheel. It was bravely decorated with swirls and whorls of icing and we had it for my husband's birthday dinner.

Lydia's Cake

10 eggs
Separate yellow from white. Mix yolks with 1½ glass of sugar. To beat white into foam and mix with yolks. (Part of white must be left unmixed.) To put into this paste 1²/₃ of glass of flour. To stir thoroughly and to add the remaining part of white slightly stirring in one direction. To pour into greased pan and bake in oven on moderate heat.

400 grams of butter [this is nearly a pound] to mix with 1½ glass of powdered sugar.

To boil 1 glass of strong coffee and *very hot* to pour into this paste.

Another glass of sweet coffee to mix with ¼ glass of brandy or wine. To cut the biscuit in ½. To soak. To put in a strata of paste. The remained part of butter paste for decoration.

[We could always get plenty of butter and sugar on our Diplomatic cards, but butter and sugar were unobtainable in the workers' stores while I was in Moscow.]

The following three recipes were given to me by two girls who are secretary and clerk respectively for an American correspondent who lives in the Metropole Hotel. These two are the ones who used to try not to laugh at my Russian and never quite succeeded. They are merry kids and very smart and I am sure that they will realize I am not being unkind when I present their recipes as they wrote them. I think they are charming and I certainly hope you do, too.

Vareniki with Cherries

[Cherries were usually obtainable in season in the bazaar. I have a sneaking suspicion that my career girls forgot the flour!]

DOUGH

1 egg, 1 ¾ glass of water, a bit of salt. The dough must be rather thick (or heavy) You to roll the dough and when it is thin enough to cut it with a glass in little round pieces. To take the seeds out of the cherries, pit them (cherries) in a sieve, place it on a bowl or saucepan, put some sugar on the cherries and leave them so for about two hours. Then to put in every little piece of dough (the dough should be made when the cherries are ready to put in the dough) about 4-5 cherries and make a varenik like this: [Here follows a small pencil sketch of a little dumpling.) Put them in boiling water for several minutes until they rise to the surface of the water. The juice from the cherries must be boiled with sugar and served together with sour cream for cold vareniki.

[When, on rare occasions, sour cream was available at the Dipstore our couriers would scurry off at an early hour with a glass jar or tin can to obtain this luxury. It was seldom to be had in the workers' stores, but often you could get it in the bazaar. Americans usually hesitated to buy it there because of the unsanitary conditions under which it was sold. You couldn't see the cans in the Dipstore. They were in a back room. This was easier on the stomach.]

Pelmeni

The dough is made just like for vareniki. To shope [I think they mean chop] fat pork, mix it with shaped onions, add some salt and pepper and put in the dough cut with a glass in small round pieces. Freeze until quite frozen. Put in boiling water. Serve with vinaigre, melted butter and sometimes with the bouillon in which the pelmeni have been boiled.

Kulick

2 kilograms of flour [about five pounds], 10 yellow of the eggs, 3 glasses of sugar, 4 glasses of milk, 400 grams

of butter, 200 grams of raisins or sugared fruits cut in tiny pieces, east, vanilla or cardamom or nutmeg, a bit of salt. The yellow of the eggs must be rubbed with sugar, then add 1 glass of warm milk, 1 glass of flour and east diluted with warm milk. Add then the remaining warm milk, flour and species and knead the dough for about one hour (not less) adding little by little melted butter. Then put in the dough the raisins and tiny pieces of sugared fruit and leave it for the night warmly covered in a quiet place. In the morning put the dough in richly buttered molds and leave it so for another hour or 40 minutes. Then bake it.

Sounds pretty good, at that, doesn't it? When I am able to get sugar enough I shall certainly try it.

In Moscow the ration book is still an omnipresent bedevilment. The Russians have a great many categories of ration books and food cards (someone told me 15 categories in all), ranging all the way from the Diplomatic category down to the Dependent's card. A Dependent's food card calls for three hundred grams of bread a day and that is all. This means that an elderly person, unable to work, or a person who for some other reason cannot work, is entitled to less than one pound of bread a day. The rest of their sustenance must come from kindly souls who are willing to share. An unskilled laborer whose monthly wages are from two hundred to two hundred fifty rubles is entitled to the following food items on his ration:

80 grams of cereal monthly
60 grams of meat monthly
20 grams of oil
600 grams of bread daily

In explanation of the above list, I would like to add that during the time I was in Moscow neither meats nor oil were available in the workers' stores.

The food allotted to a white-collar worker is as follows:

2 kilograms, 200 grams of meat monthly (4½ pounds)
600 grams of bread daily (a little over a pound, half white bread and half black bread)
600 grams of butter a month (a little over a pound)
2 kilograms of cereal a month (about 4 pounds)
900 grams of sugar a month (about 1¾ pounds)

In connection with the above list I was told that at no time during my stay in Moscow was meat, white bread, butter or sugar available in that workers' store.

Children and women soon to be mothers got extra rations, and artists and scientific workers are treated pretty tenderly in food rationing. Foreign correspondents get diplomatic rating, so we had Diplomatic food cards. My husband's was category I and my own was category II. The first-category book entitled its possessor to buy the following amounts of food during one month:

> 5 kilos of meat (a kilo is about 2 and ⅕th pounds)
> 5 kilos of fish (these fish coupons may be used for meat; this gives a first-category person 22 pounds of meat a month)
> 30 kilos of bread (this means about 75 loaves of bread a month)
> 5 kilos of sugar
> 3 kilos of butter
> 4 kilos of cereal (rice, *kasha*, macaroni, etc.)
> 4 kilos of coffee
> ¼ kilo of tea
> 13 pints of wine or vodka
> 800 Russian cigarettes
> 2 kilos of cheese
> 8 cans of condensed milk
> 4 kilos each of carrots, onions, cabbage and beets

There are other things, too, like ten boxes of matches a month, but the above items are staples.

On the first of the month when I got my books of food coupons, I used to think that we were entitled to enough food to feed an army. That's about what we had to do. We had to feed ourselves three meals a day, give lunch to a courier, dinner to a chauffeur, extra products to a second courier and give the secretary a fat monthly allowance of miscellaneous products. Any Soviet citizen who works for a foreigner would far rather be paid in goods than in rubles. In fact, he will not work for you at all unless some kind of "deal" is made with him. An ordinary Soviet citizen cannot usually buy white bread, flour, butter, sugar, coffee, cocoa, meat, or candy in his own ration store. Therefore, employment with a foreigner means an opportunity to get some of these precious things. Bread has to be handed out freely to anybody who does a small service. Our chambermaids in the hotel were tipped in bread except on holidays when they got extra rations and rubles, too.

It is confusing at first to be paying for small services in soap or bread or cigarettes, but you soon get into the rhythm of that arrangement. So it is easy to see how our enormous food allowance was soon dissipated. Before the month was over I always had to buy extra food at the Gastronom where, if you will pardon my saying so, prices are gastronomical. The business of buying food in Moscow seems at first glance to a stranger to be a formidable undertaking. But if you stare it straight in the eye and hold the thought steadily that you are master of the situation, you will find that you will not have to keep the bull whip handy, although holding a chair in front of you might be a good idea in crowded shops. Shopping for food is shopping for food in any language.

Two kinds of food shops are open to foreigners in Moscow. First is the Diplomatic Store—the Dipstore. Here you must use food coupons and here is where the old ration book tries to get its fangs on your throat.

Let us take an average day in the American housekeeper's life. The butcher is first on your list when you go marketing at the Dipstore. The butcher is a man of balanced judgment. Your conversation does not seem any crazier to him than the conversation of any woman who tries to tell him his business. He is not easily stampeded. He is tall, spare, well past middle age. He wears a long white coat. Instead of the straw hat which is the badge of his tribe in America, he wears a small dark-blue beret that sits rather skittishly on his bald head. His glasses slip around on his long, thin nose and he peers at you over them benevolently. After you have chosen a cut of meat he gives you what he darn well knows you ought to have, and that's all there is to the meat problem.

The meat in Moscow is generally pretty good, although they cut it somewhat differently from the way they do in America. After you have smiled winningly at the butcher (a hangover from America), you go and make other selections. There is the vegetable department, but the choice of vegetables is usually limited to carrots, onions, beets and cabbage. In winter, even these vegetables are scare or non-existent.

There is not much choice of fruit, either. In the autumn grapes, peaches and pears may be bought occasionally; in winter there are sometimes a few apples for sale. Green salad is always hard to come by, and occasionally there is a little celery in the store. There is always plenty of bologna, frankfurters, smoked fish and caviar, and there is seldom a shortage of cheese. Bread can always be had. Whenever chocolates and sweet biscuits are obtainable, there is a mild riot, for Russians love sweets.

Although all counters are always crowded, salesgirls, plump and placid, move like amiable blond Amazons, unhurried and benign. They regard the milling crowds cheerfully and go along serenely courteous under the never-ceasing barrage of customers' demands.

After you have decided what you want to buy at every counter, you take your completed list to the coupon lady. This lady is stout, calm, competent and kind. Also, glory be, she speaks English. She has an immediately soothing effect on the flurried foreign housewife. She is a rock in a turbulent sea. She not only knows what she is doing, she knows what you think you're doing. She takes your list and your ration book and goes to work on the latter with scissors. She takes the required number of meat coupons, makes out a little price ticket and attaches it to them and proceeds unhurriedly down the list. When she has finished, you have several price tickets attached to the requisite number of food tickets.

After putting your ration book lovingly away in your bag, you move along to the end of the line and the cashier's desk. The line is generally a long one and it takes quite a while to inch your way up to the cashier. This lady has no adding machine. Instead, she has a business called an abacus which is so simple that it baffles description. It is a very ancient instrument, holding several parallel rows of wires. On the wires are movable wooden beads. She snaps the beads back and forth, stamps your tickets and gives them back with your change. You stuff the money into your pocketbook without counting it. First, because Soviet cashiers do not make mistakes. Second, because there is not enough room in the store to begin complicated examples in addition and subtraction. When you get home, you figure it out and it's always all right. But just now you take the stamped tickets, go back to each counter where you made your selection, present the ticket and ration coupons and receive your purchases. You have been pushed around and trampled but not more than you would be at home.

There are other stores where foreigners may buy food—the Gastronoms. At these super-delicatessens no ration coupons are needed. Prices are many times those at the Dipstore. For example, when I was there, butter at the Dipstore cost about twenty-eight rubles a kilo; at the Gastronom it cost four hundred rubles a kilo.

One thing that tends to make food buying a little easier on the head is that prices in all stores of the same character are alike. There is no point in chasing around from one Gastronom to another looking for a bargain. A price is a price, so you can relax as far as that goes.

There are several of these super-stores in Moscow, some of which for grandeur and glory make the late Charles and the old Park & Tilford's look like secondhand shops on Tobacco Road.

One of the favorites is in Gorki Street. This Gastronom is colossal. Maybe the main salesroom was a ballroom in the old days, for it is spacious and lofty and stunning in its magnificence. Enormous chandeliers dripping gold crystal hang from the gilded, domed ceiling. Byzantine columns bright with gold, crimson and blue separate tall, impressive windows, many of which are of stained glass in antique Russian designs. The counters are ranged around the sides of the room and in an open square in the middle. The place is definitely nowhere to go if you are trying to diet. The very smell makes your head swim. Prices, of course, do likewise.

Meat, fish and poultry are sold in separate rooms. Bread has a room to itself, too. But in the great main room are pastries, a dozen kinds of smoked fish and caviar of great fanciness, high-grade fruit and sometimes even bananas and oranges. Pickles, cream cheese with raisins, big fat pink boiled hams, golden-brown loins of pork which have been cooked with much garlic and many spices, and countless varieties of bologna, sausage, bacon, little roast squabs, big roast turkeys and sometimes pheasants. Fancy tobacco, fancy chocolates in tinfoil and colored papers, fancy sweet biscuits, all at fancy, fancy prices.

Oh, yes, there are luxuries to be had in Moscow, but you must be prepared to pay for them. And you must also be prepared to run the risk of being trampled to death, for hundreds of other people want luxuries too, early and late, deep around the counters. It takes a strong mind and durable feet to withstand a shopping expedition to the Gastronom, but it is definitely worth it.

It takes even stronger will power and even tougher feet to withstand a shopping expedition to the bazaar or open market. It is here to the open market that the peasants of the collective farms bring their surplus products for sale. Prices here are about midway between those at the Dipstore and those at the Gastronom.

Many things can be bought at the bazaars that cannot be had at either of the other stores and no ration coupons are required. You go to the bazaars if you want potatoes, fresh fruits, flowers and sundries.

If you can imagine the crowd that would attend a sale of high-grade nylon stockings for forty-nine cents a pair, you have a clear picture of what goes on in a Moscow bazaar. The one I went to the oftenest was located out near the Circus Theatre and I often wondered what the circus had to offer that the bazaar couldn't supply. These bazaars are provided by the government as market places for the peasants. After a farmer has raised whatever crop has been assigned to him and fulfills the quota the government demands, he is free to sell whatever is left over in the public market. He can charge whatever he can get, and since what he is selling is seldom available in the workers' stores (although often the ration card calls for it), the prices in the bazaars are usually very stiff indeed and the present-day farmer is sitting pretty. Legally, only the peasants are supposed to sell in the bazaar. But every man and his mother turn up there with every conceivable kind of thing for sale, and I never saw a policeman forbid anybody to sell anything.

The bazaar is in a sort of public square, and there are several long, low market buildings made of concrete with glass roofs, standing in the enclosure. Inside these buildings, people who have meat or fresh milk for sale rent space. The theory is, I guess, that meat, fish and milk must be sold in sanitary surroundings, but if that's sanitation, I'll take vanilla. It gives anybody used to refrigerated meat and milk and clean salesrooms the willies to see the bloody slabs of fresh meat on the splintery counters, with flies flying like crazy all over everything. The smell would knock you down. I never got the courage to go where milk was sold, so maybe they do have refrigeration there. Not in the meat market, however. The meat is hacked off into ragged slabs and is pawed over by the far-from-dainty purchasers and handled thoroughly by the dirty fingers of the sellers. Only when you have been in Moscow long enough to feel the void left by good meat, or have been to the big, clean Gastronom where excellent meat is sold under fairly sanitary conditions—but at the most appalling prices—can you bring yourself to buy meat in the Moscow bazaar. But the prices are lower than the Gastronom and the meat is better, if higher priced, than the Dipstore where foreigners trade. So you come to it. And it doesn't kill you.

Outside, in the open air, booths for the sale of vegetables are arranged around the walls of the market place. Here you can buy potatoes, and nearly all vegetables in season. Vegetables are fairly easy to come by when the gardens are yielding, but after that time is past, potatoes and cabbage are about all you can ever get. But there are lots of other things you can get if you feel generous with your money. Shoes are always eagerly sought after, and dozens of people are always standing around with shoes for sale. American Army shoes usually cause a riot. (Don't ask me where they get them; once in a while even a new pair would appear.) When I first got to Moscow, a good pair of shoes would bring fifteen hundred rubles—about a hundred and forty-five American dollars. When you consider that an average workman gets about three or four hundred rubles a month, you can see what fifteen hundred rubles mean to most people. I have seen thousands of things for sale: sweaters, dresses, underwear; postal cards; books; sheet music; phonograph records; pathetic little blank books; sleazy rayon stockings; babies' hand-knit socks; pictures torn from foreign magazines, bits of ribbon and colored yarn—any little trinket or gadget that people can get hold of to turn into rubles.

Yes, every man and his mother are there and you will be crushed like an eggshell if you don't watch every step. You will be jostled and stepped on and pushed and shoved until you are breathless and nearly lifeless. It will all be done with the best good nature in the world. Everybody is in fine spirits and nobody means any harm, but there are just about fifty times more people than the space will hold and so the place is a complete madhouse. You have no room to carry your bundles, and since the reason you go to the bazaar at all is to get things that make bundles, it's a problem. It is best to hold your pocketbook very tightly, too—but that didn't do me any good. I held mine so tightly against my side that I nearly broke a rib, but when I got back to the hotel I found that some adroit character had managed to slip my change purse out of my bag anyhow. If I hadn't been smart enough to forget to put any money *into* the purse, I'd have been out quite a mess of rubles. As it was, the thief got only a flabby old change purse, quite empty. (I fooled 'em.)

All foreigners get sick and tired of the constant pressure brought to bear on them by the Russians for food. The Americans think longingly of the time when they will return to a land where a dime or a quarter is the simple payment for service rendered. Yet when you come to the end of your patience and feel that one more request for butter or white bread or soap or meat is going to make you a permanent resident of the insane asylum, one of those Russians who have been needling you beyond endurance shows up with a present which has cost his whole month's salary or which has been in his family for generations and can't be bought anywhere for any price. And he will give it to you with a flourish and such a smile and be so happy about the whole thing that you will be plunged into despair at your own lack of openhandedness and spontaneous generosity.

Association with these people assumes a family atmosphere in spite of anything you can do. Against your wishes and better judgment, you become the head of the family. You get into their personal lives even if you never meet their relatives or go to their homes and even if you cannot speak Russian or they English. You become involved with their problems and you start giving them pills and advice and tying up their physical and mental wounds.

Lydia Vyschinskaya once made a speech to our office staff on this subject. Lydia speaks no English and she is a meek, refined, cultured little woman, pretty, reticent and altogether charming. The fact that she made a speech at all shows how deeply moved she was. "When Mrs. Atkinson first came to Moscow," she told them, "she spoke very bad Russian. [I never spoke anything else, but that's beside the point.] But," said Lydia, "even though I could not understand her language, I wanted to understand *her* with all my heart, and I did!" In her gentle way she had made it very clear that heart can speak to heart without the spoken word. The social and international implications of this struck us all of a heap. The lot of us burst into tears of international understanding, and no more work was done that day.

So this is a panoramic view of the Moscow food merry-go-round as I knew it. Dipstore, Gastronom, bazaar—you pay your money and you take your choice. Three meals a day—it is a cross the housewife has to bear in any country or climate. Here it is with Russian variations. My husband always said airily, "Well, we've got to eat, you know." The answer to that one was, "Boy, are you telling me!"

Chapter 20

Eating Out

THERE ARE NOT MANY restaurants or cafés where a foreigner can stop to get a meal in Moscow. In fact, getting a meal in a restaurant is quite an elaborate task. The streets of the city are not lined with eating places. There are workers' restaurants where people employed in certain establishments may go at definite times to eat. But the business of wandering and having a bite anytime you happen to feel like it is impossible. The hotel dining rooms require ration tickets. You can't buy food in the Dipstore and eat in the hotel too. It's one or the other and you have to give up your ration tickets.

Two big expensive restaurants exist to which foreigners go when they wish to have a party outside their own homes and don't want to use the ration books, the Aragvi and the Aurora. There are one or two others, but these are popular ones. It is best to go the day before, order your meal, explain how many guests you expect to have, and pay a deposit. We had a party once at the Aragvi. It was to be a party for six people, four guests besides my husband and me. I went down with the secretary the day before and together we decided on the menu. I told the manager that I would like a table not too near the music, but near the center of the room, where we could see people.

When we arrived the next evening, I found we had been given a private dining room, upstairs, with a small balcony overlooking the main dining room. There was an air of funereal gloom over the small room. The first object that caught our eyes was probably the most amazing piece of furniture in the world. It might have been cabinet or some sort of secretary, but it was baffling and utterly overpowering. It filled one wall from ceiling to floor. It was made of black wood, carved and tortured into a thousand bumps, designs and patterns. It was a complete mystery how it had ever been got into the room, as it was far bigger than the doorway. It must have been built there. When we tore our eyes away from this monstrosity, they fell upon the statue of a panther slightly less than life-size and *in extremis*. Its lips were drawn back in a terrible snarl over rows of sharp teeth. Its anguished eyes seemed to regard us and did little to make us feel welcome.

The table, long enough to accommodate sixteen amply, had carefully spaced so that once seated at it six people could communicate only by shouting or lip reading. Two large baskets of flowers, such as are generally presented to prima donnas at opening nights of the opera, had been set in the center of the table to prevent our seeing one another. We could hear the music faintly from below. By going out onto the tiny balcony, we could see other people sitting at tables, eating cheerfully. We were encased in gloom.

To the utter horror of the manager and the hovering waiters, I fell upon the table and rearranged it into some semblance of an American board. I put the flowers on the floor and moved the silver and china so that we were at least in speaking distance of one another. I know I hurt the management's feelings because it had gone to great trouble to try to make things nice. It was not their fault that we all got the cold shivers in that funny place. All four of my guests had been in Russia for quite a long time and were much less upset than I was by the way things were going.

The food, though very elaborate, seemed not very good to me. The wines were good and it was only reasonable in the circumstances to drink as much as possible of them to try to forget. When the manager asked me to write in their guest book at the end of the meal, I thought a moment and then wrote: "I can honestly say I never saw anything like it." I will admit that this was mean, but after all you don't pay three thousand rubles (in foreign exchange about three hundred thirty-five dollars) for a dinner party to have it turn out so grisly.

I realize that my story sounds ill-tempered. I know as well as anyone that the management of the Aragvi had done everything it could to provide nice things for our party. It all goes back to the fact that the Russian standards are different from our own. The Russians always want to be "refined." I really think they would be delighted and would hold you in high esteem, if you never spoke or smiled during an entire evening; if you could manage to look somewhat disagreeable as well, and to treat not only the waiters but your guests with arrogance, you would have fulfilled their idea of dignity. The American manner shocks them. Badinage shocks them. I am sure they must indulge in lighthearted conversation and persiflage at some time themselves, but it certainly is seldom in public. They may not enjoy being bored, but they are bored very often, poor things. So if you look bored, it is no reflection on their service, but on the contrary a compliment.

The Aurora Restaurant is a much more cheerful place, although it, too, has a slightly frigid air. It is not quite so fussy as the Aragvi and you can go there without warning. When foreigners enter the dining room, the band immediately plays, "There is a Tavern in the Town," which the Russians sing very gaily. This serves a double purpose. It is first a greeting to the foreigners, and secondly an announcement to everyone else that foreigners are present.

The food at the Aurora is pretty good. We went there with a party of friends one night, and as I remember it, the meal consisted of the following: Vodka for those who wanted it; more vodka. For appetizers, little salt fish, thin slices of salami with plenty of garlic, some kind of small pickled vegetables, sliced cucumbers, and celery. A rather nice soup. Next, a salad of radishes, sliced cucumbers, celery and beets mixed together with a sour-cream dressing. Some of us had steak which is neither cut nor cooked as the Americans are used to having it and which was not very good. Some of us had chicken—boiled, I think. There were potatoes with parsley and butter, fresh green peas and cabbage. For dessert there was excellent ice cream. Coffee. During the meal there were Georgian red wine and a little more vodka. Naturally, after dessert there was vodka. An excellent meal, you say. It was. It cost us about thirty-five dollars apiece.

As far as furnishings and service are concerned, it is no injustice to lump all three of the foreign residence hotels together, the National, the Savoy, the Metropole. All are furnished in the beloved Victorian ·style. Probably no new furnishings, hangings, rugs or plumbing have been installed in any of them for a great many years. What they have done, probably what they have had to do, is to repair, reupholster and restore as best they could. The Five Year

Plans have made little or no provision for the manufacture of new household goods, and the time has long passed when these furnishings were up to date and new. I can laugh at it now, even a little tenderly, so resilient is the human nervous system, when I look back and remember how I and some of the other Americans in the hotels had to live. But it was very depressing and nerve-racking at the time. Life was a series of irritating frustrations. It is not easy for an American to forget his own standard of living. And it is not easy to remember that the standard of living in Moscow is the best they are able to provide.

I sometimes wonder at the good manners and restraint shown by the managers and hotel employees in Moscow when an American comes into the hotel. He immediately bursts out into roars of dissatisfaction. The rooms are gloomy and shabby, the plumbing seldom functions properly, the food is tasteless, badly cooked and badly served. And an American says so usually at the top of his lungs.

What the Americans are getting is top-drawer luxury compared with what the ordinary Russian citizen has, but the hotel people take the criticism quietly and do the best they can to try to satisfy their guests' whims. None of the hotels is any worse than a good third-class theatrical hotel in the middle forties in New York City. I have never heard a Russian say, "If you don't like it here, why don't you go back where you came from?" In view of the fact that none of us was an invited guest, but all of us had beaten our way in of our own free will, indeed after having begged to be permitted to enter, it would certainly well be within their rights if they made that cutting remark. The Americans who manage by hook or crook to obtain an apartment for themselves can live better than the luckless wights who have to live in the hotels. But their life is no bed of roses either. They have their troubles. At least, that's what they say. But there can be no comparison whatever between life in an apartment and life in the Metropole Hotel. Whoever survives six months' residence in the Metropole is entitled to wear a medal "V.M.H."— Veteran Metropole Hotel, with wound stripes

Chapter 21

Shops and Stores

THERE ARE NOT SO MANY so-called "open" stores in Moscow. Most of the shops are closed shops, which means that they are for the use of the workers in certain specified factories or organizations. There are three or four open department stores. The one with which I was most familiar was the big Mostorg near the Metropole Hotel. This is a five or six-story building, almost half a block square. It was built about 1905 by a firm of foreign merchants and has long been one of the most popular stores in Russia. The original building was partly destroyed by fire many years ago, and the present building is the reconstructed one. The manager told my husband that an average of forty-five thousand people passed through its portals every day. That seemed to me like an extremely conservative estimate. I have been there at all seasons of the year and I never went in the place that I was not mashed to a pulp by the mob of eager shoppers.

Christmas was something to remember, or rather to try to forget. Our own holiday crowds are nothing compared with the holiday shoppers in Moscow. Of course you understand that it is not the Christmas season they celebrate. I do not know what they call it, but it looks suspiciously like Christmas to me. The store was full of goods that looked like Christmas presents. Counter after counter was sagging under loads of what looked like Christmas-tree ornaments to my capitalistic eyes. And delightful little ornaments they were. Americans have forgotten how to make such charming trifles if they ever knew. Tiny, fragile bird cages, elfin castles, fairy fruits, glowing and shining little animals that never lived on land or sea were offered in the most abundant profusion.

There were dolls galore, and there were other toys, these definitely not up to the American standard either in workmanship or design. But I imagine that the small recipients of the playthings were just as happy as if they had been. During the war all this sort of thing vanished completely from the scene. Now came the first holiday season in many years when it was possible to buy knickknacks and nonsense for the children. Also because of the war, plenty of rubles were available for the purpose, and the rubles flowed very freely indeed. It may be possible to guide the Soviet citizens along a serious way most of the year, but when it comes to Christmastime, the floods burst the dam. The citizens of Moscow are just as cockeyed then as anybody else.

Even when Christmas was over and things had returned somewhat to their normal course, the store was crowded all day long, every day. Although the new Five Year Plan does not call for much increase in consumers' goods, it was noticeable that a small trickle of these things was beginning to flow into the store. When I first went there in July 1945, ordinary kitchenware could not be purchased. Pots and pans were precious. And even secondhand ones brought high prices in the bazaars. But after a while a good stock of aluminum saucepans, frying pans and such things appeared on the shelves and a riot ensued. The shelves were swept bare in less than a day.

When you manage to get a few pots and pans together it means that you are a solid citizen and are well established in your present home. There is a story told around the Metropole Hotel of a certain Russian girl who became acquainted with a certain Englishman who lived in the hotel, and the housing shortage being what it is and all, before you could say "knife" she had moved in with him. Time went by, the arrangement proved satisfactory to both, housekeeping began, pots and pans were acquired.

But then the Englishman was recalled and a new man was sent to replace him. As the new man was unpacking his bags, a knock came at the door. It was the Russian girl. "How do you do?" she said, and came in and sat down. Delicately, but definitely, she outlined her place in the scheme of things and the startled Englishman was confronted with the rather alarming fact that she was inclined to believe she went with the room!

He had other ideas about it. Perhaps he did not care for blondes. At any rate, bluntly and firmly he pointed out that he felt in all fairness to himself he should have a few hours to look around.

The girl was affronted. "I can cook, also," she said with dignity.

This almost cornered the Englishman, but after all, he had been around and was an artful dodger. He stated that it was his intention to eat hotel food. (Of course, that was the most flagrant and transparent nonsense. *Nobody* can eat Metropole food and she knew it.) It was all a distinct reflection on her charms and she was outraged.

She told him off, good. She stood up. "In *that* case," she said witheringly, "I shall take my pots and pans."

Electric irons appeared. I bought one for three hundred fifty rubles, and I wish to state that it was no good. It heated up slowly, did not attain at any time any great degree of heat and had a wire gadget presumably meant for a stand attached to the back that pressed wrinkles in as fast as the front part of the iron pressed them out. A cynical American friend said it was his opinion it had been planned that way.

"It is always like this," he said, "that they can be sure there will never be any unemployment in the Soviet Union. Or perhaps—" he enlarged on his theme—"they have now discovered perpetual motion." It was all right for him to make gags about .it, but he did not have to iron with it and I did.

It was of extreme interest to me how shoes came to Moscow. No shoes had been manufactured for a long time. Secondhand shoes brought fantastic prices in the bazaar. But finally a shipment came through and was housed on the top floor of the Mostorg. You might think that this caused a riot. But you would be wrong. The shoes were not just for *anyone*. They were for a favored few. If you had exceeded your norm in the factory, if the quality of your work had been particularly good, if for some reason or other you were worthy of praise and reward, you got a letter from your foreman permitting you to buy a pair of shoes. Two days a week shoes were on sale. The lines formed early and stood three deep, a whole block long. A guard stood at the door to admit a few people at a time. They went to the floor where the shoes were sold, made their purchases and departed. When there was room for more people, more were admitted. But it was a weary business waiting one's turn. Members of the armed forces were given priority. The uniformed men and members of their families formed a separate line. Shoes were never available in any great quantity during the ten months

I was in Moscow. They were always extremely expensive and compared very unfavorably with American footwear.

Shopping in Moscow has its perils as well as anywhere else. Aside from the fact that you get very weary from being crowded and pushed around, there is always the danger of having your pocketbook snatched or your pocket picked. Another thing the stores in Moscow have in common with the stores in America is shoplifters. At the door of the Mostorg and every other store there is always a guard sitting. At the Mostorg he is a tall, bearded, elderly gentleman of distinguished appearance. I often wondered what he had to do besides just sit there, bundled up in his heavy coat, with his woolen hat pulled down around his ears. I knew, of course, that his chief duty was to keep the wide door half closed. If the door were opened wide, it would be twice as easy for the surging crowd to get in. Therefore, on some Russian premise, it was his job to make entry as uncomfortable as possible.

But I never saw him do anything else until one day I beheld him in action. I was passing along on my way as usual to the Metropole when I saw him emerge from the Mostorg clutching a screaming woman by one arm. I was naturally entranced. Of course, such a scene in America would immediately attract a throng of curious spectators who would impede the progress of the main actors and fill the air with their questions. Not so in Moscow. I alone stood and watched. I alone drew closer and asked questions. The rest of the crowd, which had been morosely pushing its way into the store, and the usual hurrying people on the street faded from view at once. With frightened looks on their faces, some of them really pale with terror, they turned and melted down the side streets.

My companion, the luckless Lydia, who was carrying my purchases from the grocery store, looked as if she too would like to take wing, but not I. "What is it?" I asked her. "What in the world is the matter?" Lydia looked extremely unhappy and nudged me and urged me along. But I could not help observing that the bearded watchman had a look of extreme pleasure on his face, and that his grip upon the struggling woman never loosened for a moment. Even at that moment of excitement I wondered whether he was pleased because at last he had something to do or because he was able to impose on another citizen.

Lydia finally got me moving toward the Metropole. But she could not stop my questions. "What was it about?" I insisted. She said in a low tone, "The woman is a thief."

I remembered then that the woman had been carrying the usual shopping bag and it had been stuffed full. "And what is the guard going to do with her?" I asked. "Is he taking her to the police?"

"No," Lydia replied, "he is taking her to the cellars."

I was galvanized. All the stories I had ever heard of Russian torture came to my mind. "The cellars!" I cried. "And what will they do with her there?"

"They will question her," Lydia answered.

I let the matter drop. When Lydia spoke to me, she used a kind of pidgin language which she constructed especially for my ears. When I got back to the hotel, I told the story to our secretary in order to try to get the straight of it. The secretary roared with laughter. What Lydia had said, he explained, was that the guard was taking the woman to the *sellers*, meaning the owners of the store.

A friend of mine told me a story along the same lines, which illustrates how easily the spoken word can be misunderstood. It concerned a young girl of whom they were all very proud. She was the daughter of a very simple peasant family and had entered a certain factory as a sweeper. She was a bright child and extremely ambitious, although modest and shy. She was given an opportunity to advance and, faster than you would believe possible, she went from a completely unskilled worker to be the operator of quite a complicated machine. She loved the work and threw herself into it with enthusiasm. She became one of the best workers of the factory, and because of her background and her achievement it was decided to present her with some sort of prize. She was a popular girl and the workers decided that it would be a kind thing to have a little ceremony in connection with the presentation. This was arranged. And to make it even more impressive, they decided to have a commissar from the upper brackets come and make a speech and give the prize.

When she was told of this, the youngster nearly died from embarrassment and stage fright. But she realized that it was an honor and that it had all been planned out of the kindness of their hearts. So she nerved herself for the ordeal and agreed to appear on the platform with the commissar at the time specified.

The choice of commissar had in this case been unfortunate. He spoke a different dialect from that of the workers of the factory, but being a proud man he would not admit it. He stated flatly that he understood their dialect and could speak it perfectly. The evening came, his speech began. It was his intention to say, "Comrades, I want you to think about this young girl's beautiful life." His imperfect knowledge of their dialect resulted in: "Comrades, I want you to look at this young girl's red belly."

Naturally the audience was surprised. The girl waited no longer. Already frightened almost out of her wits, when she heard these strange words, she fled from the platform without more ado. They found her sobbing with embarrassment and chagrin behind the coat-room and could not persuade her to return or to take the prize. What the commissar did or how he felt, I cannot report. What confusion the nuances of a word can cause!

If the goods for sale in the Mostorg had been more varied, more interesting or less expensive, perhaps I would have spent more time there even though it was always so dreadfully crowded. As it was, the Commission stores got most of my trade. Whenever I had a little leisure time, I would wander through them with my friends. It was the Moscow equivalent of window-shopping. We would stand before the counters and criticize the goods exhibited or finger the fur coats and secondhand dresses hanging within reach. It was vastly satisfactory to comment bitterly on the exorbitant prices and the poor quality of the goods.

The stocks in the Commission stores are a true cross section of the life in Moscow. They are a reflection of both the needs and the desires of its citizens. If some people did not need money, things would not be brought there for sale. And if other people were not hungry for consumers' goods, the things would not be there either.

The Commission stores are really secondhand stores. It is very seldom that anything new is for sale in any of them. They are operated by the government, as is every other enterprise. When you take an article to the Commission shop, the government official there decides on what price it must sell for. You have to accept this decision or take the stuff away. The government takes a commission of twenty percent and you get the remainder.

There is a tremendous assortment of miscellaneous stuff for sale in the Commission stores. Considering the many years of hardship and stern necessity, considering the many years they have been cut off from the outside world, and considering the many years when new goods were not manufactured, I found it always a wonder that so many interesting, sometimes indeed valuable things were for sale. It was sometimes possible to pick up a real little treasure in the way of a bit of old glass, a piece of silver, a length of old brocade or a fine piece of porcelain. These things were never cheap. I don't think anyone ever bought a bargain in a Commission store. But for the most part the articles offered were well worn and, in the case of clothing and underwear, sleazy and of very poor quality.

There were plenty of used fur coats. I had always thought that Russians went around swathed in sable and ermine, since Russia seems the source of all the best furs which are for sale in America. But the plain truth of the matter is that all the best Russian furs are sent abroad and a pretty moth-eaten collection is all that remains over there. I saw one magnificent seal coat in good condition, although the lining was much worn. This number was priced at thirty-five thousand rubles, which translated into foreign exchange would have been about thirty-two hundred fifty dollars. I saw some sable skins pretty well worn also, but these too were priced exorbitantly.

One secondhand dress that I remember, a brown rayon, a rather mournful shade and distinctly homemade, even though still in good condition, was priced at twelve hundred rubles. Blouses are much in demand and you seldom see a good one for sale. Russian girls yearn for pretty underwear, but you will not find it in the Commission shops. I saw a lot of underwear for sale at good stiff prices, rayon of a very poor quality not known in America, of the most fantastic shades of morbid lavenders and greens.

Furniture is much needed and desired and appeared in the shops in some quantity. All the Russian furniture that I saw was of the most depressing mid-Victorian kind. Mid-Victorian Russian, if you know or can guess what I mean: heavily carved, with extraneous lumps and bumps on the chairs, which made them not only unsightly but probably very uncomfortable as well.

One day while I was wandering around one of the biggest Commission shops, a set of bedroom furniture was brought in by some moving men. It was a wonder to the jay birds, that set of bedroom furniture. It was made of light-colored wood, much like our own bird's-eye maple. The set consisted of several pieces, a wardrobe with mirrored doors big as a one-car garage, an enormous bureau with at least an acre of mirror attached, twin beds, and another piece which I can only describe as miscellaneous. The men set these pieces down on the floor and a price card was attached. The price tag read one hundred thousand rubles. The shoppers eddied around to observe this remarkable business with wonder. But before the moving men were able to leave the shop, the furniture had been bought and the same men carried it out again.

Another day I was in the same shop trying to work myself up into buying a small silver angel for two hundred rubles. My chief reason for hesitating was that I could not decide what I could do with it after I got it. It could not be hung up and it would not lie flat down, and what its purpose really was I was never able to decide. I was in the shop perhaps fifteen minutes and while I was there, three grand pianos were sold. So from this you may be able to gather that the Moscovites have rubles and want luxuries and the two are continually getting together.

Built opposite the Kremlin at the eastern edge of the Red Square is a great, low, glass-roofed building called the Commercial Arcade. This was erected years ago to take the place of the outdoor booths of the old market place, and although it is now down at the heel and badly in need of repair, it still remains one of the most fascinating buildings in Moscow. Inside, the vaulted roof arches over the main floor, and galleries run the entire length on each side. The light that comes down through the ancient glass is dim and only a few electric lights here and there do anything to help the illumination. The floor is of marble, broken and battered now, and small shops open off either side of the big main passageway. Each shop has its dingy little window full of dingy and badly arranged goods, but I never wandered through the old place that I was not caught up into dreaming about what it must have been like "in the old days."

Most of the little shops are "closed shops" which means they are for the use of certain organizations only. Their wares are bleak and pitiful. The windows contain an indiscriminate lot of junky stuff—mostly cards of earth-colored plastic buttons when I was there. Dozens upon dozens of cards of buttons, lying dusty and forlorn and unwanted in the dusty, dim, little windows. There were a few one-burner electric plates, a yard or two of sleazy rayon, a few bits of flashy, unattractive underwear, everything faded and tired and dejected.

I was walking there one day with a Russian girl who really lost her temper about the buttons. "Look at that!" she said bitterly. "Hundreds of buttons that nobody wants! A manager gets an order to turn out so many thousands of buttons as his norm for the year. He gets his factory to work and turn out buttons—all the same size, all the same unattractive, stupid color. Then, so virtuous, he can go home to his wife. The norm has been fulfilled, over fulfilled—by buttons nobody wants, buttons that couldn't be more unattractive. But it is easy to guess that his wife wears none of these buttons—no. She has foreign clothes and so does he. But if *we* get buttons, it's things like *that*." And she pointed a scornful finger at the buttons in the window.

She sighed. "Nobody cares about it really," she said. "They consider such things too unimportant to give any real thought. But it is one of the many places where your nerves and feelings get rubbed raw. If only they would take a little pains with us, we would be so grateful."

All around the second story a beautiful wrought-iron balcony runs and from this balcony open many little rooms which were formerly shops also, but which now serve as offices for governmental bureaus. The lights are dim within and there, as in millions of other offices the world over, the moles of the government burrow and work through the long, tiresome years.

Was the great Commercial Arcade once the scene of loud barter and exchange? Did the ladies of the town come into the bright, clean little shops to buy perfume and silks and all sorts of gay trifles? Were the gloomy halls radiant when the sun came through the clean glass roof? Were they well lighted and cheerful when the snow lay heavy upon it? Will the Commercial Arcade be restored to something of its former glory one of these days or will it be torn down to make room for a new tomb? A tomb which will stand opposite the red granite tomb of Lenin and be a twin shrine for pilgrims from all over the vast U.S.S.R.? That's what is being whispered in Moscow.... Although they say as they cross themselves and whisper it, "God grant the day be far!"

There was another arcade in Moscow, not a separate building but just a glass-roofed passageway between two rows of shops. Most of the shops in the summer of 1945 were vacant and unused. But in the spring of 1946 a lot of refurbishing and repainting went on there; and before we knew what was happening, the little shops were clean and fresh and were being filled with miscellaneous articles. We finally found out what was going on. There was to be an exhibit in the arcade, an exhibit of consumers' goods. Nothing was to be for sale; it was merely an exhibit of samples of goods which were to be produced and manufactured soon. Now these things were goods for which all Moscow was longing: kitchenware, clothing, yard goods, millinery, toys; and presumably these things were going to be sold to all comers. Some day.

But this is the way the exhibit of consumers' goods was presented to the Moscow public. The arcade ran through from one street to another. There were doors at either end. At each door two guards were stationed, plus an extra guard just for luck. In order to be able to enter the arcade and look at the samples, you had to have a pass. You got the pass by applying in writing to whatever committee was in charge of the show. When you got your pass, you approached the entrance, showed the pass to the guard, who read it carefully and passed it to her companion. When they both agreed that you were a suitable person to enter the sacred portal, you were permitted to do so. Understand me, please, when you got in, you could not buy anything. There was none of this nonsense of a public exhibit. The doors were not thrown open for the passers-by to saunter through the arcade and gape to their hearts' content. You had to have a pass to gape, and I never could understand why.

None of the shop windows in Moscow seem to American eyes to be well planned or attractive. In view of the fact that few items of merchandise are available anyway, this is scarcely to be wondered at. Now and then a window is decorated with some approximation of imagination and taste. But the same display remains for weeks at a time, getting dustier and dingier, and quickly losing whatever it originally had of freshness or appeal. All the food shops have papier-mâché displays of food: large, ruddy cardboard roast beefs, big pink hams, and bright brown bologna, orange cheeses.

There is one situation in connection with shopping, both for food and for other things, which annoys Americans almost to pieces. Even the Russians resent it, but much good it does them. This is the tiresome business of displaying things in the showcases and shop windows which are not for sale in the store. I don't know how many times I have gone to the Dipstore and looked into the showcase and been galvanized to see some rare tidbit like an orange or a pickle. Joyously I would indicate that that was for me, only to have the salesgirl say solemnly, "We have no oranges or pickles."

At first I would point an indignant finger at the oranges or pickles in the showcase and say, "What do you call that?" But the salesgirl would only say seriously, "Madame, we have no oranges or pickles."

Once I even worked myself into such a lather that I located the manager and screamed for an explanation from him. With a regal gesture he told the salesgirl to sell me whatever I sought. But it never worked again. I just had to learn that some things are "window dressing" and let it go at that. I often wondered who was it that got to eat the "window dressing," since obviously somebody did. All I know is, it was not the Atkinsons.

Chapter 22

Rackets

ALTHOUGH MOSCOW is a town of very high moral tone, and although the newspapers, magazines and radio are constantly exhorting its citizens to higher and higher levels of civic virtue, it has ten thousand rackets, just the same. A Moscow citizen is as adroit and adept at circumventing rules and regulations as an American citizen in outwitting, say, Prohibition. Anyone who is particularly skillful in this connection is known as an "operator."

There are dozens of the rackets going on in plain sight all the time, and since the Secret Police are everywhere and know everything that's going on, only two conclusions can be drawn. Either the police simply shut their eyes to the infringements of the law, or else they are in on it and get their cut. The black market in gasoline is completely obvious and is used by everybody who wants extra gasoline. My husband and I once saw the chauffeur of a private car make a deal with the driver of a city gasoline truck in the middle of a busy street. The car drew up alongside the truck and enough gas was drawn off to fill the chauffeur's tank, and away he went after forking over the necessary rubles. Nobody but us stopped to stare and nobody commented on what was evidently an everyday occurrence.

A black market in cameras flourishes in the streets outside a big state camera store within a bomb's throw of the Kremlin. Every day along the streets Soviet citizens stand selling various articles illegally. Bread, wrist watches, combs, hair nets, scarves—dozens of things are offered openly. The sellers melt away at the appearance of a police officer with all the skill of an illegal pitchman on Broadway—but they reappear as soon as the cop has passed.

There are many beggars in the streets, some of them children. Although the chief gathering place of this clan is around the churches, they stand outside the food stores, too. I used to see one boy very often. He was about twelve years old, indescribably dirty and ragged, with the skillful pose and the ancient whine of beggars from time immemorial. He was huddled in a doorway counting his "take" when I passed one day, and I lingered to watch. He had counted twenty seven rubles by the time he discovered that I was snooping, and he shoveled all the rest of the money into his pocket and left before he had finished his sums. But he had a whole fistful which he had not counted; his morning's work had netted him at least fifty rubles, I should think.

There are the prostitutes, plying their age-old trade in the halls of the hotels where the foreigners live. And there is the racket indulged in by the Red Army men who are entitled to twenty-five percent discount on purchases in the Gastronoms. They wait beside the cashier's desk and offer to pay your bill for you if you yourself are not entitled to a discount. They do so, and you and they split the difference. This service was performed for me once. I made twelve and a half percent and the obliging officer made the same amount. A nice piece of change can be picked up in this way during an afternoon.

Any service which you desire to have performed, like having your radio fixed or a pair of shoes mended, if you want an erring electric lamp repaired or if some other piece of household equipment plays you false, there is always some little man who can be induced to come and fix it. But he will always come after his day's work is over, a private and illegal enterprise which is not, presumably, condoned by the authorities. In this way a private citizen may establish a little business or himself and get not only a few extra rubles but also, in case of working for foreigners, a handout of "products"—white bread, flour, cigarettes or sugar. A dressmaker will alter a dress, a tailor will fix your husband's suit, after hours. These are a few of the ways in which the Moscovites eke out their inadequate pay envelopes. There are many other ways but these are enough to illustrate the point.

One trick indulged in widely by chilly Moscovites results in the electric meter getting cheated out of many thousands

of rubles, I should judge. During the fuel shortage—oh, yes, Moscow has them, too—it was forbidden to use electric heaters to warm cold rooms. The mother of two small children explained to me how this edict was circumvented. The wire of an electric heater is divided into its two strands. One is thrust into the wall plug, and the other is wound around the steam radiator. She assured me that in this way the electric heater would work perfectly but that the meter would not register the use of the current.

I can't vouch for this, but that's the way the story goes. Some ingenious soul has discovered this trick and it flew all over Moscow. Inspectors got wind of it and would pop in unexpectedly wherever they suspected its use. But one more person popping in to spy on him is pie for an experienced Russian and few were ever detected.

I remarked to the young mother that such carryings-on might be beneath the dignity of a patriotic citizen and she smiled wisely. "We are told that the electricity is ours, the people's; therefore we consider it permissible to cheat ourselves. We do so with a clear conscience, I assure you."

Crime Wave

They can't blame a crime wave in Moscow on American gangster movies, for the simple reason that they do not permit American gangster movies to be shown. How then explain the fact that a crime wave occurred there and in the best—or worst—American tradition, too? There was nothing about it at first in the newspapers or on the radio, but the grapevine—a very sensitive instrument in the land where the newspapers and radio give out only the most carefully selected items—the grapevine had that news and we all heard it. We were scared.

There was a gang abroad; some said that it was a group of demobilized Red Army soldiers, some that it was a gang of hooligans made up of adolescent boys who called themselves the "Black Cats." They worked in a large company, and called themselves the "Black Cats" because they went about at night and because each one had razor blades attached to his finger tips by adhesive tape. *G-rrr-ugh!*

Well, the story was that this gang would stop cars late at night on dark back streets and would open the doors and demand booty. Fur coats, wrist watches, shoes preferred, clothing taken and rubles accepted. Now the streets of

Moscow are not brightly lighted at night and long stretches are dark and lonely. When it became known that this story was true and that such a gang was really in existence, we foreigners got so that two or three cars at a time would go home from parties through the night together. Finally, we began to see mounted policemen in the streets at night where formerly a lone policeman had plodded around on foot. It became known that a regiment of cavalry had been brought into the city to put down the crime wave. Then, a few weeks later, the papers announced that the "Black Cat" gang had been arrested and the crime wave, apparently, was no more.

But robberies, although not quite such ghastly ones, continued on a smaller scale. There was a Canadian girl who worked at the Embassy, a brawny lass about six feet tall. One day, just as twilight was falling, she was going home from work when a Russian youth stopped her and asked her what time it was. She glanced at her wrist watch to tell him and as she did so he seized her hand, jerked her watch loose and fled. Up, Canada! The Canadian lass gathered her skirts about her and legged it down the street after him in a red rage. She caught him, grabbed him by the collar, snatched her watch away and shouted for the police. The police obliged and the thief was lugged off. Of course, the girl was the talk of the town and the heroine of the foreign colony. Somebody asked her how she had dared to do such a thing. The girl blushed a little as if a little abashed by her own deed. "Well, after all," she said, "that is a good watch!"

The word "hooligan" is applied to all kinds of gangsters and outlaws. It seems a little amusing to Americans. I think they really mean "hoodlum." But anybody who infringes on the law, a man who makes a disturbance in a streetcar, a boy who defaces an automobile, kids who run around in gangs through the neighborhood, raising Cain and annoying people, a chauffeur who drives recklessly, ruffians like the "Black Cats," sneak thieves, these are "hooligans."

There was the case of the American Embassy clerk who got too gay with a gypsy actress one night. He had taken her home in his car and before letting her out at her door attempted to kiss her. Or something. At any rate, the gypsy had evidently never heard of such goings-on and let out a healthy scream. By the greatest of good luck a policeman happened to be close by and he came up and rescued the maiden from the clutches of the foul American cad. After some conversation which seemed to be getting none of them anywhere, the young man got into his car and drove away. The gypsy thought it over, and two months later decided that she had been insulted and outraged and that she wasn't going to stand for it. So she went and had the young man summoned to court.

Now the Moscow newspapers do not usually print anything about crime. They have no room in their pristine columns for the puny happenings of ordinary citizens, scandalous or otherwise, unless, of course, it happens that the ordinary citizen has rendered some service to the state. A fire in the Stalin Auto Works in which several people lost their lives, and a whale of a lot of valuable equipment was ruined, was never mentioned. They said it was "not news." An accident in which an elderly woman who because of the terrible overcrowding on a bus was pushed off and run over by an automobile and left lying in the streets, unidentified for hours, was "not news." The story of the airplane bringing Mr. Byrnes to Moscow being lost in the fog and forced to hover over the airport for two hours was "not news." But the cock-and-bull story of a gypsy actress about some "insult" which had happened weeks before made the papers all right. The American, the Soviet press said severely, was a "hooligan." And they made a terrific issue of the incident.

Chapter 23

The Girls Make Good

A FOREIGNER IN MOSCOW—which to my confusion, meant me while I was there—is constantly surprised at the fields of work open to women. Of course during the war every able-bodied man and near able-bodied man was in the armed forces. But even in 1936, when I was there for the first time, almost the same situation prevailed as far as heavy labor by women was concerned. A foreigner never gets used to seeing women bootblacks and women stevedores; and women bricklayers and women working in street-repair gangs and construction gangs are always a source of wonderment. Most of us realize that from time immemorial Russian women have done heavy work on the farms, even pulling plows, and in many thousands of cases handling all the heavy physical farm work themselves. Peasant women are well used to heavy labor, but the sight of husky women slinging bags of concrete onto a truck, or flinging birch logs off a load and stacking them in piles, makes an American's eyes widen.

When I was in Odessa, waiting for the ship *Ethiopia Victory* to sail for America with my husband and me aboard, I used to hang over the rail and watch the young women stevedores working on the dock. Most of them were slim and young. The American seamen used to watch the girls working with wonder and contempt and anger. "What a country!" the boys would say in disgust.

The dock was piled high with cargo. Small wooden boxes weighing about thirty pounds each were being loaded into a freight car. The girls worked like a chain gang, with a seldom

varied pace, busy as ants. They would pick up the heavy boxes and sling them to their shoulders and walk along until they came to the freight car. Here they would stack the boxes and immediately go back, still in line, to return with another box. There was little talking and no laughter, just a steady plodding between cargo and car. I watched until I was tired. I chose one girl and counted twenty-seven boxes picked up and delivered before I got tired of just watching. The sun was pouring down on the pier and the girls often mopped their faces and necks with their neckerchiefs—but always they were walking.

The American seamen never could quite believe what they saw. There were some wolf calls and whistles, and although the girls were not unaware of this, there was no outward sign from them as they labored on. The boys knew some of the girls, and told me that after a day's work on the docks the girls appeared fresh as paint and ready for an evening's dancing with the American sailors at the International Club (called by the sailors "The Red Mill"). But the stories I heard from a Russian woman doctor were not quite so cheerful. That heavy labor takes its toll. Miscarriages are frequent, for many women continue their work after becoming pregnant, even though a Committee for Labor Protection is supposed to see that they do not. Much sterility can be traced directly to the strain of this heavy labor, and many hernias and other painful and disabling troubles result from it. The American seamen regard the whole business of women's work on the docks as highly comic. And this, in addition to the "supervised play" that the Russians impose upon a seaman at liberty on Russian soil, goes to make up the bitter anti-Soviet sentiment which nine out of ten American seamen acquire when in Russia.

"If I never have a job again," one youngster said to me determinedly, "I'll never sign on another ship that's going to Russia."

"How long have you been in Russia?" I asked him.

"Two weeks," he said bitterly, "and that, sister, is plenty."

As the ship drew away from the Russian shore, our men shouted pseudo-affectionate farewells to the girl longshoremen and they made rude noises at Russia in general. They were particularly upset about the dereliction of a large yellow mongrel dog which they had intended to adopt and bring back as ship's mascot. All during the ship's stay in Odessa the dog had been a frequent and beloved

visitor. Probably few human Russians lived as high as that dog did. The boys stuffed him with meat and chicken and pie and cake and anything else his starved and bony carcass seemed to be able to contain. The dog got so he could tell an American a mile away and would lope across the docks and fling himself upon the American with delight. The dog got to be what the sailors proudly described to me as "anti-Soviet." I saw it happen myself. When a Russian, man or woman, would approach him he would snarl and bark savagely. But all Americans were wonderful. It was truly comic to see how he never failed to know the nationality.

Yet when the time for sailing came, he could not be coaxed aboard. When one of the boys seized him and lugged him up the ladder, he went limp and hung like a slaughtered sheep, a great inert mass of yellow cur. And when he was dumped on the deck, he turned and streaked ashore like greased lightning. He had never done that before. He usually had to be booted off. But, full of American food, and warm from American caresses, with words of American endearment filling his flea-chewed ears, he streaked down the steep stairway and couldn't be found. After the hawsers had been pulled aboard and a wide strip of water showed between the ship and the shore, he reappeared and sat, tongue lolling, staring coldly at his erstwhile friends. Catcalls and groans were directed at him but he gave no sign. A Red Army soldier sauntered along the pier and stopped beside him. The dog looked up with love and smiled. The soldier put his hand on the dog's head and stroked him. The dog wagged his tail. The ship sailed out of the harbor. This made conversation for the whole trip.

It is not only in the field of heavy labor that women have a place in Moscow. The *Moscow News* (the English-language newspaper) made the following statement about women workers:

> *Before the war the Soviet Union accounted for 150,000 engineers and technicians, 33,000 scientific workers, 73,000 doctors, 4,000 locomotive engineers, 100 factory and oil-field directors, 100,000 skilled industrial workers, collective-farm managers and field-brigade leaders. During the war, women replaced men in all spheres of life and these figures soared.*

So not only do you see women functioning capably in the fields of heavy labor, but you see, every day, women traffic policemen, women driving subway trains, busses and trucks, women electricians, watchmakers, machinists. Others not so often seen, but working in great number just the same, are radio operators on airplanes, welders, factory workers, carpenters and locomotive engineers. In fact, it is easy to state flatly that the Soviet Union today would not be so far advanced as it is if it were not for the manual labor of its women.

Many workers in the coal mines are women. The mines in Stalino, for instance, have women miners—young women at that. Not all of these miners are Russians, it is true; many are slave laborers, abducted from conquered territory. Young girls from fourteen to twenty have been rounded up in enormous numbers and sent to work the Soviet coal mines as prisoners of war. Some of these youngsters have been working two years or more in the mines. When their health will no longer permit their working, they are shipped back to their home towns, broken in body and spirit. One girl I heard about was quite bald after her long labors underground, and another's legs were swollen she could no longer stand. Naturally, such miners are of no further use to the Soviet Union and are returned with dispatch.

One young girl now laboring in the Stalino mines is the daughter of an American citizen—a girl of eighteen, who has been conscripted since she was a little less than sixteen years of age. The Soviets are not too particular about nationality when they need workers.

When dreamy-eyed Communists in this country argue down my throat that Soviet Russia is the promised land, I think of the thousands of little slave girls in the Soviet coal mines and personally I am unconvinced. I wonder what the fate of those miners would be if they staged a coal strike such as Mr. Lewis engineered in this country?

There is another side of the picture. There is always another side of the picture in the Soviet Union. I have seen hundreds of healthy, hearty working girls, young, vigorous and handsome. These are the girls that fate, or hard work and loyalty to Soviet principles, brought to the capital. These are the lucky ones. The bloom on the cheeks of these Moscow working girls is seldom from cosmetics. Cosmetics, as I have said, are expensive, of poor quality, and not readily available. And yet it is no exaggeration to say that some of these husky

kids have skins like the well-known peaches and cream. Their hair is shiny and heavy—healthy, strong hair that is beautiful with the lights that only youth and vigor can bestow. It certainly is not brought about by meticulous care and a hundred strokes of the brush every night, because when I was there, there were no hairbrushes to be had and even combs were very scarce articles indeed.

Wednesday, March 6, 1946, was Women's Day in the Soviet Union and the government went all out to give the girls a great big hand. I don't think things went so far as giving women a day off from work, but there were meetings and posters all around Moscow and the newspapers published laudatory and grateful editorials and articles about what women had done to help win the war. It was a very sincere and touching tribute to women of the U.S.S.R. Here is part of an editorial which appeared in the *Moscow News* on that day;

> *Today we address ourselves to the women: to the mothers, wives, sisters, daughters who go to make up a powerful force in our society. Our first words are words of the deepest gratitude for the great exploits accomplished by women in the war against Fascist aggression, exploits unparalleled in history.*
>
> *In this war women fought bravely side by side with the men as snipers, fliers, scouts, as ambulance personnel carrying wounded men to safety from the battlefield under enemy fire, as partisans blowing up enemy trains, accepting martyrs' death without a murmur, proudly conscious of having done their duty to their country.... Yet this does not exhaust women's service in the past war. The women took the places of their fathers, husbands, sons and brothers in the vast labor front in the rear; they manned machines, built airplanes, produced ammunition, made tanks, sewed uniforms for the fighting men, did the work of men on the collective-farm fields, supplying both the front and rear with food.*
>
> *As we pay tribute to all that women have done, we do not forget that the burden of war did*

not relieve them from their duties as mothers, wives and daughters; it did not free them from their duties to the family of which woman is the mainstay.... The women endured everything. And it is to the eternal glory of our Soviet woman that she was imbued from the outset with a high sense of moral duty to her country, setting an example for the women of the world.

It is natural that the Soviet woman should be in the vanguard of the struggle against Fascism, in the struggle for our independence and freedom, for our way of life, for our system, for the great gains of October. For it is in our country that women have been truly emancipated. It is here that she has gained true equality with men; here that all roads are open to her, as to all citizens of our country.

There is no wonder then, that the world has rung with the fame of the Soviet woman, no wonder that the struggle waged by the Soviet women was an inspiration to the woman patriots of France, Yugoslavia, Poland, Holland, Belgium and other countries oppressed by Hitler. The exploits of the Soviet woman were a stimulus to the women of the capitalist countries and of the oppressed nations....

Another news item from the same paper read:

International Women's Day is a traditional holiday in the Soviet Union. On that day women are honored at meetings and gatherings in towns and villages all over the country. In fact, Women's Day functions are held throughout the week preceding March 8. In Moscow alone several thousand affairs are being arranged in theatres, concert halls, palaces of culture and factory clubs attended by women in all walks of life from factory workers to scientists.... One of these women's meetings was held in the shop of an adding-machine works. The workers assembled in their workshop after the shift to listen to a talk on International Women's Day.

The speaker told them about the great role women play in the life of the Soviet Union and about their sisters abroad, the brave women patriots who acquitted themselves with honors in the struggle against Fascist domination in many countries.

Tribute was paid to the excellent work of the women in the factory. One of those who was highly praised was Eudokia Khlystova, a middle-aged woman with three medals on her jacket who was sitting in one of the front rows....

On March 7 a big district Women's Day affair will be held in the new Drama Theatre in the Bauman district which is to be opened on that occasion.

Mimosa, brought by plane from the Crimea, will decorate the club of the People's Commissariat of the Food Industry for the March 8 celebrations which will be attended by 800 women....

Women's meetings will be held in all departments of Moscow University...the heroines of the day are honor students....

And so on.
And a third item included this:

*When the new Supreme Soviet of the U.S.S.R. meets next Monday in the Large Hall of the Kremlin Palace, every fifth seat will be occupied by a woman. In the first Supreme Soviet of the U.S.S.R. there were 227 women deputies. **Now there are** 277....*

It went on to explain how much more advanced women are under the Soviet system than they were under the Czars.

But an elderly Russian gentleman to whom I showed this item nearly frothed at the mouth when he read it. He had been high up in educational circles in the old days and he gave me the following information:

"Under the Czars, for two hundred years a married woman was independent in her property rights-we had this law, which in your Florida was passed only in 1943! No country in the world ever gave women so much opportunity for education and higher learning as Czarist Russia!...As to the enormous place that women have in the life of Soviet Russia, I can only say that married women *have* to work, in the factories, etc., since the wages and salaries of their husband are not sufficient. This has been proved by a Labor Survey made in 1942. It is also perfectly true that taking such a big part in the industrial life of the Soviet Union does not relieve a married woman from her duties as homemaker. Who ever saw a Russian husband help with the housework or dishwashing?"

And a young girl to whom I mentioned the government's gratitude and thanks said bitterly, "Certainly, they say they are grateful. But it would prove it a little better if the new Five Year Plan should include a few clothes and shoes and some furniture and other necessary 'luxuries.' I am twenty years old now and by the time the new Five Year Plan is finished I shall be twenty-five. What good will it do me *then* to have new clothes and a decent place to live? I'll be too old to care!"

Yes, the Soviets have a nice line and they certainly buttered the ladies up good on March 6. But an American woman would feel that life was pretty tough if she had to live the way most Russian woman live today—and will have to live for a long, long time to come. Some people say that with the return of the men from the war, women are to be relegated more to the background, and there are several straws showing that the wind may be blowing in that direction.

Farnsworth Fowle, who was the C.B.S. man in Moscow when we were there, stated recently in a broadcast in New York that the Soviet government is slowing down on handing out medical degrees to women. The reason given for this is "not that women do not make good doctors, but that they do not show as much talent as men for research work." At the present time seventy percent of the doctors in the U.S.S.R. are women. He stated also that women in the diplomatic services are recently being by-passed in the matter of promotions and appointments. In the summer of 1945 I heard that women airplane pilots were being deprived of their jobs, "because it had been found that they were not the equals of men in this work and that they did not function so well in emergencies." I made every effort to verify this, but was unable to reach anyone who would even comment on it officially or otherwise. During the war nearly all bus drivers were women. Before we left Moscow it was plainly noticeable that men had replaced them in almost every case. There were many women traffic policemen during the war. After its close few, if any, remained at those posts. I wonder what jobs they were given instead.

These women traffic policemen who stood at the busy intersections of the streets and boulevards were well worth watching. There was none of the vague business of jerking a thumb in the general direction that traffic was to go. The policewoman had a well-regulated and definite series of signals worked like a manual of arms. They carried stubby, white-tipped wands which they manipulated in a snappy routine fashion. Bringing their heels smartly together, they pointed the wand down the right way, held the pose a second, came to attention and faced about smartly. But the pose they assumed when it became necessary to discuss an infringement of traffic rules was international. They would saunter over to the offender, put a booted foot on the running board of the car, thrust a severe, rosy face into the car window and inquire bitterly if the driver had lost sight and hearing.

Many courts in Moscow function under women judges. A high percentage of labor delegates are women. In the elections held in 1946 more than one-third of the candidates were women, mostly doctors and teachers. There is no woman member of the Politburo, however, that tight little circle of fourteen who are the real rulers of the ruled.

One interesting candidate for election was thirty-year-old Tatanya Fedorova. In 1937, when she was only twenty-one, she worked as calker, concrete pourer and timber cutter. Nominated as Deputy to the Supreme Soviet and elected, she so caught the imagination and interest of her constituents that she received over forty thousand letters during her term of office. She said gravely, "I answered every one and still worked on the Metro (subway)." She felt, however, that she should have additional education to continue in politics and to advance in her work. Therefore she enrolled as a student in the university to qualify for the degree of Tunnel-Building Engineer. She kept her construction job and studied at night. In 1941 her diligence was rewarded by a diploma stating that she had passed the examination and now had the degree she coveted. During the siege of Moscow she had charge of the antitank barricades, and her hard-won knowledge of engineering stood her in good stead. For the gallant discharge of her duties she got the Order of Lenin and the Medal for the Defense of Moscow. Later she received two more orders and two more medals. Now, as a tunnel engineer she has charge of further Metro construction work and continues as Deputy to the Supreme Soviet. She is a slender, handsome, earnest girl, eager to serve her country in peacetime reconstruction.

The amount of actual combat work performed by women in Russia is impressive. Take the case of the woman aviator, Evdoki Bershanskaya. Before the war she was an instructor in civilian aviation. When the war started, she joined the regiment of the famous woman flier, Roskova. She started with the rank of lieutenant, but owing to her brilliant personality, her ability to work with others and her flying skill, she was finally promoted to lieutenant colonel with the command of a squadron of women aviators—the Taman Air Unit.

The girls of that squadron averaged nineteen years of age! They flew on bombing missions on the Dombas front, in the Caucasus, in Kuban, Crimea, Sevastopol and ultimately East Prussia, Poland and Germany. The girl fliers of the squadron adored their colonel. She was called "the mother of the regiment." Sixteen of these young women won the Order of the Hero of the Soviet Union. Their colonel earned twelve government orders and awards. Stalin personally thanked the Taman Unit on twelve occasions for gallantry and decisive bombing of targets.

Now, at the age of thirty-three, Evdokie Bershamkayaj, a tall, strong, dignified woman, plans to retire from military life and return home, "to knit and embroider, be a wife to my husband and mother to my twelve-year-old son." She added thoughtfully, "For a while, anyhow."

It is difficult to imagine such an impressive and forceful woman sitting happily over an embroidery frame and conducting the daily, uneventful routine of domesticity. But the people who know her well say that when not on duty with the Army, she is a very feminine person, witty, charming and delightfully gay.

Another famous Moscow lady is Zinaida Troitskayaya. She is thirty-two years old, strong, tall and modest. She has high cheekbones, blue eyes that tilt surprisingly at the outer corners. Her mousy blond hair is drawn simply back into a knot on the nape of her neck. Her mouth curls pleasantly into ready smiles. She wears no make-up of any kind and her uniform is far from new. She gives no impression of being a celebrity. But that's what she is. The reasons she is a celebrity are: 1—she is a general, and 2—she is a locomotive engineer.

Her father was a railroad man and from earliest childhood she was ambitious to become a locomotive engineer. That amused the family but did not alarm them. Children usually have wild ideas about what they want to be when they grow up. But when Zinaida graduated from school at the age of fifteen and announced her intention of entering the Institute of Locomotive Engineering, the family was really startled. She was too young to enter the university. The people there told her kindly, "We do not take little girls." Therefore Zinaida wangled her way into the Institute of Electromotive Engineering as apprentice metal fitter. Finally, she earned the degree of metal fitter, fifth grade.

Now she was ready to try for the job of headman—locomotive driver. It was necessary for her to apply to a special commission—no woman had ever wanted to be a locomotive engineer before. The commission gave the matter serious thought. It decided that if she could prove that locomotive engineering is a field in which women can function safely and well, it would provide a great additional source of labor for the Soviet Union. Granted permission to study, she received the degree of Assistant Locomotive Engineer upon completing the course, the first woman locomotive engineer in the world according to the Soviets. There are now more than forty thousand in the Soviet Union.

During the first weeks of her new work she was accompanied on every trip by two physicians of the Labor Protection Committee, who after careful observation and tests, decided that there was no reason why she could not continue the work. After one year as assistant she was rated as first-grade engineer. Her life's ambition was realized. Thereafter she drove her own locomotive on the Moscow-Leninsky railroad. During the siege of Moscow she drove supply trains to the besieged city and for gallantry under fire she was made a general. Later on she was taken off the locomotive and made chief of depot in charge of the Metro. She is pleased with her work, and proud of this assignment, but longs for the day when she can return to her real love—driving the engines.

She is married and has a little daughter who is plenty skeptical about her mother's fame. "If you are an engine driver," she said sourly to her mother, "where's your engine?"

Zinaida's manner is modest, almost shy, but you can feel that she is deeply earnest and serious. "Let our friendship begin at this moment," she said to me gravely. "Tell the women of America that we hope for friendship with them. Tell them what we are doing here. Let us work together."

For my money the general has something there.

All this may sound as though Moscow's women are a collection of Amazons, lady Herculeses and Atlases, but it truly isn't so. Even the ones who are doing what Americans consider men's work somehow appear to be completely feminine.

I was discussing this equality of the sexes one day with an American who prides himself on knowing a lot of Russian statistics. He listened to me quietly for a while and then he said, "The census of 1939 showed that there were seven million more women than men in the U.S.S.R. World War II took at least two million more men. Who is going to do the work if the women don't?"

Now these statistics proved very valuable and illuminating to me. I began to feel that the place woman had made for herself under the hammer and sickle might be due less to the progressiveness of the state than to plain necessity. I began to wonder what woman's place in Soviet Russia would be if the men far outnumbered the women, if there were plenty of men to do the unskilled labor, plenty of men studying and entering the professions and sciences. How many women judges, doctors, technicians would there be? In a country where the fundamental attitude toward women is really Asiatic, would women rise to the top as quickly if the population were preponderantly male?

And where are the big families that the state is calling for to come from? Although illegitimacy is no disgrace, indeed does not exist as we know it, under Soviet law, maybe polygamy will have to be permitted if millions of women are to have husbands and children. Or the Iron Curtain will have to be hoisted high enough to permit the influx of a few million extra males—prisoners of war or political immigrants—or something. All these thoughts went streaming through my head as the statistician and I were making our way along the crowded Moscow streets.

"Seven million more women than men even in 1939," I murmured; "two million men lost in the war!" Yet here on the Moscow boulevard nearly every other woman was ponderous and heavy with child. It really looked as though practically every one of them was about to present the state with a new little statistic. I could not help feeling bewildered. I nudged the statistician and pointed to those pregnant facts.

"What's going on around here?" I said.

Chapter 24

Shooting at the Moon

I WAS SURPRISED and my curiosity was aroused by meeting women who were locomotive engineers, sailor and such. But I think that perhaps the most impressive woman I met while I was in the U.S.S.R. was Mme. Petrova, the secretary of the Women's Anti-Fascist Committee. She granted me an interview, which in itself was amazing, and after I got there she really talked to me (through an interpreter) which was more amazing still. There was no hedging and nonsense about this pleasant woman. She was grave and gracious, serious and very kind. I talked to her for more than an hour about woman's place in the scheme of things.

"What are the women of America doing to combat Fascism?" she asked me.

Well, I didn't know. When I came to think of it, it seemed to me that we felt that by fighting Germany and Japan we were fighting Fascism, but whether or not the women of America were making any organized effort to fight Fascism as such, I didn't know. What organizations we have, I thought to myself, are fighting to advance the cause of democracy. But how could I say that to Mme. Petrova when the Russian definition of democracy and the American definition of it are as different as chalk and cheese? All I could do was turn red and gulp.

But Mme. Pettova did not press me too hard. "Tell the women of America," she said, "that Russian women are working hard for peace!"

I felt then and there that Mme. Petrova represented women who were honest and good and who seek the way to peace as eagerly as we Americans do. I came away from her office convinced that if the women of America could reach across the barriers of space and language and around the wall of totalitarianism which surrounds these sisters of ours, together we could remake the world. The only thing necessary for this co-operation and understanding would be for them to abandon their form of government and for us to lay aside ours. I'm afraid neither group is quite willing to do this.

I made a statement about this co-operation with Russian women in an article I wrote for the *Woman's Home Companion*, and I received several letters asking me how to go about writing to Mme. Petrova and trying to begin some kind of friendly relationship with the Russian women. A lady who wrote one such letter said she could not resist trying to get something of the kind started, although, she added wistfully, "It may be shooting at the moon." I gave her the only address I know. I don't know whether any good results have been achieved, but certainly Mrs. Samras tried.* Here is her letter:

> December 2, 1946
> Mme. Petrova, Chairman
> Women's Anti-Fascist Committee
> Moscow
> U.S.S.R.

> My Dear Mme. Petrova:

> Through Mme. Oriana Atkinson, an American writer to whom you granted an interview in 1945, I have learned of you and the desire of your organization to help establish a war-free world.

> Many of my friends and I have discussed the possibility of making known to women in other countries the American women's desire for peace and in some way of co-ordinating our efforts to press those who assemble to plan and negotiate for peace so that they may undertake their task with greater responsibility and perhaps with greater haste.

> There is a common heart beating in the breast of all women—it is love for home and

family. Women, especially mothers, are near to the simple elementary aspects of life which, though not easily recognizable, are the fundamentals of the whole of life, in all its intricate combinations.

That women want peace is becoming better known every day. For us war is heartache and despair. There is no glamour or adventure in it.

Can the women of Russia and the women of America work for world peace in unison? If our countries can be bound more closely in spirit, the influence would soon permeate other countries. Could we exchange with you writings on this subject of peace and women's relation to it; or would it be feasible to exchange lecturers to discuss the topic?

I am the mother of one child and the bearer of another—the wife of a Hindu, a native Indian. I have a keen sense of responsibility toward my children and the need of making their world a friendly one. But first I am a woman who, like millions of women in this country and over the earth, abhors suffering, pain and unnatural death.

We have little knowledge of the best way to proceed, but American women are strongly moved to try to proceed. Where and how should we begin?

Very sincerely,

(signed) Mrs. Evelyn K. Samras

Chapter 25

Family Circle

WHEN ALL IS SAID and done, I believe it is as wives and mothers only that most of the women of Moscow would find their ultimate satisfaction. I know many who would trade any "career" they may have made for themselves for the simple life of the homemaker. They are weary of two jobs—in the factory or office or whatnot by day, and coming home to wrestle with the difficult problems of housekeeping at night. To stand in a long line for bread and other rations after a weary day's work is fatiguing and depressing. To struggle with the evening meal and to tend to the children, plus the necessary house cleaning and the laundry, done with cold water and poor, if any, soap, is enough to break the spirit of even so strong and gallant women as the Moscow housewives. They are tired; they do not complain, but they feel deeply that with the end of the war they deserve better things than the new Five Year Plan seems to hold for them. They gaze into the future with brooding eyes. "What can you do?" they say with a shrug. "What is there to do but endure?"

It must be admitted, however, that even if the necessary "consumers' goods" have reached a vanishing point, the government has done much to restore the institution of the family to more solid ground. On coming to power, the new Soviet government was lavish with divorces and made abortions easy to obtain and cheap. Life became a merry-go-round for a while; marriage partners were easy to get rid of and remarriage was easy as pie. The family as a solid institution was laughed to scorn by the government, and family relationships and affections were ridiculed as bourgeois nonsense. But somehow it didn't work. Although the people embraced this new freedom with enthusiasm, they found to their surprise that family and home had deeper roots than they or the government had realized. And today the government is as conservative as Queen Victoria ever was, although more helpful in many ways. Nowadays the family is cherished by the government, given official blessing and subsidies.

In order to lend additional solemnity to marriage and impress upon people that it is a very serious step, one deserving the most serious thought, new instructions regarding the registration of marriages have recently been issued. Marriage parlors have been provided exclusively for marriage registrations, furnished and fixed up more appropriately than the gloomy cells used for other civil acts.

Physical examination of either party is not required, but both must affirm that they are free of venereal disease, and if it is later found that a false statement has been made in this connection, it is punishable as a crime with a sentence of up to five years. The age of the woman must be at least sixteen and that of the man eighteen.

After being admonished of the seriousness of marriage, registration of the couple is made and a certificate is issued in the presence of a representative of the Soviet of Deputies and Workers. Managers of enterprises, farms and industries are expected to provide the couple with transportation to the registrar's office and help the married pair to obtain furniture and household goods. (Quite a task.)

Many people are having church ceremonies in addition to the civil registration. The Orthodox ceremony is long, colorful, elaborate and solemn, involving the use of incense, candles, crowns and music with two priests officiating and admonishing the couple. People thus married seem to expect to stay so.

Alterations in the divorce laws were made in July 1944. Divorces, formerly so debonairly and easily obtained, must now be secured publicly in court, though if a closed hearing is requested, the court may grant it. It is no longer a simple matter of a post card to get a divorce. To start proceedings, the following demands must be met: application for divorce must be handed to the People's Court, stating the reasons why it is desired; a fee of one hundred rubles must be paid. The wife or husband must be called to the court and told of the action and a list of witnesses submitted.

An advertisement of the court action must be published in the local paper and paid for by the person bringing the suit. The court must make every effort to reconcile the couple. If this is not possible, the court must establish who is to have the custody of the children and who bears the expense of their upbringing. The division of the property and the giving of the premarriage name to the person who desires it are also settled.

So you see there is no Tommy Manville stuff about this. The Soviet Union today wants its citizens to get married seriously, to stay married if humanly possible, to have a lot of good healthy children and be a credit to the Soviet system of life.

Abortions are now illegal. Motherhood has been recrowned. Women receive the following pensions and payments for bringing up children:

To the mother with two children, on the birth of a third child one payment of four hundred rubles is made, but she gets no further monthly allowance as is the case with mothers of four or more children. (Four hundred rubles amount to a month's wages for many people.)

To a mother of three children, on the birth of a fourth child a down payment of thirteen hundred rubles is made and a monthly allowance of eighty rubles is given.

To a mother of four children, on the birth of a fifth child a down payment of seventeen hundred rubles is made and there is a monthly allowance of a hundred and twenty rubles.

And so on, by easy stages until the birth of a tenth child, when a down payment of thirty-five hundred rubles and a monthly allowance of two hundred and fifty rubles are granted. This happy lady then gets also the Order of Mother Heroine, which nobody, least of all I, will deny that she has earned.

Down payments are made at the birth of the children but the monthly allowances do not begin until the child's second year. They continue until the fifth birthday of the child only. This money is for the exclusive use of the mothers and children, and the fathers have no claim whatever on it.

Unmarried mothers get help from the state when the paternity cannot be determined or when the father cannot be found. An unmarried mother gets a hundred rubles a month allowance for one child, a hundred fifty rubles a month for two children, and two hundred a month for three or more. There's no use having more than three illegitimate children, because evidently the state by that time is beginning to lose faith in your morals and it won't raise the ante any higher. None of these payments, by the way, is made until the children are two years of age. If, however, the woman marries but not the father of her children, the allowances are continued. If an unmarried mother wishes to place her child in an institution, the institution is obliged to receive the child and bring it up fully at state expense. The mother may reclaim the child any time she so desires, and she naturally gets no allowance for the child when it is in the institution.

Mothers in Russia nowadays are being given prenatal care and good progress is being made in maternity care in hospitals. Infant mortality has been greatly reduced and much study is being given to reduce it still further.

An American woman I knew in Moscow who was going to have a baby went to a Russian prenatal clinic for examination and care. She was in bouncing health, and was continuing with her job. The Russian doctors were astonished. "According to our Soviet laws," they told her, "you are entitled to maternity leave before the birth of your child. We will give you a note to your employers and they will be forced to permit you to take this leave." She thanked them gravely and went back to the American Embassy and told her cringing employers that they were bloodsuckers and dastards. Then she went to her desk and worked until the day before her baby was born. "We are a toff people."

Efforts are being made to provide living quarters where individual families may have some privacy and maintain a real family life. The housing situation in Moscow is a scandal to the jay birds. (Although the Russians make every effort to see that foreigners are taken care of, it is simply an impossible situation. The American Embassy staff consisted of one hundred and eight while I was there, but no matter how they rearranged and squeezed, there were always three people without lodgings. The only way this situation could be met was to send three people off on errands to Vladivostok or Archangel, keeping them on the road and out of Moscow for weeks at a time.)

Red Army men who have been stationed away from their wives and families are being transferred as fast as possible to their home sectors. The newspapers are full of editorials inveighing against the men who have taken up with lights-of-love during the separation period and calling upon them to go home to mamma. And bitter scorn is heaped upon the head of any mamma who also took advantage of the enforced separation and got a little careless herself. The Soviet Union wants its citizens to be serious about life and that's what most of them are.

"Serious" is a popular word in Moscow. If you say somebody is a "serious person," you can't pay a bigger compliment. You mean that he is a solid citizen, dependable, worthy. This is a little difficult for Americans to grasp. One of the young American girls who worked at the Embassy met a young Russian man at the home of a mutual friend.

"Are you a serious person?" he asked her distrustfully.

"Absolutely not!" she assured him, jealous of her reputation as a wit and a good companion. She was amazed when he drifted away from her at once. He was taking no chances with a wild American dame.

Chapter 26

Just Outside the Family Circle

IF, AS SOMEBODY once said, civilization is to be judged according to the status of women therein, the Soviet Union is in the top drawer so far as civilization goes. In theory. According to my own observations, Moscow women have a far greater place in the daily business of life than the women of, say, New York. But Moscow is a man's city and the Soviet Union is a man's world.

In America one feels the influence of women every moment. In Russia, in spite of women's hard work, their participation in every scheme of life, their penetration into every nook and cranny of Russian existence, the Soviet Union remains a man's world, dominated and controlled by men.

Of course during the war nearly all the men were at the front, and Moscow, like every other city in the world, nearly became a city of women. But after the war, when the men began coming home, it was still noticeable that they seemed to prefer the company of other men to that of women. In the two expensive restaurants which are the most popular ones in Moscow, the Aurora and the Aragvi, the parties at the tables were predominantly parties of men. Many times one would see a man sitting alone at a table. This did not prevent his going over to tables where foreigners were dining and asking the foreign women to dance with him. It was really a nuisance, and the Americans particularly got so they refused. The American men would say, "Where's your own girl?" There were always a smiling shrug and a compliment for the American women, but we certainly used to wonder why they didn't bring the Russian girls out for a night on the town. Russian men seem to have a grand time together with a kind of hail-fellow, stag-poker-party atmosphere that indicates they neither want feminine companionship nor miss it.

There is some blatant homosexuality about in Moscow, particularly among the Army officers. I am usually completely unaware of this kind of goings-on and it has to be as plain as the nose on my face before I notice it. I can give one example of it, however, that was so open and bland that even I could not remain blind to it. A young Russian girl I knew met a young soldier home on leave and fell very much in love with him. They made a date, and she was certainly one excited and happy girl. Ever a soft touch where romance is concerned, I offered to lend her a few doodads to wear on this tremendous occasion, and she gaily stripped my meager wardrobe bare. They were to dine and dance at the Moscow roof garden— truly enough to delight anybody, for it is the gayest and most frivolous spot in town. In summer there is an open-air garden on the roof, and there is a band and a dance floor and colored lights and a view out over the sprawling ancient city. No wonder a young girl whose life is the usual drab existence of a modern Moscow maiden was enthralled at the prospect.

So we decked her out, and she went off with her big dark eyes shining and her hair combed à la Americaine, in a page-boy bob, gleaming like waxed ebony. She skimmed along, with her feet hardly touching the ground, giving out sparks of youthful vivaciousness. About ten o'clock I met her in the hall, coming to my room to return her fine feathers. She was unable to restrain her tears and when I asked her in astonishment what in the world had happened, she told me the following story.

Everything had gone as planned and they had been shown to a fine table and the evening began in wonderful style. But even before their food had been served, even before they had danced together on the tiny, crowded floor, a Red Army officer had come over to the table and asked to join the party. My little friend had been flattered, although a little annoyed at having the evening thus upset. But it soon became apparent that she was not the attraction, but rather her boy friend. The older man had made profuse compliments to the youth, and had finally asked him point-blank to accompany him home.

The boy had accepted, much to the girl's amazement, and he and the officer had brought her to the hotel and left her there without more ado. The Army officer had patted her kindly on the shoulder in farewell. "You are a lucky girl to know such a pretty boy," he told her, "but just remember, we Georgians like pretty boys, too."

The girl was completely amazed and entirely bewildered. She couldn't understand it at all, and finally decided that her boy friend had been afraid to refuse because of the other man's superior rank. This may have been true. I did not try to enlighten the child, because I could see she would not have understood me if I had done so. She went off home, in a deep-blue Russian mood of complete despair, but holding to the hope that the boy would phone her the next day and make a date for the two remaining days of his leave. He did phone, but only to explain without much apology that he was going to spend his time with his new friend and that he would write her a letter when he got back to his camp. She never saw him again that I know of, and she never recovered from the blow to her pride, either.

The relationship between the sexes in Moscow is always puzzling to Americans. One of the first things an American woman misses is the electrical nonsense that is breath of life to Americans. Of course, America is a woman's country— every other nation, bar none, has made fun of us for years because of what they call "woman domination." You can't sell an automobile jack or a keg of nails or an electric dynamo in this country unless your ads show a smiling, leggy girl emphasizing how wonderful the product is. An American girl would think she was prematurely senile if she were not whistled at on the street, and all of us, including those of us who are whale bait, keep mentally supple by the simple expedient of batting nonsense around with whatever man happens to be handy.

But the Russian man's attitude toward women seems to be coldly biological. Russian men just don't seem to *like* women. Even in the springtime, in the public squares and public parks, the usual horseplay between the boys and girls seems to have this cold animalism about it. The plain fun of just being together doesn't seem to be there. A truck driver, in Russia, is somebody who drives a truck.

He doesn't take time off, endangering the lives of pedestrians if necessary, to whistle at some cute chick passing by.

I have seen hundreds of darling young girls, rosy arid creamy with the glamour of youth, plodding along the

streets, and the young men never gave them a tumble. The relationship between the young fry has all the heavy restraint of a diplomatic tea party. For this reason, Russian girls are delighted to make the acquaintance of Americans who always have a "line" and who, in the vast majority of cases, would push their best man friend into the river, if necessary, to spend an evening with a luscious girl. In Russia men and women, boys and girls, work cheerfully shoulder to shoulder, but the old American moxie never enters into the question at all.

Many Russian men have a very charming way of kissing your hand—or even the inside of your wrist—which is pretty thrilling for the moment. But American women have the feeling that it is only window dressing, for a Russian will boot you off a bus as soon as look at you and the idea of opening a door for you simply never occurs to him. I remember once I was battling along the street, against a cold wind and snow, and came breathless to the entrance of the Metropole Hotel. For some reason the revolving door was not in use and I had to go to a smaller entrance at one side. I was with a Russian girl and we were puffing and blowing and half weeping from the cold. Just inside the door stood a tall Russian officer, who watched our struggles to open the door with cool interest, making no effort to help us. I looked at him in astonishment—and then the probable reason occurred to me. "Poor man," I said to my companion, "he's blind!"

"Blind!" she said savagely, trying to pull the door open against the wind. "He's Russian, that's what *he* is."

Some Russian girls told me that their cavaliers had a sweet trick of kissing them on the shoulder, just at the turn of the neck, which they much appreciated. But they are pretty bitter about the general attitude of the Russian male. "Sure, we have equality," one Russian married woman told me, "equal rights to go out and kill ourselves fulfilling a norm all day and then the right to come home and do all the cooking and housework and give the children the proper parental influence." If you are honest, you must regard the basic equality of the sexes with respect and astonishment. Russian women are not treated as queens, as friends, as beloved companions by their men, nor regarded as something very special to be worked for and protected and treated with lavish generosity and tenderness as American women are. It has long been admitted, unhappily however, that it is only a very rare woman of forty or over who can find a job in America during normal times. In Russia thousands of middle-aged women are contributing to their country's welfare and are finding self-respect and dignity in doing it.

None of this, however, makes the ladies want to be spinsters. Nobody wants to be an old maid in Moscow any more than anywhere else. Most of the young girls have their eye out for a husband and if they can manage to snare a high bracket, an "intellectual," a politician or, even better, an officer in the Army or Navy, they consider themselves blessed.

I asked one teen-ager what her hopes in that connection were, and she said, giggling, "If not an' American, then a Red Army officer." I asked what about marrying a humble young man of her own age and class and she said, "Pooh!" She elaborated a bit for me on the subject of Americans as husbands. (There were not a few American officers and enlisted men in Moscow at the time.) Americans, she told me, are wonderful. They buy you presents and give you food and they are so *gay*. And so *naughty!* And, she added, she had been told that an American husband would often help with the housework. Imagine! No Russian would dream of doing such a thing. And Russians have no taste—as lovers they are incomparably stupid. An American lover—oh, dear me!—God could give no greater blessing. But a Russian, she told me, has a technique like a rooster. American women do not know how to treat such treasures of husbands as the Americans are. A Russian girl would work her fingers to the bone for such a one.

As a matter of fact, Russian girls do nothing of the kind. Once they are safely married to these American jewels, the great majority of them turn arrogant, grasping, nagging and eternally rapacious. They marry less for love of American husbands than for a chance to get to America, that flowing land of liquid gold. Some of them manage to get visas; many do not. But I know some American boys who wish they had cut their throats before they took as wife the sharp and clever little "Gimme girl" who knew a good thing when she saw it.

While I am on the subject of the "Gimme girls," the ones who make up what the cynical American enlisted men called "the chocolate-bar babies," meaning, of course, the girls who are pliable for chocolate bars or other handouts, but in a nonprofessional way, I might as well tell what I know about the real professionals. There is an often repeated phrase in the U.S.S.R., "We have no prostitution." It is seriously explained that the basic reason for prostitution has been removed—economic necessity. They will tell you that there are thousands of jobs open all the time and that there is no need for any woman to sink to the level of bartering her body for food. One can only draw the conclusion, therefore, that the bevies of young floozies who operate without let or hindrance in the halls and lobbies of the hotels open to foreigners, or in America House, the headquarters of the American Army in Moscow, are plying their trade for fun. Any foreign male can be sure of being solicited either in person or by phone. And a dizzier lot of bedizened and painted females would be hard to find in any country.

I have been told that the penalty for this business is extremely severe. If so, the darlings of delight seem blandly unaware that they are playing with dynamite. The dazzling mirage of reward in the shape of silk stockings, or foreign food and trinkets, seems to outshine the glowering possibility of having to chop wood in Siberia. Americans say facetiously, "It's against their Constitution to indulge in prostitution," but it's being indulged in, just the same. All is not purity and patriotism in the land of the Soviets, even though they may want it to be so.

All hotels open to foreigners are full of the "May I? girls." A "May I? girl" is one who phones to a foreigner's room just about as soon as he has set his luggage down on the floor. The phone will ring and the gentle Russian voice will ask, "May I come up?" The boys who have been around know what it's all about and either postpone the appointment, accept it with alacrity or refuse coldly, according to how they feel about it. Ignorant young men are apt to acquiesce out of politeness and then they are going to be like a puppy trying to get rid of a porcupine quill.

Since the Secret Police are everywhere and know everything, it cannot be argued that they do not know all about this activity. Whether the girls are permitted to do this and are required to pay for the privilege, or whether it is a government activity and they are definitely sent out by the police for whatever information they may be able to obtain—who knows? But the fact remains that few foreign males ever leave Moscow without having been "solicited" many times by the floozies. Oh, yes, there's prostitution in Moscow, all right, and even though it may be forbidden by law, the eyes of the law seem to be pretty tightly closed where the "May I? girls" are concerned.

Chapter 27

A Spinster, Some Mud larks and a Widow

BUT TO RETURN to the subject of spinsters—I did meet one career girl who assured me solemnly that she vastly prefers her job to marriage. This young woman is twenty-five years old and is now and has been for four years second mate on a river steamer. This is little Tamara Nesterkena, a serious, quiet and very determined young lady, indeed.

Tamara was born in Smolensk and is an only child. Her parents had decided that teaching was a good career for their daughter and accordingly she went to the Pedagogical Institute. But only for one year. She didn't care for the Institute and she didn't like the idea of becoming a teacher, so she enrolled in technical school. For some reason she is unable to explain, she decided to study commercial river navigation, which included purser's work, bookkeeping for boats, keeping records and such things. On graduating, she obtained a position aboard a river steamer, but once again she became dissatisfied with the work given her and she enlisted as a common seaman. Before her first season as seaman was over, she had been promoted to bos'n. She took some technical training and was soon promoted to second mate.

Now she is in what she proudly calls "the best ship of the Moscow-Gorki line," the *Gregori Pirogov*. Gregori Pirogov was a famous bass singer in the Soviet Opera. His family, touched and happy at this beautiful little ship's being named for their boy, have adopted the *Gregori Pirogov* and help keep the ship's furnishings up to date and spotless. A group of theatrical artists also have come to consider the ship their special care and send presents and games and musical instruments to the members of the crew. They come aboard when the ship is in Moscow to furnish "cultural leadership" for the officers and crew. Pirogov's brother Alexander takes a great interest in the ship and its affairs and helps to organize theatre parties for the crew and to cement friendship between them and the people of the Opera House. So it is really easy to believe Tamara when she says that life aboard that ship is homelike.

Tamara is already eligible for captaincy on second-class ships, but she prefers to remain with the beloved *Gregori Pirogov*. The vessel takes some freight, crated goods mostly, but can carry four hundred passengers in its pleasant little cabins. The ship's run is between Moscow and Gorki, and it makes the round trip in twelve days from April to mid-November. During the winter when the river is frozen, the ship is repaired and refurbished.

Tamara's work fascinates her. Her mother, however, is not quite so fascinated. She is content, since her daughter seems to be so happy, but she says wistfully, "How does it sound to say my daughter is a seaman?" But that's just what she is—and a good one from all reports I heard. She seems overconscientious to me. "I am eligible for captaincy," she explained carefully, "but I do not wish that responsibility at present. One must know the river like the floor of one's own room. Day and night the responsibility is heavy upon you." So with six years' experience in river navigation, she remains in charge of a crew of thirty-two men sailors, the only woman officer on the ship. She receives the cargo and supervises the stowing of it.

The men of the crew do not resent her, she told me shyly, because they realize that she knows her job. They respect and like her and they all associate comfortably together when she is off duty. She has a cabin of her own and a private office of her own and the ship is her real home. She loves it dearly. "When I step off the ship and go ashore," she told me, "I always look back at her and feel a kind of relationship—ownership almost—with her." She cannot understand why more girls do not take up that kind of work. "I don't mean just as stewardesses and waitresses," she explained. "I mean really to be sailors. It's grand!"

She has day duty only, a trick of eight hours. She knows each member of the crew as if he were a brother—all his family affairs and troubles. She wears her plain little uniform

proudly and although by no stretch of the imagination could she be called a pretty girl, her plain little mug is so earnest and sweet that it touches your heartstrings. She has often been offered shore jobs, but she will never leave the river. When ashore, she states flatly that she has all kinds of illnesses, but when she is plying up and down the river, she is as sound as an apple. Yet life aboard a river steamer is not all smooth sailing. The high winds often making landings dangerous and tricky; if the captain did not know his business, the small ship might easily overturn. "Imagine that!" she said. "To lose the ship!"

I met only one or two women who had lived in Moscow before the Revolution and most of them were loath to talk about life in the old days. One elderly lady, however, gave me glimpses into the life of that time. She said no lady would *dream* of wearing ready-made clothes. Indeed, there is still a very definite feeling in that direction; Moscow ladies much prefer to have their clothes made to order, although in present circumstances they will wear anything they can lay their hands on. No lady, said my elderly informant, would have *dreamed* of going on the street without her gloves. That seemed to be about the sum and substance of her remarks and they were, I must admit, not very enlightening. "Are you better off now than you were before the Revolution?" I asked her. (She could scarcely be worse off than she is now, but I asked her anyhow.) She looked a little frightened at the question but she took a deep breath and answered me. "All I know about *that* is," she replied bitterly, "that before the Revolution, I *ate*."

The old women in Moscow were fascinating. The really old women, the old folks you see in the churches at Mass, or standing before the church steps, hands outstretched, begging, the old women on the park benches or feebly sweeping the streets at the crossings—these must be reservoirs of memories and tales from the ancient past. The beggars alone would be worth a year's research. They are such comfortable old mud larks, bundles of unspeakable rags, but settled down into the slough of beggarhood with complete contentment. They are like flocks of old and skinny crows come to rest on the steps of the church. They never seem to care whether they are given alms or not. They extend their filthy old hands absent-mindedly, really unwilling to take time from jabbering with their fellow beggars. They seem to be just about the only people I saw in Moscow who were

not bustling about urgent affairs.

These are the people who probably have Dependent's food cards—or maybe none. It doesn't seem to worry them that their card calls for only a bit of bread and nothing more. They look as though they have got used to living on nothing and, never expect to have anything else. They have no piteous whining attitude. They seldom show you stumps of palms or sores on their feet or other dreadful malformations as do the horrid beggars of Persia—or New York. They don't cringe. The just pull their rusty old shawls around their heads and make the best of life. And the churchgoers shell out the rubles to them graciously. The poorer the church the better the pickings, I noticed.

I have heard some strange sounds in my life, but I never heard anything stranger than the laughter of the beggarwomen on the steps of the old churches of Moscow. It is as thin as frog music, as frail as a breeze in an old reed marsh. They cackle and laugh together, the old beggarwomen. It may be that when you are down so low that you can't go lower, when you know that to expect any kindness of life is sheer insanity, when good food, warm clothes, a decent bed are as far removed from your orbit as the moon or Mars, then perhaps as compensation you get a kind of tattered serenity that enables you to exist and laugh a little while you are doing so.

Yet in Moscow, as everywhere else on the face of the globe, character comes through. While some of the oldsters take to poverty with a smile and a shrug, others combat what would seem to be their obvious destiny and fight through to better things. There is, for instance, the case of little Mme. Vera Arnold. I met her quite by chance, and fell victim to her charms without a murmur. She must be nearly eighty years old, and it would take two of her to make a shadow. She is elfin, talkative, full of vitality. In fact, meeting her is a little like stepping on a live wire. She sat before me, a minute bundle of nondescript clothes, with her small muddy felt boots crossed jauntily. You could see that she had neither the time nor the desire to pay attention to anything so futile as personal adornment. I found out later that she had no time for anything but nonsense. Her conversation was a torrent. And this, peeled down to the essentials, was the story of her lives.

As a young woman she had been studious and ambitious. Her education had been an excellent one and on her graduation she became associated with the worlds of science and mathematics. Finally, her main work placed her in charge of the Sector of National Economy and she became editor in chief of a scientific journal called the *Statistic Review*. As a sort of side line, and to use to advantage any spare moments she found being wasted, she held the chair of mathematics in the University of Kharkov. These activities continued until she became of pension age, and when she was eligible for pension, she retired. Her pension was tiny, of course, as is usual with the pensions of educated people who have given their best years to educating others. But, at a time of life when most women's chief interest is in keeping a sharp eye out for the possible advent of grandchildren, a trick of chance placed her lively little feet on a brand-new path.

The Soviet government was planning to produce·a film of a semi-scientific nature on the history of agricultural implements. She was called in for consultation. This was the beginning of her new career. While in conference with the film committee, she had a brilliant idea that was really the germ of a new form of art. Seething with inspiration, this elderly little firebrand designed and planned a gay, fantastic (but, incidentally, highly informative) series of pictures which she called *From the Stick to the Tractor.* She made real characters out of inanimate agricultural implements, animated them and wrote a snappy little script for scenario. The film was such a pronounced success that she soon became a kind of Soviet Lewis Carroll. Her second film was called *How Ships Are Salvaged,* and again she supplied a simple, jolly script.

But her heart was really not with movies. She had an idea that she wanted to work with and for children and that the motion-picture form was too complicated really to teach them. Yet children believe photographs more than they do sketches or paintings.

Mme. Arnold had had some experience with young children in kindergarten work and had found that the mind of a child can be reached and stimulated by the use of dolls and puppets better than by pictures. So, taking these two pieces of information, and adding them together, she arrived at her new art form—photographs of dolls and toys, arranged in story form.

She buys the dolls, as a rule, but sometimes she makes them. All the little toy animals which she later has photographed she makes herself from bits of fabric and paper and wood. She makes scenery, too, to illustrate whatever script she has chosen or written. After "actors" and scenery are finished, she sets them up on her writing desk, arranging the poses and adjusting the lights properly. Then her friend and fellow worker, the photographer Ziuzin, gets ready his camera and together they make the series of photographs which tells an enchanting story and brings new delights into the lives of the children.

She has been knee-deep in this work for seven or eight years now and has manufactured, arranged and written about forty different scripts in that time. Some of the originals have been used by the government as a kind of painless propaganda—one, for instance, was used to break down the bitter resistance of small boys who do not take kindly to being bathed and made otherwise decently presentable. Another very famous one is based on a beloved old fairy tale called "Little Masha and the Bear." Mme. Arnold happened to have this series of photographs with her when I met her and I was fascinated by it. The little doll Masha was photographed in the most delightfully innocent and naïve poses with her protagonist, a woolly and foolish Teddy bear. The whole story was acted out in a delightful series.

Any child would have been filled with joy at the opportunity of being able to "read" the story by means of the small photographs. And that's just what they are allowed to do. They may hold the cards and look to their heart's content while the teacher tells the story which accompanies the pictures. Prints of the pictures are in many of the kindergartens and schools in Moscow as well as in the House of the Pioneers—a Children's Palace of Play.

I asked Mme. Arnold whether she would be permitted to give me a few of the charming photographs to bring home and she said gaily, "Why not?" She promised to bring them back the next day, but I never saw her again, nor was I able to reach her through any of her friends. But even if she were not permitted to visit me, I feel fairly sure that she will go on and on to better and better ideas, always provided, of course, that she doesn't just fly to pieces in the excitement of it all.

That, then, is the story of one elderly woman and how she guided her destiny.

I met a good many women while I was in Moscow—actresses, sailors, locomotive engineers, doctors, secretaries, couriers, women in public life, artists, grandmothers, brides, chauffeurs—a whole world of Moscow women. And, now that I stand off and look the situation over, I find that I think they are just like women anywhere. There are good, serious, hard-working women, and there are floozies.

There are self-seeking, selfish, cruel and contemptible women, and gentle, self-sacrificing wives and mothers. Two things they all have in common however: 1—desperate hope for better times, and 2—desperate hope for peace.

Chapter 28

Small Fry

WHEN COLD WINDS BEGIN to blow around the Kremlin walls, the streets of Moscow are full of over-upholstered gnomes. They are the children of Moscow who are being tenderly protected against chill and frostbite. You may be sure that there are some pretty snappy fashions among the members of the younger set: pointed pixie hoods, brilliant woolen scarves, knitted caps, stout felt boots, bright mittens and padded jackets or heavy little woolen coats—all strained to bursting over heaven knows how many layers beneath.

But even though the little ones are swathed almost to immobility, this does not prevent their demanding and getting paper cups of ice cream from the shivering vendors on every street corner. A treat is a treat, according to the children's viewpoint, and the temperature has nothing to do with it. It is a brave sight to see them trotting along spooning ice cream into their mouths even though their cheeks are blazing red with the cold.

"Everything for the children," said a Russian gentleman to me as he watched the scurrying crowd.

A little investigation proves that he is right. The children occupy a very large part in the general scheme of things. Not only are their physical needs being well provided for. The cultural program is enormous. Two important newspapers in Moscow are published exclusively for young readers. The *Komsomol Pravda*, a daily, with a circulation of four hundred and thirty-four thousand, is a serious newspaper for the young adults. The *Pioneer Pravda* is published once a week for children and its circulation is four hundred thousand. The copy of *Pioneer Pravda* which I examined and had translated seemed to me to be an excellent newspaper for children. (I am not talking about the content of the articles, or their political implication.) The paper is a four-page tabloid-size publication. There are plenty of sketches and photographs to liven it up. On the front page was a long article about a super-youth named Volodya. Volodya was able to perform a prodigious amount of good work daily. His lessons were always perfect, he was always neat and clean, he was his mother's staff and stay, and nobody knew how in the world he was able to do it. But Volodya said it was all very simple. The reason he was able to do all this: every minute of his day was planned.

There were several carefully selected and edited news items concerning politics and Soviet progress in science and agriculture and there was a small article entitled "Do Your Friends All Go to School?" The article, severe in tone, pointed out that education is a priceless thing and that everybody should take full advantage of it. If by any chance any young person's friends did not attend school (could it be they meant somebody is playing hooky?), the newspaper pointed out that it was the duty of its readers to report such goings-on to the authorities and see that the culprit went back to school.

There were articles on art and photographs of two paintings were shown with the artists' names and a short biographical sketch of each of them. There was a poem, with a little information about the author. There was a long article about the celebration being held in one of the schools in honor of the birthday of a famous Russian poet. The back page was devoted to games and puzzles—a crossword puzzle and an illustrated article on "magic" tricks. There were a detailed scientific article and an article on how to make a bookshelf, with drawings to illustrate the way. There were a short story about animals and an installment of a serial called "The Phantom of the Blue Cave." There were no comic strips at all.

It seems to me that it might be an excellent idea for some enterprising American publisher to print a daily newspaper for children. Certainly the ones I saw in Russia were extremely popular and seemed to fill a need.

There are several children's theatres in Moscow which the architects have scaled down to the size of their patrons. The state grants a yearly subsidy of three million rubles to the children's theatres and provides busses for the children

Oriana Atkinson

who live in the outskirts of the city. There are also three puppet theatres for children and one children's movie—with films especially produced for children—and one traveling vaudeville theatre that visits the schools.

The children's theatres co-operate closely with the schools and produce programs suitable for different age groups; Fairy tales for the very youngest, from nothing to seven years; others from eight to fifteen years receive stronger fare. The fairy tales of Marshak and *The Snow Queen* by Schwartz are among the spectacles provided for the youngest patrons. For children of the fourth, fifth and sixth grades of school, Gabbed's *Town of Foreman* and *The Spring Bird*, which is about the 1905 Revolution, are given.

For members of the seventh grade and older children, Ostrovsky's *Poverty Is Not a Vice*, Katyev's *Son of the Regiment* and Michbaikoff's *A Happy Dream* are in the repertory; also Shapvalov's play *Two Volunteers* about the American Civil War, showing how the Russians fought on the side of the North.

A Sunday matinee for the fairy-tale group is a fascinating affair. Two familiar and beloved stories by Marshak, *About the Goat* and *The Little Room*, are acted by a permanent repertory company, some of whom have been with the children's theatre for thirty-five years.

In fantastic costumes and with weird make-up, the little plays are acted at a gentle pace and with sweeping gestures that bring the audience intimately into the action. The children are frequently consulted about the action of a play and they shout their preferences and prejudices freely.

When the earnest, hard-working, little goat wanders into the den of the ferocious wolves, you can cut the apprehension of the audience with a knife. Many feel impelled to cover their eyes and ears. And when the inevitable happens and the innocent goat is horribly devoured, there isn't a dry eye in the house.

Before I went to Russia I had not been inside a schoolhouse for—let's say twenty—years and I never felt better in my life. I never passed a school but that I walked a little faster and drew a great free breath and thought how wonderful it was that I was outside looking in. But when I got to Russia, I had the opportunity to write an article about Russian children and, of course, you can't write about children without investigating their schools. So I found myself poking my nose into schools and talking to schoolteachers. Even then I kept

telling myself, wasn't it grand that I could walk out of the school any time I felt like it; and if anybody started to give me a physics examination or to quiz me on algebra, all I had to say was that I was unfamiliar with the language.

The school buildings in Moscow seem to me to look about like public-school buildings in America. There is no average school building. Some look older than others and, to tell the truth, I was inside only two. They had the same atmosphere that schoolhouses in America have. They were clean, but they looked as though they took a good beating from the hands and feet of the youngsters. The buildings seemed to me to be like the American counterparts, fighting against terrible odds to keep sanitary—and to keep one brick straight on top of the other. This is only my imagination, of course, for the schools *were* clean and *were* adequate, but the vibrations of youth and its terrible vigor seemed to emanate from the walls, and you could feel the abundant vitality that was held in leash there.

One headmistress who impressed me deeply was the principal of Public School Number 183. When I first saw her, I felt as though she were a character straight out of Charles Dickens. She is a very tall, big woman, severe, austere, really a little frightening. But talking to her, even through an interpreter, I got a terrific respect for her. I could see that she regarded her life's work of teaching as a tremendously important thing. And I could see that she was well qualified to be at the head of that school. I always have the deepest respect for anybody who can manage kids. My own method is to give them whatever they yell for at once and let that end the matter. Anything for a quiet life. I could see that this woman knew better. And without knowing very much Russian, I could see that the children who managed to graduate from her school would be worthy citizens and good scholars, too, if I'm any judge.

This lady's name is Maria Petrovna Kourshavkova—a big name for a fine, big woman. And even as I feared, Mme. Kourshavkova found me wanting in manners and proceeded to show me what I should have known without her lesson. She had taken me and the interpreter to her office, where on the wall behind her desk hung several pictures of great men, including a picture of Franklin D. Roosevelt. In order to emphasize that Americans carry freedom of speech everywhere with them, I smiled at the picture and remarked, "Plenty of Americans, you know, were bitterly opposed to President Roosevelt's policies." My interpreter ceased to translate. "Go on," I said to her. With a sick smile she did so, and to my astonishment Maria Petrovna Kourshavkova turned a dark red and stared down at the top of her desk. Then I realized that what I had done was not to demonstrate that I enjoyed freedom of speech. I had committed a breach of etiquette in criticizing a leader. Nobody cared about my political views. They just wondered what kind of school I had gone to.

Public School 183 is a large five-story brick building, clean and attractive. Although the amount of heat supplied in winter is not great, it is enough to take the chill from the air. In a conspicuous place on the wall hang the "Rules for the Pupils," which are standard in all Moscow schools. They begin: "Every student must stubbornly and insistently apply himself to his education in order to be of real use to the state." The list contains the rules of conduct for the model pupil, both at school and at home. If all of them are scrupulously

adhered to, Moscow will soon be perfect. There are the usual pictures of Lenin and Stalin, and a statute of Stalin as a young boy stands on one of the stair landings.

A visitor is kept nodding like a Chinese toy to return the shy and delightful greetings of the children. Demure and modest, the little ones trot along in single file murmuring a polite word that it would be churlish to ignore.

Grade Three, scrubbed and shining, was having a penmanship lesson when the foreign visitor entered. The pupils rose and stood courteously for a moment and then resumed their labors. The copybooks upon which they were working were marvels of neatness—not a blot in a classful. Grade Three breathed heavily, frowned intently and bore down hard on their pens. The results were beautiful and clear.

Above the third grade the classes are not coeducational. "We found it to be a success, this separation," said Maria Petrovna Kourshavkova. "The girls have become more feminine and quiet and have concentrated more wholeheartedly on their work." Certainly the girls in the chemistry class were feminine and quiet, although a sharp-eyed investigator could perceive a slight tendency to giggle. They were performing some miracle or other with test tubes and Bunsen burners. The chemistry laboratory is well supplied with equipment and, like all other classrooms, well lighted and comfortable. I was not shown either a gymnasium or a playground.

From thirty-five to forty-two children make up the average class. The small children attend school from 8:30 A.M. to 2:00 P.M., and the older children from 2:00 P.M. to 7:30 P.M. There are a reading room and a circulating library for the use of the children. The number of volumes is not large but they are much used. Shakespeare, Jack London, Kipling, Ernest Thompson Seton and some other foreign authors have been translated into Russian for the older grades.

All the school children receive a daily ration of fifty grams of bread and sweets with tea at school, sometimes hot porridge. They have special ration cards to meet the needs of growing youngsters. They may always have butter, even at times when butter is not available for grownups, and sugar also is supplied. And children of the eighth, ninth and tenth grades have a bread ration of four hundred fifty grams daily, which is one hundred fifty grams more than the younger children. There are special milk stores for children where they get a special ration, when milk is available.

Education is compulsory from the seventh to the fifteenth year. The elementary schools have a ten-year course, tuition-free except for the eighth, ninth and tenth years when a fee of two hundred rubles (about sixteen dollars) is charged. The children of servicemen and women, war orphans and children whose people are unable to pay anything, are taught free.

Some schoolbooks are supplied, but since at present there is a shortage of books, many of the children are expected to use textbooks in the public libraries. So much home work is given that sometimes the older students have to work until eleven and twelve o'clock at night to keep up with their grades. A wide range of subjects is taught: Russian, English, French, German languages, Russian literature, European literature, American literature, ancient history, Russian history, modern European history, elementary astronomy, physics, mathematics including algebra and geometry, biology, chemistry, botany and the history of the Communist Party. There is also a program of military training, slightly different for boys and girls.

Every school has a Pioneer and a Young Communist League in which the children receive their first grounding in political knowledge. Both of these groups maintain summer camps and an extensive athletic program, but their chief function is political guidance.

There is another serious organization composed of older children. This committee draws members from the Pioneer and the Young Communist Leagues of the schools and factories. Some of its functions are cultural. In the main, however, this too exists for political guidance. During the war its chief work was to instill in the young people hatred of Fascism. Now they are beginning a program of international relations and mass social work. Members exchange letters with children and young people of Britain and America. It is hoped to build up international understanding and friendship by this means.

Here is a Russian description of the function of the Young Communist League in 1932. I was unable to get a more modern outline of the organization. There may have been some changes made since that time, but if there have been, nobody I asked about it would give me an official statement.

"The Young Communist League affirms its solidarity with the Russian Communist Party. The principle of the League is to disseminate the

principles of Communism and to draw the youth of the working class and the peasantry into the work of building Soviet Russia.... The Y.C.L. has never diverged from the correct political line.... It has collaborated wholeheartedly with the Party on all undertakings.... it has taken the initiative in the movement for socialist emulation and for increased tempo...successfully leading the movement...for high-pressure work at the bench."

The Pioneers, the younger children's group, was started to educate the children in the spirit of Communism, "social-labor education." They are given useful political, cultural and physical training. Their motto is: "Be ready to fight in the workers' cause!" The reply to this challenge is "Always ready." They have a special uniform, olive-drab, and a badge and red neckerchiefs. The members are "children of working-class parents between the ages of ten and sixteen."

The children between the ages of eight and ten years are "Little Octoberites," and they have a group of their own.

The standard of education in Moscow is very high. Not only do the parents and the teachers set high standards, they maintain an urgent, almost hungry determination that the children shall excel.

As I say, I met only two headmistresses, but these and the schoolteachers I saw struck me as being just about tops in what educators should be. They had a reserved, dignified and calm manner and they seemed to be thoroughly devoted to their work. The children regarded the teachers with friendly eyes and spoke to them without restraint or servility. And the manners of the school children were charmingly old-fashioned, highly conventional and pleasing. The whole atmosphere of the schools was serious. The students were there to learn and were very thankful to have the chance. Many, perhaps most of them, were obtaining an education which their own parents never dreamed of. It is my guess that in the length and breadth of Moscow there is no horsing around in the schools.

When the children graduate, they deserve to graduate. They have been well taught. But there is a large program of political indoctrination, even in the primary schools, which seems to me to go far beyond inculcation of love of country and pride in their land. A child who graduates from a Russian public school emerges a well-disciplined young member of the Soviet state in addition to being a well-educated youngster. He is a firm believer in the saintliness of Lenin and in the infallibility of Stalin. Complete devotion to the precepts of his government and hatred and suspicion of "capitalism" are deeply ingrained in his mind.

One little girl who came to my room to pay me a very short visit turned to her mother in wonder and said, "Why, she is a very nice lady. I can hardly believe that she is a capitalist." In the schools as in every other walk of Moscow life, the state is the important thing and individual education and culture are definitely subordinated.

During the war many children were permitted to work, but now it is said no one under fifteen years can have working papers. A program of education for working youth is provided. There are night-school classes for working children. Although attendance is not compulsory, it is expected, and classes are well attended.

There are hundreds of day nurseries all over Moscow. Many apartment buildings have their own nurseries, with nurses and food provided by the state. Every factory has a nursery for the children of the workers, either in the factory or in a building close by.

Weather permitting, the parks are always full of children. The parks have a supervised-play program. A walk through any Moscow park recalls the general park atmosphere of New York. There is an incessant, insane activity among the children, the same molecular madness that always possesses children at play in America. Sandboxes are well patronized when the weather is pleasant, and the customers are not above whamming one another over the head with small shovels or any other blunt instrument.

Crosswalks are usually covered with the mysterious chalk patterns of some international hopscotch. Little girls, whose game is interrupted by pedestrians, watch anxiously lest the marks be erased by stupid adult feet. Little boys, who have warlike games with sticks for guns, make the air shrill with the familiar *rat-a-tat* sound in imitation of machine-gun fire.

There are few perambulators. The factories making these gave way to armament factories during the war. The very youngest children, wrapped like mummies, ride serenely in the arms of their elders and peer out at the passing show like solemn baby owls.

The children of Moscow seldom cry. When they do, they cry in an absent-minded kind of way with no real interest in whatever is causing their tears. There seem to be few of the temperamental bursts of rage and nerves that we are accustomed to in America. Moscow children seem to be so fascinated by the routine of daily life that they have neither the time nor the inclination to indulge in tantrums.

The attitude of the Russians toward their children touched me very deeply. Aside from what the government is doing for children's welfare, the feeling of adults toward children is understanding, warm and protective. It is as though the memories of the hardships and the tragedies of their own recent past have filled them with the desire to shower upon the little ones the greatest possible happiness. They seem eager to paint the lives of their children with only the brightest colors and to provide them at all cost with whatever luxuries of life they are able to obtain. The purges of 1936 are still vivid to most adults. The famines and horrors of the war years are still clear. In their attitude toward the children you see the hope that the young ones may be spared such misery and such terror.

As for the children themselves, I could never quite analyze their attitude toward life. Although most I saw seemed healthy and normal, I sensed in them an unchildlike watchfulness and quietness. They seemed to be observing life all the time, so eager to participate in every passing moment that they could not waste time weeping. I can't say that they were stolid, for I have seen exhibitions of the craziest child play accompanied by screams of delight. But it is as if they had inherited a knowledge of many dark things—like the age-old knowledge of little helpless animals who learn how to freeze immobile at some signal from the mother and to wait ice-silent until the danger is past.

I never heard the unreasoning roars of rage with which our American children hold us in subjection. I never saw a Russian child have to be bribed into good behavior and I never saw a Russian strike a child at any time. The children seem to have an urgency toward obedience and placidity in their relationship to the adult world which I cannot explain or describe. It is not meekness or fear but a kind of acceptance of law.

People usually ask me whether Russian children differ from American and European children and then they get very mad when I tell them what I think. As far as I have been able to judge, the very little children differ from ours and the adolescents do not differ much. The little children seem quieter than ours, less nervous, gentler. The Russians seem to dote on babies and treat their littlest ones with an almost overwhelming amount of attention. Yet it does not seem to "spoil" the children, nor make them show-offs or brats. Some of the Red Army men who returned from Paris or Berlin brought their youngsters tiny, luxurious fur coats and they looked very cute in them and tremendously important. Naturally, the small fry who were that lucky were regarded openmouthed by less fortunate comrades and were definitely cocks of the walk. On the other hand, I heard parents of adolescent children say that they had acute headaches trying to solve the problems presented by their maturing young. They quite frankly applied the adjectives "fresh," "insolent," "hard to handle" and "bad-mannered" to them. The parents seemed to find themselves as mystified and upset by their teen-agers as we puzzled and well-meaning Americans are by ours. But at least no American parent was ever told off quite the way one Russian father was. He was trying to discipline a headstrong young daughter, and she said to him firmly and coldly, "Do not forget, please, that I am a Soviet citizen and if you attempt to punish me I shall report you to the police."

If the above observations seem somewhat contradictory, it is just one more instance of the fact that Russia is a land of contradictions. Little Russian children seem to me to be angelic. Most of the older ones seem to me to be normally human. A few, like the young daughter I told about, are undoubtedly little devils.

Moscow has high principles and strict rules for children, but even so, the children break out into nonsense at the drop of a handkerchief. Some of them hitch onto busses. Some make faces at policemen. They fall into fountains in the parks in summer and they are attracted to the melting snow puddles in winter as iron filings are attracted to magnets. Although they belong to serious political groups and read serious books and newspapers and are guided in most of their activities, both in and out of school, they scuff out their shoes and they slide on the ice on the seat of their pants. Their vocal cords are usually strained to the limit of endurance. If you could haul them away from play long enough to scrub off the surface grime, you would find underneath the face of the Soviet future.

The spooky corridors of the Metropole Hotel through which timid adults scurry as fast as their legs will carry them, are always full of small fry who seem to find these tunnels enchanting.

Take the fourth floor, for instance, which is the one I know the best. To reach Room 467 it was necessary to turn off the main lobby into a long inner hall from which rooms open on both sides. There were no windows in this hall and the tiny electric lights illuminate the shadows only dimly. Yet here happy children play all day and often far into the night. They race and howl, ride velocipedes, strain their eyes over picture books, cut out pictures, play with dolls, drill toy soldiers and scream current events into one another's faces. Some of them go to school, but many of them, being only temporary inhabitants, stay long hours in the halls. It is the center of the children's lives, their loved playground where they have their real being.

Evenings are the best time. During the day there is usually a moderate amount of activity in the hall, but after school, around four o'clock, there begins the gathering of the clans and from then on, until twelve or one o'clock at night, there is a crescendo which at its height can rattle the windows and make ordinary conversation in the rooms impossible. Of course, by closing the double doors and watching your companion's lips closely you may be able to understand what is being said, but during the summer, when it is necessary to leave the door open, you're a gone goose. Just take a walk and let it go at that.

No one complains, except humorously, about this riot, nor have I ever seen anyone in authority do anything to stop it. Maids, porters and other passers-by step carefully around the scattered toys and move gingerly and apologetically around the game formations, to the accompaniment of anxious looks or scowls from the children. Bedtime, or what would be considered bedtime in America, never interferes in the least. No parent ever opens a door and calls, "Bedtime, Sascha"or "Mischa." The children race and roar until one by one they drop like ninepins because of physical exhaustion. For sheer animal vigor I have never seen anything to compare with it.

No adult ever pays the slightest attention to them. They sort themselves into age groups and hurl themselves into play with the intensity of wild animals. They settle their own disputes and arrange their own affairs entirely by themselves.

Although in my goings to and fro I often saw crashing falls and assorted accidents, the children involved seldom wept or complained. There always seemed to be such a mad urgency not to miss a trick that the hurt child would fling himself back into the maelstrom at once, even though he might be pale from hurt or shock.

The only time I ever saw any of the children subdued or bored was at a Christmas party which had been arranged for them. It was a kind of costume party and each child had been supplied with a costume of a sort, whether by parents or supervisors I do not know. The party was held in the main dining room of the Metropole. In the green light which filtered languidly down through the big glass-domed roof, the children, arrayed in rags and tags of fancy dress, milled around unhappily. An old red-fox furpiece had changed one little boy into a fox; a ratty beaver coat made another one into a bear. There were ballerinas, dolls, chefs, gypsies and soldiers, effects all achieved with scraps of materials and dabs of fur. It was amazing what those few scraps could do. But the children were depressed and they eddied round and round the famous little fountain in the middle of the dining-room floor and looked as though they wished they were dead.

On a platform at one end of the room where sometimes a band played, a woman was thumping cheerily away on a piano. Grandfather Frost—Santa Claus to you—officiated in the middle of the floor. He was the skinniest gentleman of his kind I had ever seen and his white suit billowed about him in empty folds. In Russia, the land of the admired poundage, it did seem a little strange. He was also a very disgruntled and cross Grandfather Frost, for he glared at the children over his beard as if he hated the sight of them. He held a wand; at least I suppose it was meant to be a wand—it looked like a bed slat and he looked as if he wished to heaven that just one of the children would make one false move. But none did. They plodded around obediently, peeping a little song in the feeblest of tones. They were pale with boredom but they kept bravely on. Only a few little boys had pulled away from the herd and were off in a far corner joyously engaged in gouging one another's eyes out. These alone gave any indication of the zip they could muster if they chose.

When I left, the children were tapping their feet timidly and clapping their hands gently to amuse a toothy teacher who was nodding brightly and trying to prod them into some semblance of life. She should have seen the fourth-floor gang later that night, when, free from her supervision, it got going on something which—to judge by the savage yelps—was probably called "Disemboweling a Nazi." She'd have been surprised.

As I have said, many of the children are only transient residents, pausing for a day or a week or two because their parents are on their way somewhere else. But there are several old inhabitants whom I got to know by sight although we never passed the time of day in the halls. I used to be astonished at the healthy appearance of these children. It was impossible for them ever to have a drop of fruit juice or any of the things that sweating and fearful mothers in America are always pouring down the throats of their protesting young. The children of the Metropole never got any fresh air and nobody ever worried about germs or dirt.

I remember one infant who at the time I lived in the hotel was about fourteen months old. His mother used to swathe him in shawls and blankets as if she expected to take him to the North Pole by dog sled. Then she would tuck him into a rickety perambulator, tuck a few more covers over him in case of frostbite and roll him up and down the corridor outside my room. And yet, divested of his wrappings and seen in his working clothes, he was like a lump of pig iron. He used to come staggering out into the hall in his free moments and take his place unsteadily at the tail of whatever game was going on.

In the insanity of play the stampeding children would slam into him and he would be hurled against the wall or to the floor by the impact. He never cried. He would shut his eyes and wait until he crashed and then would experimentally roll his head to find out whether it was still operating. If he felt that he was badly hurt, he would retire mournfully but silently to his parents' room and come back when he felt sufficiently recovered.

He was too young and too little to be anything but a nuisance in the games and he knew it. But he was stolidly determined to be in on them and I must say the other children stood him very well. When they ran, he ran, he knew not why. When a line was being formed and players chosen or counted off, he was always on deck. He was extremely adhesive, this chunky baby, but he had such a winning personality that he was generally beloved. I have seen a big boy scoop him out of harm's way and put him gently back on his feet after some crisis was past. Sometimes one of the older girls would set him on her hip and carry him as she dashed about her game.

When he wearied of the fast pace of his elders, he would wander off on adventures of his own and he was usually very lucky. I have seen him poised unsteadily at the top of a steep stairway, peering curiously down into the gloom, but somebody always reached a hand to grasp him by his soggy pants and haul him back to safety. He was a serene and healthy little boy, being reared without benefit of elaborate health program, and by the look of him he will grow to be six feet tall with a chest like a barrel.

In direct contrast to this charming infant was the Scourge. He was the most sinister character I met in the Soviet Union. He was about eighteen inches high and perhaps four years old. He had a face like a baby vulture with small baleful eyes and a tiny hooked beak of a nose. He would appear at my door at strange hours of the day or night clad in a minute striped jersey and a pair of pants that looked like two one-cent stamps. Although I always took a firm stance and blocked the doorway with my not inconsiderable bulk, he would bare his fangs at me in a cold grin and drift by me somehow like an evil vapor.

Once inside the room, his eyes, darting everywhere, would inevitably come to rest on the one nook where a bit of candy or a sweet biscuit was secreted. When I coldly refused the tidbit, being filled with complete revulsion for the creature, he would settle down to await my ultimate collapse with the air of one who has an eternity at his disposal. Bribed to depart, he would turn the ransom over in his minute claws, handling it with contempt. Urged, untenderly, to leave, he would turn his skinny back on me in disdain and go, leaving me speechless with fury.

All the kids hated him. He would wander into a group of older children who were engaged in some activity which, until his appearance among them, had been a highly successful enterprise. In a split second silence would fall upon them. This tiny despot would stand in silent contempt among them and would either stroll away in disgust, leaving the game spoiled, or would rearrange it according to his taste. It would have been perfectly simple for one of the big boys or girls to take him by the back of the neck and toss him out of the way but I never saw it happen. It was perfectly plain that they loathed him and he seemed to glory in it. His strength was as the strength of ten, spiritually, it seemed. He was a dark, skinny enigma, with destiny held tight in his sallow fist. He was one cold blob of concentrated power, and I warn the Politburo that this brooding atom is sullenly awaiting the moment when he can seize the reins of government and plunge his country into the most dreadful revolution it yet has known. I do not know where this rodent has his lair, nor who brought him forth, since, obviously, nobody would ever claim him. But somewhere in the Metropole Hotel the energy is at large which will one day plunge us all howling into chaos and old night.

Another child evidently knew me before I knew her. One day as I was hurrying down the hall, intent upon my own affairs, something launched itself at me out of the shadows, clutched me around the knees and coiled in a soft mass around my feet. I let out a shuddering roar. I had long expected to be the victim of some nameless horror in that corridor, but still it was a shock. I stood stock-still and awaited my doom. Up out of the blackness rose a picked chicken of a little girl, eyes wide with terror. She threw herself at me and burrowed her head into my stomach. So, after my quaking nerves had subsided, I concluded that she was only trying to be affectionate. It had nearly been the death of us both, and I figured we could both use a stimulant. Therefore I took her with me into my room and gave her a handful of withered raisins and patted eau de cologne on her forehead. Seen in the light the little one looked like the Little Match Girl.

She was about seven years old. She was very frail and pale and shy. Her little face was triangular like a kitten's, her big eyes were honest and grave and good. She was wearing a ragged, patched dress of gray Canton flannel, too short and too tight for even her skinny frame. Her feet were thrust into soiled, much worn, felt boots, and her head was shaved until it was almost as bald as an egg. The fact that one cheek was bulging with raisins spoiled the picture a bit, but I knew her for the Little Match Girl just the same. She curtsied to me and bobbed her little shaved head and disappeared, leaving me bemused and nostalgic. But not for long.

In about five minutes she was back again, leading the Chunky Baby by the hand. She hissed something at him out of the side of her mouth and he obediently extended one grimy, fat paw, palm upward. He also gurgled what both he and I understood to be the Russian equivalent of "Me too." Since the raisins I had were fit only to be tossed against a lady's window at midnight, I gave him a handful. My Little Match Girl pounced. She snatched all the raisins away from him, popped one into his surprised soft mouth, and pulled him after her out the door, which she carefully closed.

But it didn't stay closed long.

Word had got around that I was a soft touch and this time Matches was accompanied by the Scourge and two other friends. I said, "Beat it," in English and they understood. The Scourge fixed Matches with a beady eye and she curtsied. "We shall return tomorrow," she said. And they did, too. My life became a living hell. When the mob numbered seven kids, all standing with outstretched palms, I decided it was too much of a good thing. I said, in Russian, "I do not speak Russian." They consulted among themselves. They smiled forgivingly at me. "Not necessary," they told me and stretched out their paws again. Two pounds of raisins could not hold out very long under this combined assault, so finally I gave Matches the bag which now had only about three raisins in it. A long sigh went through the crowd. They took the bag and vanished.

Matches came back off and on after that, but a piece of bread and butter or a slice of salami wasn't the same. Gradually her visits ceased. I did not see her again until the day of the Christmas party. She was skimming along the hall, done up in a flimsy white cheesecloth number, representing either a ballerina or a fairy, I'm not sure which. Her hair had grown out quite a lot and covered her whole head with delicate tiny tendrils. She had a crown of silver paper, and her bare arms and legs were indigo with the cold. She carried a little wand with a minute blob of tinsel at the tip and her cheeks were scarlet with excitement and her eyes were blazing like stars. This was no Little Match Girl. This was Cinderella.

There was one other little girl who was only a temporary resident. Her mother knew someone who lived in the Metropole, and she used to bring the little girl to the hotel to give her a bath, since her own apartment had no bathing facilities. I met them several times in the hall and once I invited them to come into my room to get a piece of American candy for the little one.

They came, timidly and reluctantly, and when the child got into the center of the floor, she lay down and elevated her fat legs, exposing the seat of a grimy pair of drawers to our astonished gaze. She showed no immediate inclination to get up or to change her position. There seemed to be nothing we could do about it, so we sat down to wait until she decided that perhaps there might be other ways of greeting a hostess. Her mother and I had a halting but pleasant conversation in pidgin Russian and ignored the child.

Gradually and watchfully, she got to her feet and began an inspection of the foreign lady's room. There was a long mirror in a wardrobe door and to this she drifted at once. Her mother shrugged helplessly. The little girl upped herself onto her toes and bowed to her image, spreading her shabby skirts and smiling and nodding like a ballerina. Then she twirled away in a series of feathery whirls and returned to the mirror, flushed with enchantment at her own proficiency. She rolled coquettish eyes at me—but she really didn't see me at all—I was an audience, a whole great theatre full of breathless adorers. Holding a fold of her little skirt, she stepped daintily around the room, caressing and touching ever so lightly anything bright or colorful that caught her eye. Never for an instant did she drop the pose of actress.

Her mother flushed red with annoyance. "Twenty-four hours a day it goes on," she said angrily. "That devil will never stop dancing and nodding. Me she treats like a slave!"

"Does she study dancing?" I asked. "Are you planning to let her become an actress?"

"Indeed not!" cried her mother. "An actress, indeed! She has never even been inside a theatre!"

There was a little flowered handkerchief of mine lying on a table and the youngster touched it with reverent fingers. With a great, hearty burst of generosity I handed it to her and said, in Lady Bountiful's voice and with Lady Bountiful's smile, "You may have it, dear."

The child regarded me with loathing. Her eyebrows drew together in a frown of displeasure and she said, coldly and haughtily, "Not necessary, thank you. I have much more beautiful things than that!"

"What a dreadful lie!" her mother shouted. "Take the lovely handkerchief, you silly girl."

With incredible delicacy the four-year-old lifted the filmy square of cotton and dropped it scornfully into the wastebasket. A queen rebuked a forward subject. Her mother blushed again. We were at an impasse. I tried the candy. The little girl looked at me, her great violet eyes soft with pity.

"I have pounds and pounds of better candy than that," she said airily and went to look at her mischievous smile in the mirror.

"Well, come, then," said her mother in despair. "We will go home to where you have all these wonderful things." She took her daughter by the hand and went through the little hallway to the door.

"Excuse her, please," said the mother. "I am sure she really wants the handkerchief and the candy, but how stubborn, how stubborn!"

The ballerina rose on the toes of her dirty little felt boots, holding her mother's hand in one of hers. Then she turned to me with a gesture of such airy grace that she seemed to be made of disembodied joy. She blew me a kiss from the tips of grubby little fingers and flashed a forgiving smile at me.

"Good-by," she crowed, "good-by, little darling. Come to see me in my beautiful house and I will give you gold and diamonds." As the door closed behind her, I heard her silvery laughter.

Chapter 29

Spontaneous Demonstrations

ONE THING in which the Soviets really excel is in the planning and execution of great public "demonstrations." Their parades on Youth Day, May Day, the Anniversary of the October Revolution and on other holidays set aside as days of national rejoicing, are planned to the tiniest detail, rehearsed until perfect and result in a show of splendid impressiveness. The first time a stranger in Moscow sees one of the great "demonstrations," he is sure to get a tremendous thrill. But after he sees four or five, the edge begins to get a trifle dull. The over-all scheme is dramatically sound; the plans have been made and carried out flawlessly. But it is the same every time. As an American said who had been in Moscow too long, "If you've seen one, you've seen 'em all."

The parades in Moscow are not *for* the people, they are *of* the people. Everybody gets into the act. By half past seven in the morning the streets are cleared of vehicular and pedestrian traffic and no one is allowed to leave the hotels or the houses. The houses are practically empty anyhow, as all the inhabitants are already in their places, wherever their places in the line of march may be. The great Red Square, center and heart of such activities, has been swept and garnished and is brilliant with banners of screaming red, hung in straight lines of bunting from roof to ground on every building fronting the Square. The guards are posted. Nobody is going to be able to sneak into Red Square unless he passes through five or six lines of guards, stationed at intervals of about twenty-five feet, beginning at the corners of the boulevards which converge on the square.

An onlooker who finally gets past these grim gentlemen must show his identification papers, plus his "*propus*" or invitation, to at least five different watchful soldiers. The pass is read word for word. The passport is read word for word, the passport picture is compared with your own face, and not carelessly either. No chances are taken that you might intend to cause serious trouble. "They don't allow no fooling around in there." Nobody is allowed to watch a parade from a balcony or a roof top. Armed guards are stationed around to prevent that, too.

The Metropole Hotel is situated about four or five long blocks from the Red Square, and we expected to watch a certain parade from the balcony of our room. We were advised not to do so by American friends who said that it was not permitted. We were astonished, but inquired of the Intourist whether we might not go out on the balcony to watch. They said, "No." In view of the fact that we had heard a story about a young Russian who had gone up to the roof of a near-by building with a camera to take some distance photos of the parade one May Day, we stayed indoors. This young man had happily found a fine view and had settled himself and his camera for a pleasant day's picture taking when he observed two armed guards approaching. He began to have his doubts as to the desirability of staying where he was, but he never got a chance to explain or to change his mind. Without speaking or questioning him in any way, the two soldiers pushed him off the roof, into the courtyard below. So we stayed inside.

A "demonstration" usually lasts all day. Every factory has its contingent of marchers, carrying patriotic banners and red flags. Every office and bureau and shop and store is represented. This, plus the tremendous representation of the armed might of the Soviet Union, results in a parade of at least a million people, some say even more. With uniformed soldiers carrying rifles or drawn swords, or carrying rifles with fixed bayonets; with tanks, and antiaircraft guns and trucks; with sailors, cadets and cavalry units; with bands; with airplanes roaring overhead, Moscow rises up and pours itself through the streets that center in the Red Square. All day long there is the sound of marching. There is singing, a deep, sinister roar of men's voices beating out the tune in time to the heavy tread of feet.

In the Red Square, on top of the dark red granite tomb of Lenin, the leaders stand reviewing the vast flowing mass.

In perfect alignment the tanks roll by. At the precise second they were planned, the cavalry move by on the sleek and shining matched horses. With never a moment's hitch or hesitation the armed battalions pass. *Might! Strength! Power!* The disciplined cadence is beaten out against the ancient stones of the Red Square.

And then the workers come—the untrained marchers in the ragtag and bobtail of their shabby clothes. They come by the hundreds, by the thousands, by the tens of thousands, men and women, young and old, carrying the banners of their country—"GLORY TO STALIN," "GLORY TO THE GREAT SOVIET PEOPLE," "SOVIET DEMOCRACY Is THE HIGHEST TYPE OF DEMOCRACY."

They have been standing in line since dawn. Perhaps it is four o'clock in the afternoon by the time they pass the reviewing stand. They plod along, devotedly, if a little wearily, turning their faces toward Stalin and the others like sunflowers to the sun. On and on they go. On and on they come, without music for the most part. In silence they fill the streets from curb to curb, march into the Square and away. There is none of this business of people lining up along the line of march to watch and cheer. The marchers are the only moving beings on the streets. The Red Square is the only place where you can see a parade in Moscow and you must be an invited guest to get there.

One day I met a Russian .girl I knew and she looked very tired. "What's the matter?" I asked. "You look pale."

She smiled slyly. "I *am* tired," she said. "All last night I was rehearsing for a spontaneous demonstration."

The Sports Parade was a marvelous example of this meticulous rehearsing. Young people from all over the Soviet Union had been brought to Moscow to take part in the festivities. Physical-culture clubs, camps, workers' organizations of all kinds were represented and the unbeatable Russian flair for dramatic presentation was allowed full play. We watched from the grandstand of the Red Square that day, stood and sat and watched until we were weary.

It was impossible not to be impressed by the grade of material the Soviets presented to our eyes. Husky, hardy, healthy, sturdy, the youths and maidens stepped out like clean, vigorous animals for the inspection of their leaders. The young girls are much heavier and more muscular than our American girls, not so long-limbed and lithe, but strong, vigorous, vital. Their costumes had been planned with great care. Modesty, combined with the greatest possible freedom of movement, seemed to have been the watchword. And as they swung along, heads high, bosoms high, faces alert and bright and hair shining in the sunlight, they were good to look upon. A touch of theatre here and there did nothing to detract from the general picture. For instance, one group of about a hundred teen-agers, dressed in blue rayon blouses and snug little shorts of the same color, had been screened and matched so that they were exactly the same height, had exactly the same color of hair, and they had all been painted the same rosy sun tan.

The young men were attractive, too. Faces set, nary a smile, just set, grim faces, they too swung along for inspection, with strength and vim. The muscles of their brown arms bulged in the sunlight. Their firm, hard legs looked as though they could carry many a long and weary mile. In a similar group of young Americans, you would be able to sense the humor, the feeling that "this is all good fun," but not in Moscow. These stern youths carried oars, or weights, or Indian clubs and such things, but you felt they would rather be carrying a rifle or a bayonet. They didn't look mean, but they surely looked tough; and when one contingent of six-footers passed, wearing loose trousers and sandals, their naked torsos bronze and shining and their heads shaved close and bald, most of the foreigners present got a real turn. These boys seemed to glory in their ugliness and in the sinister air they had. It is perhaps just as well that they did not know that the whisper "galley slaves" went around the grandstand where the foreigners stood.

That day of the Sports Parade was a big day in Moscow. Our own General Eisenhower was a spectator and stood with the highest of the Soviet leaders on the tomb of Lenin. He was greeted by applause from the foreigners present, but none of the Russians knew who he was. There was no announcement of his presence, naturally. We watched the parade for hours, and then our weary feet could take no more. Braving the scowls of the guards, we withdrew and walked back to the Metropole Hotel. At the edge of the Square, trying to peek between the legs of the cordon of soldiers, was a dirty, tattered boy about twelve years old. He had only one leg but he hopped along nimbly with the aid of a crutch. The soldiers, furious at such an exhibition of poverty and weakness, chased him savagely down a side street, where he was soon comfortably lost to view.

Chapter 30

Holiday Time

MOSCOW USUALLY GIVES the impression that life is a most serious business, but sometimes the Moscovites have holidays. These holidays are less times for merrymaking than for rest. Most of the Soviet citizens have to plug along pretty continually, and when it is legally permitted, they relax like jelly. All the food stores close for three days and the factories and shops are closed, too. The program for holidays is what might be called "supervised play." The government says, "Play now," and gives them their amusements. The city puts on gala dress, red banners and red flags, bunting and inspiration slogans and pictures of their leaders, but it is always the same costume. It is like the performance of a play when the same scenery is taken out of the storehouse and put back on the same stage. It is enchanting the first time you see it, but when you have seen it once or twice the decorations kind of lose their appeal.

Small stages are erected in public squares of the city and on these stages free vaudeville shows are presented. Actors are assigned to the street circuit, and all day long and until about ten o'clock at night under the big portable spotlights mounted on trucks, the little stage shows go on. Passive crowds stand quietly observing; seldom is there laughter or applause. They just look and murmur gently to one another.

I stood in such a crowd, before such a show, for several hours, during the "Celebration of the Anniversary of the October Revolution," November 7, 1945. I remember some of the acts. There was an elderly, raucous-voiced gypsy singer, in colorful gypsy costume, who came out and shouted her songs to the accompaniment of the piano which was provided for the artists on the stage. She was evidently what Americans would call "an old-timer," and she knew her stuff and tried very hard. The silence of the audience could have been cut with a knife. She did her act and retired with a swirl of gaudy petticoats, and not one feeble clap of the hands rewarded her.

There was a strong-man act—I do not think the men were actors, although I cannot be sure. Somebody told me that they were from various factories; they had worked up the act among themselves. My chief reaction was that before long they would all be in the hospital for hernia operations, but the crowd didn't seem to share my apprehension. They were interested to a small degree. They watched closely, and occasionally there was a murmur of approbation, but no applause. The burly young men took turns lifting various metal bars of increasing weights, the trick being to grasp the heavy bars by the ends, lift them waist-high and then to arm's length above their heads. Their muscles strained and bulged and they puffed plenty. I tried to tell myself it was none of my business, but I couldn't help thinking that if I were their mother, they wouldn't be permitted to do any such thing. Finally, one husky swung a behemoth of a bar shakily above his head and let it crash to the floor and nearly fell down beside it. His opponent got it only waist-high and had to give up. So the other gent was the winner. People grunted some when he took a purple-faced bow, but, on the whole, I would report that they were glad to see the last of him.

There were children in native costume, looking very cute and somewhat scared, who stepped off to the tinkling tune of the piano and did what is known as a "folk dance." There was a spatter of applause in deference to their youth, but nobody hollered "Hurray." Nobody hollered anything. But suddenly the crowd surged forward. There was a happy hum, a sound of real anticipation. The kids in the audience who had been standing around, slightly blue from the cold, trampled on the feet of their elders and horned through the crowd with youthful enthusiasm. They lined up close to the edge of the platform and chattered among themselves gaily. This act was something they had seen before and it was evidently going to be good.

A tall, shabbily dressed man, with a black fur hat (what we call a shako, I guess), appeared, smiled broadly and took a bow. He was applauded wildly. He retired for a moment and

then reappeared with an assistant carrying an owl that sat grumpily on a metal stand. The crowd roared. The owl gave them a dirty look and shut his eyes, as if the sight of them was more than he could bear. The crowd laughed and the man went into his spiel. He was evidently giving a natural-history talk, but one spiced with humor and burlesque. It went over big. The attendant retired and returned with a live moth-eaten eagle on another stand and the talk went on.

In turn, the man showed, beside the eagle and the owl, an ostrich, a raccoon, a fox, a wolf and several other animals which I have now forgotten. It wowed the people. They really loved it. The animals were not required to do any tricks at all; they were just on exhibition and the turn was probably chiefly educational. But interlarded with the zoology notes were jokes and stories which the listeners swallowed with delight. The hit of the act was a pudgy little bear cub who stood up on his hind legs, held bits of bread in his paws and exposed a round expanse of fat, furry little belly to the enraptured onlookers. They *adored* him. Real, deafening applause ended the act, which only made the one that followed seem dopier than ever. This was a group of very nice, clean young men from some factory who had come to sing for the merrymakers. The merrymakers looked at them with something just the near side of loathing and took their offering in absolute silence. By this time I was frozen to the marrow and I pushed my way out of the crowd and went back to the hotel. I could see the rest of the show from the balcony, but I never heard any applause again such as the animal man got. One or two of the other acts were rewarded with a *spat-spat* or two.

The Moscovites do not celebrate Christmas on December 25 as we do. The Russians get into the holiday spirit about December 25 but it spreads over into New Year's, and December 31 was New Year's Eve, as with us. Christmas trees, carefully called New Year's trees, were erected in many city squares and a dazzling sight they were. Under the sifting snow and beneath the pearly light of the Moscow sky, these New Year's trees were centers of glory. Each tree was at least fifty feet high, a real old giant, and it was decked on almost every twig with shining and imaginative little ornaments. At night the trees were lighted up with hundreds of electric bulbs twinkling like stars through the falling snowflakes. Around each tree a tiny, fantastic village of painted booths had been erected, where hot tea and hot rolls stuffed with rice or ground meat were sold. Toys, too, were for sale and the omnipresent raspberry syrup which is the Moscovite's idea of soda pop. They consume this in gigantic quantities, with every evidence of relish. It is sickly sweet and deep red in color, and I suppose is really no worse than what we drink here at home in equally appalling amounts.

The picture presented by these little villages of painted booths, bright against the gray of the squares, crowded by bundled-up people wearing padded jackets and felt boots, with fur hats or shawls over their heads, is a sight straight out of olden times. It is an illustration for a story beginning, "Once upon a time, long, long ago, there was, in a very ancient land...." To visit one of these little fairs is really to feel that you are an actor in a very old and many-times-repeated tale.

As the clock's hands pointed to twelve on New Year's Eve 1945, my husband and I stood together beside the Kremlin clock tower and heard the old bell ring in the New Year. It was a crystal night, and the snow was white on the ground all around, heavy on the branches of the evergreen trees that stand arrogantly before the Kremlin wall. The snow powdered our shoulders and the shoulders of the guards, and came twinkling slowly out of the dark sky like cellophane snow in a Christmas pantomime.

We stood there together, listening to the brazen notes slashing through the still air and we thought how Times Square must look and sound on this first New Year's of peace. Here in the Red Square the only sound was the sound of the bell, and although there were perhaps twenty-five people in its vast expanse, there was no joyous shouting, indeed no sound of a human voice.

My husband and I exchanged our New Year's greetings and then we both looked around for others to wish a Happy New Year. In Russian, the greeting sounds like "C-novem godum." So we hollered "C-novem godum" to anybody who would listen. Nobody paid any attention to us. My husband was determined that somebody besides me should know of his vast store of hearty good will, so he descended upon the guards who stood stonily before the Kremlin Gate. "C-novem godum," he said chippily, in the best Bostonian Russian. The guards looked at him as if they thought they probably had a job on their hands. But the beatific smile which my husband had on his face was too much for even such well-trained soldiers to resist. They bowed. It was not enough. My husband stretched out his hand and, with some misgivings,

one of the guards shifted his rifle and shook hands. They let it be understood that that would be about all from us.

We were a trifle dashed, but we plowed off into the darkness, determined to be gay. We walked around the entire Kremlin, stepping into drifts to our knees and shouting "C-novem godum" to everybody we passed—and we passed very few. One or two replied, without enthusiasm. Some did not answer at all, but stared at this evidence of bad taste on the part of barbarous foreigners. A traffic policeman alone and lonely at the intersection of two broad streets, standing like a snow statue under the pool of light from a lamppost, saluted us with grave dignity but did not wish us a Happy New Year. Within the walls of the Moscow houses there were doubtless many gay parties and much vodka was probably being guzzled in honor of this propitious hour. But the streets were echoingly empty, the few people who were abroad showed no signs of joyousness; only two crazy Americans went sloughing through the night howling "C-novem godum" to the cold Russian air.

The schools of Moscow arrange big parties for the children at this holiday time. I attended one at the House of the Columns, a magnificent public building of classical architecture near the Metropole Hotel. It was the New Year season and the children came trooping through the snowy streets to see the wonders that had been prepared for them. In the great rotunda of the building an enormous evergreen tree—some said it was eighty feet high—had been erected. There must have been about ten thousand little ornaments glittering on it. The tree was strung with lights, and the youngsters, who were brought in relays by their teachers, crowded around it, marched to music, sang, stamped their feet, clapped their hands and were enchanted.

Circus actors and actors from the Children's Theatre performed on the big stage. On the broad circular corridor around the central part of the building, what amounted to a small Coney Island had been built, with sliding boards, small Ferris wheels and games. The *décor* was strongly reminiscent of Disney, with bright-colored animals and gnomes and dwarfs and fairies painted on the walls. Gigantic figures of red-nosed fat ladies and other amusing people were towering here and there in corners. On small stages at intervals along the hall, magicians played their old games before crowds of sharp-eyed little customers who watched every trick and were usually able to catch the abashed charlatans red-handed.

Bands played familiar tunes. There was singing. The party lasted more than a week, and to judge by the sleepy-eyed children who went home through the snow clutching paper hats and bright toys, the excitement was terrific and the entire affair could honestly be counted a success.

Tickets for this entertainment cost thirty-five rubles and are obtained through the various factory and trade organizations or are given as prizes to children who have high scholastic standing. Thirty-five rubles is not a trifling amount when your parents' income is low.

Comparatively few people in Moscow have radios, but at busy street intersections there are radio loud-speakers. Any important announcements of interest to the Moscovites are made over them. The signal calling attention to such an announcement consists of the first few bars of the "Soviet Song of the People."

"Broad is my native country," ring out the notes, "broad is my native country," over and over until everyone's attention is focused on the radio.

The rest of the verse goes as follows:

> *It has many woods, fields and rivers.*
> *I know no other land*
> *Where a man can breathe so free.*

The time that I was most interested in the public announcements from this central radio system was on the Soviet V-J Day. America had heard the news two days before. The Moscow citizens had to wait.

I happened to be standing near a Metro station when the theme song began to sound and the crowds hurrying to the subway began to collect and stood waiting to hear what the announcement might be. When it finally came, it proved to be that the war with Japan was ended and that finally peace had spread her wings over the whole world. There was not a sound in the Square. Nobody cheered; no great sigh of joy or relief went through the crowd. Even before the announcement was finished, people were off again about their affairs, crowding into the subway, climbing onto the busses, scurrying along the streets.

To say that I was amazed is to put it very mildly. I knew very well what such an announcement would bring forth in the streets of America. It seemed to me that even as I stood there in the streets of Moscow, I could almost hear the great joyous roar of the crowds of my native New York. My eyes stung with tears of happiness and my throat tightened with an overwhelming sense of relief. I looked around for somebody to share my enormous, thrilling emotion. Nobody glanced my way. I said testily to a Russian I met, "For heaven's sake! Aren't you people glad that the war is over?"

My companion said sullenly, "What difference does it make to us, peace or war?"

About nine o'clock the next night it began to be rumored that something might take place in the Red Square around ten o'clock. The public system loud-speakers at the street corners soon began to announce something of the kind. So, with my husband and Edgar Snow and Farnsworth Fowle, I went to the Red Square to see what would happen. Plenty happened. The sky, cold, cloudless, vast, spread dark and wide over the Kremlin and the ruby stars glowed in the light of the full moon.

"What a perfect night for V-J celebration!" I murmured.

"Don't be silly," said one of my companions sharply. "Stalin would not permit anything else!"

At any rate, perfect was certainly the word for it. There was a crowd in Red Square—but not a big crowd, not a rushing, surging, pushing, shouting, hilarious mob, by any means. A lot of quiet people, but the big Square was not nearly filled. And then the theatricals began. From somewhere behind the Kremlin wall guns began to speak. The deep booming came slow and deep at carefully spaced intervals. And as each thunderous roar shattered the still air of the night, a thousand colored, floating, falling stars would burst against the sky. At the exact instant that the sonorous cannon resounded, the fireworks exploded and made the old Red Square into a place of wonder and delight. From some concealed spots in carefully selected places, great shafts of searchlights shot across the dark. They met in the sky, crisscrossed into patterns, vanished and reappeared.

The three hundred twenty-four guns behind the Kremlin wall sounded twenty-four times. And all this time the people stood quietly, watching gravely, murmuring now and then to one another, but standing for the most part silent. And when finally the Grand Salute was over and only moon-made light over Moscow remained, they began drifting away and soon they were all gone and the Red Square was once more empty under the cold sky. Thus peace came to Moscow. Though

she cannot be said to have come in like a lion, long may she remain, just the same.

I was not in Moscow at the time of V-E Day. On that day, I am told, the Russians really rejoiced, spontaneously and gaily. Crowds poured out into the streets, and congratulations and general delight exploded. Americans around the Embassy were embraced and kissed, and one luckless American youth was seized and tossed high in the air by the Russian celebrants. I never saw any such goings-on. I never heard a spontaneous cheer, I never saw a crowd gather voluntarily, I never saw joy unconfined for any reason whatever.

Chapter 31

Disa and Data

I FIND that I have a few assorted and unrelated notes accumulated on various occasions during my life behind the Iron Curtain. I am including them in this chapter because, after reading them, I feel that they may touch upon some aspects of life in Moscow that I have not mentioned before. I decided to call this final chapter "Data" and let it go at that. But after listening to Mr. Jimmy Durante one night on the radio, I decided to call it "Disa and Data." And at this point let me say that there is nobody even remotely approximating Mr. Jimmy Durante in the whole theatre of Soviet Russia. I saw only two comedians worthy of the name while I was in the U.S.S.R. and they certainly constitute no challenge to Durante or anybody else in the American comedy field. I was amused by many things in Moscow, but not by the Russian comedians.

Well, Russia's a big picture and the more you look at it the more you see. You won't deny that there are a thousand things which are good. Every day you learn things to arouse your admiration and respect. You cannot fail to be impressed by the vigor and hope and determination all around you. The Russian people are good people.

Most of the recreations offered the Soviet citizen are solid and serious. The music that comes pouring out of the public radio system is usually classical music and very good most of it is. Most of the theatres present classic plays. Many of the books published are classics. Many of the movies are documentary films. The Soviet people are being educated and made culture-conscious heavily and unceasingly.

Yet cheerfulness will keep creeping in. You can get your fortune told by cards, by tea leaves, by water reflection, by black rats, by birds, by psychic manifestations. Within two kilometers of Moscow there is a woman who guarantees to influence your lover—by means of his photograph—so that he will never look at another woman but you. I didn't know this when I visited her and unfortunately I did not have my husband's picture with me.

People understand that if you drop a fork, a woman is coming to call; but if you drop a knife, it will be a man. You have only to tell a sympathetic listener what you dreamed last night to have the dream interpreted for good or ill. If you break a mirror—well, you know what. Russians love ghost stories and grisly supernatural tales and have a good store of them which they will relate with relish and enthusiasm. You will find to your amusement that many of the old saws and proverbs with which we are familiar have Russian counterparts and that many old jokes which are part and parcel of the life in America are known and that many of our oldest jokes have been in circulation in Russia for years.

❧❧❧

I had always had the idea that in Russia the state was the sole owner of property, but I learned that a private citizen may own his own apartment or his own house and the land on which it is built; that, moreover, he is allowed to rent this apartment or house and keep the rent thereof for himself. He may make a will leaving this property to his heirs. On the other hand, my Russian friends said, "Of course, we understand that in America you may own a house but not the land on which it is built." I told them that this was absurd, that certainly we may own land, but they did not believe me.

❧❧❧

June 22, 1941, may prove to be the most important date in modern Russian history. That is the date on which Germany attacked Russia, thus ending by force Russian isolationism. Future events may prove that it was really the day when the Iron Curtain cracked.

In 1939 Sir Archibald Sinclair said, "We cannot achieve victory without Russia but we cannot find a point of contact with her." U.N., please copy.

I asked one Russian girl what she considered the greatest contribution made by America to the welfare of mankind. (That is the sort of thing you talk about in Russia.) The girl gave the matter not more than one minute's serious consideration and then she smiled impishly and replied, "Scotch tape."

One of the few aspects of Moscow life which I found downright soothing and which I thought I preferred to the American way was the absolute lack of advertising. *No* advertising. None? Well, one. The only advertising sign I saw the entire time I was in Russia was a sign painted on the side of a building calling on people to buy government bonds.

When I first got there, this lack of advertising rested my head. I was delighted not to be exhorted on every side with slogans and earnest pleas to buy this, that or the other. Nobody asked anybody to buy anything for two reasons: 1—there wasn't much to buy, and 2—*if* you bought anything, you bought it from only one source, the government.

There is no private enterprise and no competition. If you want some buttons, you get buttons that government factories have manufactured. If you want clothes, the department store on A Street will have the same clothes as the department store on B Street and at a government-arranged price. There were very few clothes to be had; I am merely using this as an illustration.

Also, since consumers' demand so far outstripped government supply, there was not the slightest need to advertise anything, and, as I say, at first I found this a distinct relief. I conducted a poll among the Americans I knew in Moscow and everybody said that he was very glad indeed not to have advertising assault his eyes and his mind every hour of every day. People said that they hadn't realized how annoying and fatiguing the whole advertising business had become until suddenly they didn't have to put up with it any more. My husband was particularly delighted. His ideal of life, to let him tell it, is Thoreauvian. The Simple Life for him. He would like to live like an anchorite, in a cell-like room, with the utmost austerity. Why he always chooses the most comfortable chair and the softest bed is something he disdains to answer, and if I were to serve the sort of food that he oddly fancies he likes, his pitiful screams could be heard beyond the Great Divide. But anyhow, that is the way he talks and the lack of advertising was right up his alley.

Magazines and newspapers in the Soviet Union do not contain any advertising and, of course, we seldom got any newspapers from home, let alone magazines. Once in a while somebody would get a periodical by mail and it would be passed around until it was tattered and torn. I found, somewhat to my astonishment, that when a copy of the *New York Times* came in, or an old *New Yorker*, what I pored over was the advertisements. They seemed to me a vivid illustration of the way life is conducted in the States and I wondered if people were really wearing such things, and had access to such house furnishings and edibles as the merchants were imploring them to buy in the ads.

One evening, my husband was engrossed in the latest magazine which had been circulating around the foreign colony. It was dated September 1944, although this was in the spring of 1946. He, who reads things like *Early Elizabethan Literature Trends* for fun, was lost to the world in the *Woman's Home Companion*. After about half an hour he raised his bemused eyes to me and said rather tentatively, "Why don't we have a pink bathtub?"

So that's all the good it did a socialist government to try to impress upon us the life of the worker. It succeeded only in making us determined that if we lived to get out of the Soviet Union, we would plunge knee-deep into the most utterly luxurious life the United States was able to offer and maybe even go into debt a little to arrange it.

<hr/>

You very seldom see a dog in Moscow and comparatively few cats. This is easy to understand when you consider that there was hardly enough food for the Moscovites during the war, to say nothing of feeding pet animals. But I have heard that the Russians are eager to get strains of thoroughbred dogs started, and that if you have a dog and can prove, by papers, that it is a thoroughbred, you can get special rations for it. Which reminds me that I never saw a Russian wolfhound while I was over there. This was another blow to my ideas about Russia. I thought people went around in sables playing balalaikas and leading borzois. But all I saw was just people going around. I never saw sables, and I never saw wolfhounds, and the only balalaika I ever saw was in Eddie Gilmore's apartment and that one had all its strings busted.

The best example of the old law of supply and demand operating in Moscow is, I think, found in the bazaars. There are no price ceilings. But the fact that his neighbor is right beside him, selling the same kind of stuff, determines what the price shall be. A farmer would have all his produce left rotting on his hands if he tried to get more for it than the lowest price in the bazaar. I don't know how it is determined, but I do know that the prices for, say, potatoes, never vary much in one day. You can't hope to get much of a bargain as far as price goes; all you can do is to shop around for quality.

In view of the fact that there are such acute food shortages in Russia, it seems that the Russians are somewhat wasteful. Any American housewife setting up housekeeping in Russian is surprised at the way food is wasted. What I mean is, the Moscovites do not plan as carefully as we do and any Russian cook uses materials with a pretty lavish hand. They have only scorn for cutting corners or making use of leftovers when working for Americans anyhow.

Yet in this connection I saw a strange contradiction. One day in the bazaar, when there was a lot of good fresh beets for sale (fairly unusual), I saw the beet tops twisted off when somebody bought a bunch of beets, and thrown carelessly into the mud to be trampled under foot. I was shocked, thinking that fresh beet tops should surely be cooked and used for greens, especially in a land where greens are so scarce. But the next day I saw booth after booth selling beet tops only. No beets were visible. The idea that the beet tops were picked up out of the mud at the end of one day and sold the next did not hold water, for the tops were fresh and clean and very definitely could not have been the trampled ones from the day before.

❦

The first "banquet" that I was invited to was given by "Voks," the organization for international cultural relations. They had a pleasant concert and afterward a buffet supper. The tables were groaning under an array of the finest dishes imaginable—pates and sliced turkey and roast beef and pork and salads and desserts, enough to make your eyes glisten anywhere. I wouldn't eat anything. I glumly sipped a glass of red wine and brooded.

Outside, in the rainy night, thousands of good Soviet people were plodding their weary way home to suppers of cabbage soup and black bread; thousands were standing in lines, waiting to buy a loaf of black bread which might be all that they would get to eat that night.

The idea of my having all that food while others, better entitled to it than I was, were going miserably hungry, choked me. I did not understand how "Voks" had the face to set out such an array of luxuries when their own people starved.

Later in the year I was invited to a reception at Mr. Molotov's. This was the same, but on a far, far grander scale. I pushed my way ravenously to the table and began slapping slices of pink ham onto my plate and covering it with thick layers of turkey and beef in the celebrated manner of Dagwood Bumstead. On top of this I balanced pates and caviar and at one side I tenderly adjusted bits of roast pork and lamb. I thought to myself "Dear me, too bad some of those folks outside can't have a snack of this."

Six months of rationing had somewhat weakened my moral sense, I'm afraid, because none of that good food stuck in my throat at all. In extenuation I think I should add that I realized I was being a pig. But the realization didn't keep 'me from my swinish pleasure.

❦

The Soviets say proudly, "Illiteracy has been liquidated." According to many reports I heard deep inroads have been made into it. But the definition of "literacy" belittles the overall picture somewhat. If a citizen can write his name, he is counted as "literate." A little story which appeared in one of the Russian magazines illustrates the fact that even the Soviets smile about this so-called "literacy."

It seems that the manager of a factory, glancing over the pay roll one day, was horrified to discover that one of his workers had not written his name, but had simply made an "X" mark to indicate that he had received his money. This meant that the manager's factory was not one-hundred-percent literate—a situation not to be tolerated.

A committee of three had been appointed to liquidate illiteracy and his "X" proved that their work had not been efficiently performed.

The committee was called out on the carpet and denied vigorously that any illiteracy remained among the employees of the factory. "X" was summoned. When he appeared, the committee fell upon him and berated him and called on him to admit that he could write his name. He said he could. When confronted with the damning evidence, he smiled broadly and shrugged his shoulders. "I was a little drunk that day," he said gently. A breath of relief was exhaled by the ·committee, and the manager, hearing an excuse which anybody could accept as valid, smiled with relief also. Everybody shook hands all round.

"Just sign your name here," said the chairman of the committee, "and prove to all of us that you are literate."

The accused man smiled. He shrugged his shoulders. "I'm a little drunk *now*," he said.

Thereafter, when his "X" appeared on papers, everybody sighed hopelessly and said what a pity it was that "X" was such a lush!

❧ ❀ ❧

Before going to Russia I had not had any pineapple juice for I don't know how long. In Moscow I saw plenty of Libby's pineapple juice for sale in the Gastronoms for one hundred fifty rubles a can. Foreign exchange would make this cost an American about twelve dollars; taking three hundred rubles as an average monthly wage for a Moscow citizen, a can of Libby's pineapple juice would cost him about two weeks' pay.

I was raving around one day about the general shiftlessness of workmanship in Moscow, in the presence of a Russian who spoke some English. I suppose it wasn't very polite of me, but there comes a time when politeness goes by the board. Everything in the hotel seemed to be falling to pieces and nobody would fix it so it would stay fixed; a housewife's nerves became raw.

This acquaintance felt a little insulted, for which I can hardly blame him. "You have not really come into contact with our good workmanship," he said, and I was in no position to contradict him. "Now, take for instance when I was in the Army," he went on. "There was an example of good workmanship which will just prove to you that it exists. Somewhere or other, one of the boys had got hold of an American magazine called *Popular Mechanics*. It is wonderful, that magazine, and there was an article in it which described how to make a small stove out of a shell case—after the shell has been used, of course. Now it so happened that we had a great many used shell casings around, doing nothing, going to waste. In the magazine was a detailed plan for the manufacture of this stove—diagrams, measurements, everything. Naturally, I was able to translate all, and this boy—really, he was very smart indeed—made one of the stoves. It worked! It came out fine!

"And then, of course, all the fellows got to work and within a short time we had a regular stove factory going and the peasants around there bought them as fast as we could make them and we made a lot of money. So, you see, with nothing but the plans from that magazine and our own imagination, we made very good stoves indeed. It just proves that we have inventiveness and good workmanship as well as anybody."

Some Americans have the idea that Russia is aiming at a classless society. She may be aiming at it, but I know she hasn't got it. Russians admit this freely. There are desperately poor people, and people who are privileged to live very well. It is meekly accepted that big shots get privileges the masses cannot hope to obtain: privileges in food, money, living quarters and automobiles. I have seen thousands of people very poorly dressed. I have seen children with holes in their shoes and ragged clothes, whose pinched faces showed lack of proper food, and whose whole personality revealed neglect and poverty. I have seen hundreds of well-dressed citizens, hale and hearty and content, and their children were well dressed and hale and hearty too. I have never seen, in America, people in such rags as I saw every day on the streets of the capital of the Soviet Union. Yet once I saw a shiny new Zis automobile completely upholstered in red fox fur and the uniformed chauffeur had a snappy red fox hat to match. There are people at both ends of the scale of living in Moscow as elsewhere.

I have never known a society where such innumerable strata of rank exist. Everybody is fanatically aware of his own place in his own class and is intent on impressing the fellow just a little lower down the ladder. There's no use beating about the bush. Russians are arrogant to one another and, oftener than not, downright mean. Take the small world of an office. Among the employees, the secretary is top dog and is usually unspeakably arrogant to the others of the staff. (This does not apply to our Mr. Zellikoff.) But the couriers, who are next below, receive this meekly enough. They have their chance to be arrogant to the porters and chambermaids. I don't know whom the porters and the maids find to snub, but they surely find somebody. The least bit of authority makes a Russian incredibly overbearing. Russians with whom I was well acquainted astonished and abashed me by their attitude toward those who were in their employ or who were, for the moment, under their direction. Women who spoke to me in the modulated and gentle tones of ladies would turn on a waiter or a maid and give out like a virago. A domestic servant who is unlucky enough to be employed by a Russian is sure to be ground into the dirt. In this country anybody who spoke to an employee as the Russians do would soon be the bewildered possessor of a black eye or a bloody nose. Employees in Russia expect to be treated with superciliousness and brutality.

If you don't treat a waiter or a porter like a dog, he thinks you are a fool and begins to treat you like one. After a while Russians who are employed by foreigners get used to being treated with respect and, after a short interval when they try out their own wings and try to bully their employers, they get so they understand the situation and enjoy the dignity accorded them. But democracy as we understand it simply does not exist. I took Lydia Vyschinskaya, our courier, to a concert one night. Lydia knows a lot more about music than I do and she makes a very pleasant companion to boot. Sitting next to us was a Russian woman we both knew, and she was embarrassed and outraged at the fact that I had Lydia with me. (A courier!) She was distinctly uncomfortable and embraced the first opportunity to detach herself from us and get with people of her own class. I thought this comic and absurd. Lydia, although a little crushed by the snubbing she received from this regal lady, nevertheless meekly seemed to feel that it was the normal course of events and that nothing else was to be expected.

Nothing seems funnier to an American than the swanking around of some of the Red Army wives. It's like a musical comedy. These women, many of them from extremely humble stations in life, certainly make the most of their new exalted stations. Riding to glory on the stars and orders earned by their husbands in the war effort, they go top-drawer in a very highhanded way. Making the very most of every priority accorded to officers of the armed forces, they sweep through Moscow in a tornado of bad manners and evil tempers. Their reputation among the Russians is not an enviable one, and of course Americans think such nonsense outrageous.

The metamorphosis that takes place in some sweet Russian girls once they manage to acquire American husbands is something else rather marvelous. A girl who has had to "make do" all her life, suddenly becomes the most exacting and acquisitive human imaginable. Nothing satisfies her, and her standards immediately become so high and her needs so enormous that the puzzled American begins to wonder whether, after all, he has not done this princess an injustice by making her his wife. Trying to satisfy the demands of some Russian wives is, to coin a phrase, like spitting into Niagara.

The fellowship of man is a thing foreign to the Russian character, except in the very rarest of cases. The milk of human kindness flows sluggishly in that land of the Great Human Experiment. To put it very bluntly and inelegantly, over there it's dog eat dog.

Chapter 32

Peace in Our Time

AFTER THE WAR WAS OVER and the celebration of
V-J Day was past, the topic of a lasting peace was everywhere
discussed. Russians asked me with dreadful earnestness
whether I thought there would be a war between America
and Russia. But I, Yankee-fashion, turned the question back
to them.

"What do *you* think," I asked. And this is what they told
me.

One young woman, an ardent Soviet patriot, said briskly,
"Nonsense. What have we got to fight about? You have
nothing that we want and we have nothing that you want.
Why should we have a war?"

A man who had been in the Red Army said, "There will
be a war between the two countries within five years. It is
inevitable. The world cannot exist half slave and half free."
Meaning that we Americans are the slaves and that the
Russians are the free people.

An intellectual said, "Yes, there will be a war but not for
twenty years. There will always be wars as long as there is
capitalism."

Many ordinary citizens, mostly the women, wrung their
hands and said fearfully, "Oh, God, I hope not!"

Nobody that I spoke to thought that there *should* be
a war. Everybody said deeply and sincerely that he hoped
there would *not* be a war. But that does not mean that if
the leaders of the Russian people decreed war, the whole
Russian people would not be solidly behind the leaders. I
never saw the slightest indication that the people would not
support the leaders whatever their decision might be.

And war-weary and exhausted as the Russian people are today, if their beloved Mother Russia were threatened and invaded, they would rise once more and beat the invader from their soil. But who's going to invade Russia? Certainly not we. And who else could?

Now I am not a sibyl, and I never have had any intention of trying to hand out weighty decisions about American-Russian affairs. Frankly, I do not feel qualified to enter that troubled and thorny field. Yet "Can there be peace between America and Russia?" is such a burning question and I have heard it discussed in Moscow so often by serious and informed people and looked at from every possible angle, that perhaps I should set down some of the things I have heard. It has been said that Russia is war-weary; that from a purely physical standpoint Russia does not want war now. Three things vitally necessary to the waging of a successful aggressive war are lacking in Russia today. There is a shortage of food. The transportation facilities are in a bad way; they lack sufficient railroads, trucks and so on. And they lack the basic materials of war; the munitions and all the other death-dealing devices must be replenished in great number.

But then the question is asked, "When Russia recovers her strength; when her people have had a breathing spell; when the horrors of war are somewhat dimmed and a little forgotten; when the materials of war have been replenished and the country is rearmed—what then?"

To this question I have heard this answer: "If Russia continues under her present leaders, and those leaders conform strictly to the lines laid down originally for the Communist International, then war is inevitable."

But the United Nations Organization is in there pitching and on this we must pin our hopes. For the first time Russia is giving some indication of wanting to co-operate with the rest of the world. She has snarled and quarreled and thrown monkey wrenches—but she hasn't walked out. She's still in there with the other fellows, and if she were going to get out, she would have done so before now. Russia has now accepted the United Nations Organization as a cardinal point in her internal policy. Through the press and over the radio she is now representing the United Nations Organization to her people as an essential part of the world security program.

But somehow Russia has got to be educated to other facts of life. She must be made to understand that the United States is a friend. It is not going to be easy to convince her and it can never be done through appeasement. A high-ranking American diplomat said, concerning this matter of educating Russia, "We must proceed not along lines of appeasement, not along lines of otherwise empty gestures of good will, but along lines of understanding, firmness and patience."

We have men who understand Russia, who sympathize with her and who wish her well, at the same time holding the best interests of America firmly in mind. Such men should be employed to treat with Russia and to try to convince her that the United States has nothing but good will for Russia in her heart. It is not enough to send good men. We must send good men who understand Russia.

The same American diplomat I have quoted above said further, "What is needed is patience, patience above all."

Now patience is about the last thing an American can bring to bear on this, or any other, subject. We are a highly inflammable and highly impatient people. The best illustration of the difference between the American and the Russian approach to the subject of our international relationship is the way an American and the way a Russian reads his newspaper.

A thoughtful American, after reading the day's news about our Russian affairs, throws down his paper and shouts, "Well, that settles it! We're in for it! There's no fixing things up now!" But a Soviet citizen, carefully reading the government-controlled news on the fourth page of his newspaper, says slowly, "Well, these are *today's* developments."

Americans are completely unable to go slowly. Russians must examine and ponder, must move with great deliberation.

If the Iron Curtain could be raised so that Russians might travel freely abroad and so that Americans might travel freely in Russia, that would be the longest step possible toward international amity. It is perfectly true that Russians traveling in this country would find out that our standard of living is far higher than their own. Probably there are thousands who would prefer to remain here and enjoy it. But there are other thousands who are deeply patriotic and who love Mother Russia in spite of her shortcomings and her faults. Many would be happy to return to their homeland and take the news of our good things of life back simply as an inspiration to others. And they would be willing to work harder than ever to bring this good life to their own country.

Americans traveling in Russia would doubtless he amazed and annoyed at the low standard of living there, but they could not fail to be impressed by Russian valor and by the determination of a great people to advance and climb and progress and build and achieve. Americans never begrudge other people the good things of life. They wish warmly for everybody to be as well off as they are themselves.

How could it fail to be for the greatest good, this mingling of two great peoples? Tourist ladies from Montana might scream with outrage at the condition of Russian toilets; but they would meet Russians who were so jolly and good, who were such plain family people, that the Montana ladies could sense at once the honesty and the decency and the friendliness. Gentlemen from Texas would be astonished to find themselves in a land where Texan distances and spaces are dwarfed. New Yorkers would find to their astonishment cities cleaner than theirs and full of theatre buildings superior to their own. Citizens of Florida and California would find in the Crimea a climate as balmy and benign as theirs. Truly, if the people of America could meet the people of Russia in free, frank, friendly intercourse, it would prove to them both that two fine, strong nations have many and many a common interest and many and many a reason for understanding and peace.

Our own Secretary Byrnes summed it all up pretty neatly when he said, "The maintenance of peace cannot rely upon the magic of any document, but what is in the hearts and minds of men."

So pull up that old Iron Curtain, Uncle Joe! You come over to our house and we'll go over to yours. Let's all get together. What have we got to lose?

Oriana Atkinson

About the Author

ORIANA ATKINSON is a native New Yorker who has traveled widely—Russia, England, France, Ireland, all over the United States, and around the world on a freighter. She lived for a year in Moscow and her experiences there produced a best-seller, ***Over at Uncle Joe's: Moscow and Me.***

Mrs. Atkinson is also the author of three novels about the Catskills: ***Big Eyes***, ***Twin Cousins*** and ***The Golden Season***. Her most recent book was ***Manhattan and Me***, a New Yorker's book about her home town.

She has written short stories and articles for magazines and newspapers. Her husband, Brooks Atkinson, is drama critic of *The New York Times*.

Mrs. Atkinson says of herself: "My hobbies are really not pursued; they more or less stand still and wait for me. I like trying to learn the Russian language; raising roses; reading all kinds of strange things; and going to the theatre."

Obituary Oriana Atkinson
August 8, 1989

The New York Times

ORIANA ATKINSON, a writer and the widow of Brooks Atkinson, a former drama critic of The New York Times, died of pneumonia on Monday at the Huntsville (Ala.) Hospital. She was 94 years old and had lived in Huntsville for 14 years.

Mrs. Atkinson was the author of eight books of fact and fiction, two of which were best sellers. "Over at Uncle Joe's," published in 1947, was a personal account of her life among the Russians in wartime and postwar Moscow in the 10 months she spent there with her husband.

Her 1954 best seller, "Manhattan and Me," lightly described the changes that had occurred in her native New York since the time she had grown up in Greenwich Village. In the book, she wrote that although New York was the least beloved of cities, it was the most desired. She also wrote poetry and articles for The New York Times and other publications.

The Atkinsons maintained a farm in Durham, N.Y., in the Catskills, where they lived after Mr. Atkinson's retirement. Later, for health and family reasons, they moved to Huntsville, where he died in 1984 at age 89. They had been married since 1926.

Mrs. Atkinson is survived by a son from a previous marriage, Bruce Torrey MacIlveen of Huntsville; two grandsons, James Torrey MacIlveen of Decatur, Ala., and Dr. Robert Bruce MacIlveen of Portland, Ore., and six great-grandchildren.

CPSIA information can be obtained
at www.ICGtesting.com
Printed in the USA
BVHW041542190819
556237BV00007B/116/P

9 781640 660045